The Process of Psychoanalytic Therapy

Models and Strategies

About the Author:

Emanuel Peterfreund, a graduate of the University of Chicago School of Medicine, was trained in psychiatry and psychoanalysis in New York City. He is a member of the New York Psychoanalytic Society and is Associate Clinical Professor of Psychiatry at the Mount Sinai School of Medicine. His last book was *Information, Systems, and Psychoanalysis;* he is also the author of numerous articles on clinical and theoretical issues.

The Process of Psychoanalytic Therapy
Models and Strategies

EMANUEL PETERFREUND, M.D.

 THE ANALYTIC PRESS
1983

Distributed by
LAWRENCE ERLBAUM ASSOCIATES, PUBLISHERS
Hillsdale, New Jersey   London

The Analytic Press

Distributed solely by

Lawrence Erlbaum Associates, Inc., Publishers
365 Broadway
Hillsdale, New Jersey 07642

Library of Congress Cataloging in Publication Data

Peterfreund, Emanuel, 1924–
    The process of psychoanalytic therapy.

    Bibliography: p.
    Includes index.
    1. Psychoanalysis.   2. Psychoanalysis—Case studies.
I. Title.
RC504.P47   1983   616.89′17   82-20668
ISBN 0-88163-003-9

Printed in the United States of America
10 9 8 7 6 5 4 3 2 1

to Ory
and to Bob, Mike, and Karen

Contents

Preface

This book is offered as a contribution to the understanding of the psychoanalytic therapeutic process. It is an effort to update the state of the art. Its content is basically clinical, and it is addressed to those who work with patients and are constantly asking themselves: What is going on? What can I say or do that will be helpful? I am attempting to make a clinical statement, articulate a clinical point of view, advocate a clinical approach.

My training at the New York Psychoanalytic Institute over 20 years ago left me with the conviction that what is called Freudian analysis has very different meanings for different analysts and that the findings of these different analysts could in no way be compared. One basic theme of this book therefore is that a wide range of approaches—all deemed to be Freudian—have been and are being practiced. It is in attempting to specify and characterize these various approaches that I hope to have something new, useful, and relevant to say to practicing clinicians. I do not know of any previous effort made in this direction. Indeed, Ishak Ramzy, as late as 1974, tells us, "Unbelievable as it may sound, in the whole vast library of psychoanalysis—clinical, theoretical, technical or applied—there are hardly any references which outline the logical guidelines or the methodological rules which the analyst follows in order to understand his patient."

I myself have never understood why the wide disparity in the processes called Freudian have never been stressed and articulated in the literature. One possible explanation—and a not altogether satisfying one—is that the psychoanalytic process seems to have been transmitted largely by word of mouth rather than by the written word, and the literature on the process is therefore but a poor reflection of what actually takes place in practice. This oral tradition is exemplified by the courses we take as candidates, our continuous case seminars, our supervised cases, and, of course, our personal analysis. Certainly, my own understanding of the process came originally from my analysis, as well as from teachers and supervisors such as Otto Isakower, Edith Jacobson, Annie Reich, and others.

Two decades ago my interest in basic aspects of the psychoanalytic process—which I see as the interaction of patient and analyst, two highly complex systems that constantly influence each other while changing over time—led me to the general problem of biological order, organization, control, and adaptation, and then to an information-processing and systems frame of reference (discussed in my 1971 monograph *Information, Systems, and Psychoanalysis*). I found this general frame of reference to be very congenial because it had greater explanatory power than psychoanalytic metapsychology and was far more consistent with contemporary scientific thought.

Although an information-processing frame of reference is the barely visible but ever-present theoretical scaffolding of this work, my personal interest in this approach receives little attention in this book. The book can therefore be understood by those who are neither interested in nor familiar with an information-processing model, or who do not accept it. Whether the reader conceptualizes human development in terms of traditional theory or on the basis of an information-processing model is not of primary importance when the focus of attention is on the clinical interaction of patient and therapist.

I wish to thank the following publishers and editors for permission to reprint excerpts from the titles listed. Bibliographical details are given in the reference section at the end of the book.

International Universities Press: Beck, A. T., *Cognitive Therapy and the Emotional Disorders;* Brenner, C. *Psychoanalytic Technique and Psychic Conflict;* Greenson, R. R., *The Technique and Practice of Psychoanalysis;* Kovel, J. "Things and Words: Metapsychology and the Historical Point of View."

The Editor of the *International Journal of Psycho-Analysis:* Kohut, H., "The Two Analyses of Mr. Z."

The Editor of *The New England Journal of Medicine:* Blois, M.S., "Clinical Judgment and Computers."

The Editor of the *Psychoanalytic Quarterly:* Greenacre, P., "The Primal Scene and the Sense of Reality."

Clinical material appearing in chapters 1, 8, 9, and 10 was discussed in different form in *Information, Systems, and Psychoanalysis,* and in "How Does the Analyst Listen?"

I wish to express my thanks to Milton I. Klein, Joseph Reppen, and Emanuel Rice for their helpful comments on various drafts of this book.

My special thanks to Rosemarie Sand for her invaluable help. Knowledgeable in both philosophy and psychoanalysis, she read numerous drafts, offered thoughtful criticism, and provided me with ideas, suggestions, and, most important, encouragement.

Certainly my thanks to Natalie Altman for her editorial devotion to this work which went well beyond the call of duty.

To Paul Diesing I am indebted far more than my references to him in the text may suggest. Diesing's book *Patterns of Discovery in the Social Sciences,* although published in 1971, did not come to my attention until 1977. His ideas have not only reinforced and supported my own, they have also opened up new paths for exploration and elaboration.

One of the many merits of Diesing's work is his demonstration that every discipline has its own legitimate methods of inquiry, and that the social sciences (including participant-observer and case-study methods such as psychoanalysis) cannot be evaluated from the narrow stance of "science" based essentially on classical physics or of "science" defined according to an experimental ideal that is inappropriate for clinical experience.

Finally, a personal word. Dr. Lillian Malcove, who died shortly before this book was completed, was my second analyst. She understood that analysis can truly be a process that leads to discovery. To her my sincerest thanks.

Emanuel Peterfreund, M.D.

Nature is going to come out the way it is, and when we go to investigate it we shouldn't predecide what it is we are trying to do, except to try to find out more about it. . . . People ask me if science is true. I say no, we don't know what's true. We're trying to find out, and everything is possibly wrong. . . .

I can live with doubt and uncertainty. I think it's much more interesting to live *not* knowing than to have answers which might be wrong. I have approximate answers and possible beliefs and different degrees of certainty about different things, but I'm not absolutely sure of anything.

Richard Feynman
The Listener,
November 26, 1981.

The Process of Psychoanalytic Therapy

Models and Strategies

Introduction

The subject of this book is the psychoanalytic process. I am concerned with what goes on between patient and therapist, with the issues of discovery and the effectiveness of psychoanalytic treatment.

My focus is on psychoanalysis, but much of what I have to say is applicable to psychoanalytic therapy and to general clinical psychiatric practice as well. To simplify exposition, I make little distinction between psychoanalysis and psychoanalytic therapy although I recognize that important distinctions do exist. Hence, the words *therapy* and *analysis* are used interchangeably.

The distinction between *clinical theory* and a *theory of the therapeutic process* must be stressed. Clinical theory refers to a body of ideas used by the psychoanalytic clinician to order, organize, understand, or explain his data or his findings. Clinical theory includes such concepts as conflict, defense, repression, infantile sexual development, self- and object representations, unconscious processes, and the like. A theory of the therapeutic process refers, first, to the patient-therapist interaction, the mode of inquiry or of investigation used by psychoanalysts, the very way whereby we understand something about a given patient. Second, it refers to the way the patient is treated, to the activities that may lead to an efficacious outcome. In our theory of the therapeutic process we have such concepts as resistance, transference, therapeutic alliance, working through, interpretation, free association, and so on.

1

As will be discussed in the first part of the book, what is generally considered to be Freudian psychoanalysis actually consists of a wide range or spectrum of processes. In order to simplify exposition I shall be speaking of two types of therapeutic processes: *stereotyped* and *heuristic*. The fundamental aim of stereotyped approaches is to apply an accepted body of clinical theory to the patient being treated. These approaches have generally been thought to represent "classical" Freudian analysis. The fundamental aim of heuristic approaches—heuristic in the sense of serving to discover or learn—is to initiate and foster a process whereby patient and therapist work together to learn, discover, and understand as much as possible about the individual patient.

In the first part of the book I present clinical illustrations of stereotyped approaches, using my own cases as well as those of others. This highly critical section is followed by a more constructive one in which I describe a heuristic approach to psychoanalytic therapy. The general concept of heuristic strategies is discussed, followed by a discussion of the concept of working models—a term borrowed from Bowlby (1969) and which is similar to what cognitive psychologists call schemata and to what psychoanalysts call mental representations. In the context of case illustrations the characteristics of a "good" or effective hour is described. I then give a detailed description of the strategies I have found to be useful.

In specifying what I consider the optimal characteristics of the psychoanalytic process, I am especially interested in the nature of psychoanalytic inference—how we go about *discovering* something about a patient. What is the optimal way for fruitful hypotheses to be generated? How or why do we select any given hypothesis for testing from innumerable possible ones? Discovery and hypothesis formation bring up the crucial but much neglected issue of psychoanalytic evidence. Few analysts—Rubinstein (1976, 1980) is a notable exception—even recognize the importance of evidence and the need to confirm or substantiate our hypotheses.

The processes associated with discovery are usually ones that also make our treatment effective. This book concludes with a series of long-term follow-up reports from patients the reader will have met by way of the illustrative data in the body of the book.

I wish to emphasize that the approach I advocate is not original. The heuristic approach is new only in name. Many of the strategies to be discussed will sound familiar. Indeed, I hope that much of what I say will strike a chord of recognition in the experienced clinician. What is new in this work, as mentioned in the Preface, is the attempt to specify, characterize, and articulate what "good" analysts have been doing for a very long time to initiate and foster a process that leads to discovery, a process which simultaneously helps the patient.

In brief, as the title of my book suggests, the focus is on the *process* of psychoanalytic therapy—the nature of the models and strategies used that lead to *discovery,* especially the discoveries deemed to be uniquely psychoanalytic and Freudian. I am investigating our very mode of inquiry or method of investigation—the source of psychoanalytic knowledge that forms our clinical theories. I use the term *discovery* to include both a hypothesis about events—an inferred connection or relationship, for example—and the evidence to support or substantiate the hypothesis. Thus, hypothesis plus evidence constitute discovery.

PART ONE

STEREOTYPED APPROACHES TO PSYCHOANALYTIC THERAPY

1

Stereotyped Approaches: Examples from Personal Experience

Mrs. A.

Mrs. A. was one of my early cases, one conducted under supervision. Her case typifies the many experiences that led me to begin to question the scientific basis of much of clinical psychoanalysis and the validity of many widely accepted clinical generalizations. Also, it was cases such as Mrs. A. which led me to begin to specify the nature of acceptable psychoanalytic clinical thinking.

Mrs. A. was a young woman who sought analysis for a host of symptoms including intense anxiety, depression, and episodes of tachycardia. Inexplicably, her pulse rate would often exceed 160 per minute, accompanied by difficulties in breathing. She suffered from severe and crippling hypochondriacal preoccupations and fears of death. Especially prominent were fears of breast cancer, fears of imminent heart attack, and fears of aging. Her anxiety had become so great that she was taking barbiturates around the clock to calm herself. She decided that treatment was urgently needed when her agoraphobia increased to such a point that she was not able to leave home alone.

Her initial history revealed that she had had serious difficulties throughout her life, fears of getting a mastoid infection when young, ever-present fears of death. She became nauseated when out on dates. When she first began to work, in her teens, her anxiety was so intense that she had to be accompanied by her mother to and from work. In general, she felt friendless, alone, ugly, and unloved. She felt that she was never able to "connect" with people. Psychological testing confirmed that she was profoundly disturbed, and possible hospitalization was advised. She was nonetheless accepted for low-cost psychoanalysis at the Treatment Center of the New York Psychoanalytic Institute, after having been initially turned down. It is important to emphasize that Mrs. A.'s treatment started before modern psychotropic drugs were in use.

The patient was the older of two children; she had a brother 3 years her junior. The mother was portrayed as chronically irritable, angry, paranoid, lacking any affection or warmth. She had had several major depressive episodes during the patient's life. One occurred after the birth of the patient; one, which lasted about 6 months, occurred after the birth of the younger brother. The most recent episode began on the very day that the patient started treatment.

The beginning of the analysis was hardly auspicious—a desperate patient clinging to analysis as her only chance for life, feeling lucky to have finally been accepted for a low-cost analysis. And here was her analyst, 3 years her junior, obviously inexperienced, and exactly the age of her despised brother. The situation was an explosive one as the patient tried desperately to hang on to the analysis while simultaneously trying to deal with her highly ambivalent feelings toward me. In the very first hours before beginning supervision, I found it necessary to deal with the transference. I interpreted almost immediately that she was afraid of being overwhelmed by her feelings, was afraid that she might break down and cry, and thought that I was too inexperienced to handle her. The patient agreed with me completely and elaborated on these anxieties. My supervisor, however, was critical of what I said to the patient. She felt that it was much too early for the patient to be dealing with the transference, too early for her to be preoccupied with me. The supervisor felt that the patient should be talking about her husband, since he, according to the supervisor, was probably the cause of the patient's difficulties. The supervisor told me she had a hunch that the patient was ill because her husband was "making her do a perversion."

It should be emphasized that I had been taught that Freudian analysts worked from the surface, worked with the immediate experience that patients present. Mrs. A's feelings about me were at the forefront from the moment the analysis began. Indeed, they seemed to be at the forefront in a most explosive way. But the supervisor was telling me to disregard the presenting material. Furthermore, my early interpretations, though accepted and elaborated upon by the patient, were deemed to be serious errors. Finally, when I repeatedly asked the supervisor about the evidence for her inferences made about the patient's husband, the answer was always "Experience." The supervisor had had 20 years of experience and therefore understood what was going on.

Having no immediate alternative, I had to go along with my supervisor. Under the guise of interpretations, I suggested ideas to Mrs. A according to the instructions given me, especially ideas related to the husband. Actually, these efforts were in great part attempts to organize the chaos presented by the patient. Because of her desperate need to hang on to the analysis and not be thrown out, the patient picked up my suggestions and tried to deal with them. When, at the supervisor's insistence I said to Mrs. A., "You are preoccupied with me as a way of avoiding your real problem, namely, your husband," Mrs. A. would dutifully tell me something about her husband, and then say, "Now what?" Actually, she was only dancing to our tune.

As could be predicted, the analysis went downhill very rapidly. The main issue, the transference, was not being dealt with. The patient was principally concerned with how a beginner and so young a man could handle someone who felt as ill as she did, literally ready to fall apart. She felt that I was her only link to life, but she feared her own internal chaos, feared breaking down and becoming totally out of control, feared being able to overwhelm me completely and even sexually seduce me. She felt that only a God-like, very experienced, senior, special person could help her and bring the external controls that she felt were necessary to organize her.

After a few months, the supervisor decided that the case was not analyzable, because of a "persistent, unresolvable, brother transference," and suggested that I discontinue treatment. I disregarded this advice, left the supervisor, and radically changed my approach to the patient. When on my own, and before acquiring a more congenial supervisor, I stopped giving Mrs. A. subjects to deal with under the guise of interpretations. I asked for "free associations" and tried to deal with whatever came up spontaneously. I stayed very close to the surface and dealt actively with the explosive transference. Naturally, she was puzzled and bewildered by the change in technique. I was now trying to analyze her need for cues about what to talk about, whereas until now, I had been giving her such cues. Mrs. A. reacted to the marked change in technique with the following dream: "I am on a stage giving a performance, but I cannot go on because the prompter is gone." She then told of a performance at age 7 when she had trouble speaking because she could only perform on cue. Indeed, the "prompter"—the supervisor—had gone, and I think that the dream gave convincing evidence for the idea that the patient had been merely a puppet, acting a role in response to the totally artificial format imposed on her.

Although the treatment was very stormy, the situation turned out to be relatively salvageable, and I was able to work with this patient for about 9 years. However, I was able to achieve only limited success.

As time went on it became increasingly clear how ill the patient truly was. Indeed, in retrospect, in all of my years of experience I have rarely seen, outside of a hospital setting, a patient so anxious, so constantly in terror, so unable to find a moment of peace. She lived in a constant nightmare; death, destruction, cancer, heart disease, abandonment, and consequent total helplessness—all were either always happening or were just about to happen. She lived in a tenuous world, one that was constantly changing, an unreliable, unstable, unpredictable world, one that could not be trusted. She had to be ever on guard to detect the changes in the outer world in order to protect herself. Terrible things could suddenly happen for no obvious reason—someone could get violently upset and angry over the slightest offense and abandon her. She often saw herself as a rat scurrying around, trying to survive in a terrorizing world. "Survival" was the theme of her life and one of the main themes of the analytic treatment.

Mrs. A. saw herself as totally vulnerable, utterly helpless; inner urges could engulf and overwhelm her. She saw herself as a total "zero," and her body as nothing but debris or "flotsam." Indeed, she saw her body as made up of totally disorganized, disconnected parts with no apparent central regulatory mechanism. She felt that her body parts were only loosely joined together, and each part could go off on its own, totally out of control. The reality of having extra-systoles and attacks of tachycardia served as living proof to her of her disorganized, malfunctioning, bankrupt image of herself. She feared orgasm because then her body could literally "burst and fly apart." She never knew how to predict what might happen to her. She feared, for example, that she might become ill in a crowded department store, faint, and then be trampled upon and destroyed by a deaf and oblivious world.

An inner image of death and stagnation permeated her life. Her mind, she felt, was basically "dead and stagnant." She could not think, she felt; she was too inept to communicate with or contact the outer world, which could only turn away from her with "glazed and unseeing eyes." Her bowels were dead, she felt, and so were her genitals. She felt that she was empty and dead and that life for her had actually never begun. She was born a defective and born into darkness. Mrs. A. saw herself as a dazed, glassy-eyed child, living in a bombed-out world. She once said to me, "I am nothing; I offer nothing; I am just tolerated; I interfere with people; I am a bother and a nuisance; I intrude on the peace of people; I am tolerated only out of charity. I am all dead; I must create a superstructure, a façade to conceal the nothingness. I always copy and become like others. I don't know who the real me is."

I felt from the beginning that much about this patient could be understood by recognizing how ill her mother was and how traumatic were the patient's early life experiences. In addition to her multiple depressive episodes, the mother, according to the patient, "could not hear," and was intolerant of any opposition. "Bad" behavior "killed" her, and she constantly threatened abandonment. She was subject to very rapid mood changes, and very early in life the patient learned to be attuned to these moods, always alert for any sign of a breakdown. She had vivid memories from age 3 of a weeping, depressed, dejected, sad mother, with dull, glassy, unseeing eyes. She once described her early life as, "This dead mother, this dead house, this dead city."

The patient's early life was fraught with anxiety. At age 4 to 5 she would frequently awaken at night feeling that something was in her throat, that she might choke, and that she might not be able to open her mouth. In later years these fears took on the specific form of a fear of lockjaw. At age 5 to 6, she fantasied that she could make her dolls come alive and transform them into real living babies. The early years were characterized by violent quarrels with the mother, "white rages" over everything, especially over toilet training. Apparently the patient was chronically constipated as a child, received frequent enemas, and was constantly threatened with their use.

From the history and from what I learned as the analysis progressed, I had every reason to believe that Mrs. A.'s anxiety was unusually total and primitive and had to be dealt with accordingly. I was struck by the illness of the mother and the massive and overwhelming rage, anger, frustration, deprivation, and helplessness that probably characterized the patient's early years. Her anxiety was not that of a simple hysteric, and, if any sort of therapeutic process was to be established, I felt very strongly that she could not be treated as one. Certain reassurances and gratifications had to be allowed, and certain frustrations avoided. To have frustrated her when she needed to hear my voice to reassure herself of my benign presence would have been to duplicate what her depressed mother undoubtedly had done.

Several years after the beginning of this patient's treatment, I presented all of the foregoing material plus a great deal more at a case conference. After reading my extensive case report, one discussant, a young analyst of about my level of experience, concluded that I had completely misunderstood the patient. It was clear to him that she was only trying to seduce me through her anxiety, and he felt that she had succeeded in doing so, judging by my response to her. He informed me in no uncertain terms that he would have repeatedly interpreted her sexually seductive efforts regardless of how she replied and no matter how long she continued to resist.

A second discussant, a prominent senior training analyst, also viewed the material from the standpoint of late infantile sexuality. He reasoned that, inasmuch as Mrs. A. had mouth and throat symptoms beginning at age 4, she was obviously struggling with fantasies of devouring her father's phallus, and her interest in dolls and babies undoubtedly had to do with her wish to have a baby from her father. He did not understand why oedipal issues were not discussed in my case report.

A third discussant, a young analyst who was trained with me, responded to the same clinical presentation differently. He suggested that the patient's symptoms at age 4 might have been related to her mother's depressive episode during the previous year, following the brother's birth. He wondered if the mother had been closed-mouthed and unable to respond during this depressive episode.

In general, as is probably clear, my own understanding of the case was quite consistent with the ideas of the third discussant. It seemed probable that at age 4 the patient had been struggling with violent aggressive feelings toward her very ill, psychotic, depressed, silent mother. Throughout her life, she tended to develop mouth and throat symptoms when confronted with similar conflicts. It was also my understanding that her interest in dolls and babies probably had to do with fantasies of making her "dead" depressed, silent mother wake up and come alive. It also apparently had much to do with her attempts to wake up and restore her own "dead" withdrawn self.

What we have here, then, is a veritable Rashomon situation. Five "Freudian" analysts coming from the same psychoanalytic institute have almost as many understandings of the same data. It cannot be said of the supervisor that she was working with a stereotyped approach. Indeed, it is not easy to find a label for her approach; I can only call it idiosyncratic. She saw a totally unworkable case, and I never did find out the source of her inferences about the patient. Certainly, her suggestions about the patient's husband, the supposed cause of the patient's illness, did not come from any existing clinical theory. Equally certainly, these ideas had no obvious relationship to the patient's life. Indeed, years later when the patient was finally able to talk about her sex life, she said she felt that her husband was far too inhibited, not free or "perverse" enough to arouse her. Furthermore, the supervisor had abandoned one of the basic principles of Freudian analytic technique which we are all taught, namely, that one works from the surface with whatever the patient brings up.

In contrast to the supervisor's idiosyncratic approach, the first and second discussants approached the case in what I am calling a "stereotyped" way. Both disregarded the early traumatic history, the mother's psychotic depressions, and the ominous clinical picture. Both reasoned directly from existing clinical theory based on genital-oedipal themes, disregarding everything that did not fit these ideas. Both viewed the patient as though she were essentially a well-functioning simple hysteric and not profoundly ill. For the first discussant, everything was "sexual" and therefore the patient's anxiety represented merely her sexual seductiveness. The second discussant understood the clinical material from the standpoint of theoretical stages of development, all, of course, sexual and oedipal in nature. Both discussants worked with very limited models of development and psychopathology. Neither one thought about the patient from within the unique and specific case material she presented. The first discussant even suggested that I pay no attention to whether or not the patient understood and accepted the sexual interpretations that he advised; he saw lack of understanding or failure to accept interpretations as merely manifestations of resistance. For him, the issue of evidence for a hypothesis and constraints or "checkpoints" in scientific thinking—issues to be discussed throughout this book—apparently had little relevance.

In contrast, the third discussant was conceptualizing the case from within the patient's experiences. He undoubtedly had a full, flesh-and-blood experiential model of the patient which he extended imaginatively on the basis of his understanding of infantile experience. Both he and I saw a profoundly ill woman, but to some extent accessible. We both saw early trauma and the devastating consequences of real events on the patient. The type of thinking that the third discussant and I were both using is essentially, I believe, heuristic in nature.

I might add, in this context, that the first discussant once presented a case of a woman who had a deep feeling of emptiness and loneliness. The analyst decided that her feelings of emptiness referred to castration—the absent phallus. He offered this interpretation to the patient who did not at all understand what he meant. Despite repeated interpretations along these lines, there was no change in her symptoms. The analyst, recognizing that the interpretations had no obvious effect, concluded that the patient was resisting and that this very resistance was evidence that women never give up their phallic wishes.

Now, it may or may not have been true that the patient's feelings were related to phallic wishes and castration anxiety. This hypothesis is certainly a legitimate one, but it is only a hypothesis. That the hypothesis was totally unconfirmed and not understood by the patient should have indicated to the analyst that he might be on the wrong track in his understanding of her symptoms. Surely that would have been the correct scientific position. Instead, he took the failure to get confirmation and her failure to understand him as evidence for yet another unconfirmed hypothesis, namely, that women never give up their phallic wishes.

I believe this analyst never really viewed his ideas as only hypotheses; for him, his stereotyped ideas were ultimate truths. Actually he learned little about the patient's inner experiences when she reported feeling empty; what the phenomenon meant to her was, in truth, never analyzed. There was no process leading to discovery in this case.

The example just given illustrates another, most important issue—namely, how clinical ideas can become fixed in psychoanalysis when the underlying evidence is actually scanty and perhaps even nonexistent. As far as I could see, the analyst in this case was using self-deceptive, self-confirming, circular reasoning. His method could only lead to reinforcement of his a priori convictions; his ideas could not be refuted because his method did not allow them to be.

To the extent that psychoanalysts use preconceived ideas to arrive at their formulations, self-confirming and circular reasoning to buttress these formulations, and neglect the important issue of evidence, it is quite legitimate to raise serious questions about any psychoanalytic clinical theory derived from such an approach.

Mrs. B.

Excerpts from another of my early cases, again a supervised one, further illustrate my thesis. A young woman, Mrs. B., entered analysis with a variety of symptoms, including general anxiety, especially severe separation anxieties, and obsessive thoughts of killing. The diagnosis was anxiety hysteria.

My supervisor translated these symptoms directly into some supposedly well-established formulations, and the analytic work was predicated on the assumption that the obsessive thoughts of killing indicated a conflict centering on sexual and masturbatory impulses of a sadistic nature. The early "analysis" of the symptom was conducted under the assumption that the answer was already known. Insofar as an assumption about the meaning of the symptom was made at the beginning of the analysis, the task of the analysis was to get the patient to recognize the truth of the assumed meaning. This was to be accomplished by making the assumed meaning real, concrete, and specific, and by waiting until the patient stopped resisting and began to see the light. The analysis was not treated as an investigative procedure, as a process leading to discovery. The meaning assigned to the symptom was never treated as merely a hypothesis for which evidence might or might not be forthcoming.

I learned how easy it is to be led astray in an analysis and how easy it is to make things seem to fit into a formula. I discovered that by making innumerable unsubstantiated assumptions one can find an astonishing amount of "evidence" to back up just about any one of them. In this case, the patient's fears of going crazy and her violent impulses toward her husband became further "evidence" for the meaning assigned to the symptoms. And it is terribly easy to begin to think of patients as being resistant when they refuse to understand or accept our supposedly profound ideas. Fortunately, Mrs. B. was wise and healthy enough to "resist" my efforts to interpret her symptoms along the lines indicated.

It took me several months to realize that I actually understood very little about Mrs. B. I did not know what "killing" meant to her—the private connotative meanings. The phenomena—her fears of killing—had never been analyzed, and I understood little about its emotional and ideational context or the accompanying physical experience. When I realized that I had not begun an analytic process leading to discovery, that I had not fostered a process to generate and organize information relevant to her symptom, I was able to separate myself from the supervisor's approach. I dropped all preconceived notions and began to work in a more productive manner. The approach that I had taken had inhibited any true analytic process; in a real sense, I had been resisting the analytic process. I now had to convey to the patient the necessity to associate, to observe, and to allow expression to apparently irrational and disordered ideational and emotional experiences related to the symptom. Because of my supervisor's approach, the patient had never been "educated" into the analytic process. I had to convey to her, for example, the necessity for understanding the total context of a symptom, as regressive and as frightening as that might be—and it proved to be both regressive and frightening. With the change in my approach the patient began to work more productively.

We discovered that Mrs. B. was terrified of experiences during which she felt that she was not in the world, that she did not exist, and that she had no connection to other people. In these states, she could not sleep; she felt that she was falling apart; she felt vague and unreal, and everything appeared to be unfamiliar. She was afraid that she might lose complete control of herself and perhaps even go crazy. It was at these times that she became preoccupied with her obsessive thoughts of killing. The symptom therefore had very little to do with the meanings originally and arbitrarily assigned to it. In fact, the symptom proved to be difficult to analyze, and although progress was made, our understanding of it remained limited.

I have described this case because it illustrates how the original assumptions about the symptom and the entire analytic attitude made it impossible to establish any true analytic process. Of great clinical and theoretical importance is that the early analysis of the symptoms was carried out in a totally stereotyped way, based on the assumption that all symptoms are related to genital and oedipal conflicts, and that preoedipal issues require little consideration, especially in neurotic patients. Finally, it was implicitly assumed that real experiences in early life have little pathogenic significance. These clinical theoretical ideas were never treated as hypotheses for which evidence might or might not be forthcoming. In this case there was no process leading to discovery.

One may reasonably argue, and colleagues have done so, that there was nothing "wrong" in my initial assumption about the meaning of Mrs. B.'s fear of killing. What was "wrong" was my failure to correct it quickly enough. But this argument misses the point. I came to recognize that starting an analysis with specific stereotyped assumptions about the meaning of symptoms is totally unnecessary and far from an optimal approach. The optimal approach is, instead, to gear one's thinking to the establishment of an investigative analytic process, a process that can lead to discovery.

To state the matter somewhat differently, when a patient tells us of fears of killing, we face a situation of great ambiguity. Fears of killing can have innumerable meanings and causes. Until we know something about the particular patient, we have no reasonable basis for selecting one of these meanings or causes. And I certainly do not know how one could progressively test all of the possible meanings.

As an analytic process is set up, however, new, relevant information is generated; hypotheses can be formulated and tested; complexity, uncertainty, and ambiguity can be reduced. As a result, the number of possible meanings or causes of the fear of killing is markedly reduced. We then have a chance to arrive at specific meanings or causes for the particular patient.

2

Stereotyped Approaches: Examples from the Literature

To support and develop my basic theme I turn now to case material reported by other psychoanalysts, with full recognition of the dangers in evaluating and responding to an hour reported by others.

It is extremely difficult to present analytic material convincingly: confidentiality issues must be taken into account, and only a fraction of what is understood about an hour or about a fragment of an hour can be presented. It is impossible to address every question in any case presentation. Moreover, the given case material may not be presented from the perspective of interest to the critic. Whereas a critic may have questions about evidence and the confirmation of hypotheses, these issues may not have been what the reporting analyst was focusing on. Furthermore, and this is something that often seems to be misunderstood by many critics of analysis, much of what we know and understand in every area of life, including human communication, simply cannot be conveyed by words. How does one communicate in words the experience of love, the sensations of orgasm? Few of us would go to a tennis instructor who has never played the game and has only read about it; nor would we choose a surgeon whose knowledge comes only from texts but who has never performed an operation or even witnessed one. And few of us would take seriously the musical criticisms of one who has only read about music but has never heard it played. We all implicitly recognize that language is basically a pointer to most kinds of experience, not a substitute for it, and cannot capture the full richness of any given experience. A critic responding only to written presentations of a case can therefore easily be unfair to the reporting analyst. It is especially dangerous for a critic to attempt to "reinterpret" clinical material reported by someone else because there is so much that the critic does not know about the case.

Despite all of the difficulties and dangers, I nevertheless think that critical appraisal of psychoanalytic material is in order. Psychoanalysis must in some way make its data and its procedures public, and if we claim any special exemption in this regard we cannot expect to be taken seriously by the general scientific world. Analysts who, very admirably, are willing to present their clinical work and thinking in some detail must be prepared for criticism. If the criticism is honest and thoughtful, psychoanalysis can only be enriched thereby.

Case Report By Greenson

I begin with material from an analytic session reported by Ralph Greenson in his highly regarded and widely read textbook on the technique and practice of psychoanalysis (1967, pp. 143–145). I believe it is typical of a great deal of psychoanalytic work done that I refer to as stereotyped. Greenson's subject is the importance of analyzing resistance before content, and of surface before depth. (I have numbered Greenson's paragraphs to simplify my later reference to them):

[1] A woman patient, Mrs. K., in her fourth year of analysis begins an hour by telling me the following dreams: (1) "I am being photographed in the nude, lying on my back in different positions; legs closed, legs apart." (2) "I see a man with a curved yardstick in his hand; it had writing on it which was supposed to be erotic. A red, spiny backed little monster was biting this man with sharp, tiny teeth. The man was ringing a bell for help, but no one heard it but me and I didn't seem to care."

[2] Let me add here that this patient had been working in the last several hours on the problem of her fear of her homosexual impulses, which she connected to her clitoris sexuality as opposed to her vaginal sexuality. Now that she had achieved the ability to have a vaginal orgasm, she was more daring in exploring these areas. Furthermore, she had never really felt her penis envy and had only recently realized that her attitude—I'm glad I am a girl, I would have failed as a man— was a defense against a deep-seated and as yet untouched hostility to the man's penis. If we know all this, it is obvious that the manifest content of the dream is a continuation of these themes. Being photographed in the nude refers to problems of exposure as penisless. The man with the yardstick whom she ignores apparently represents her analyst. The red monster he is struggling with could represent a projection of or a revenge for her feelings about the male genital.

[3] The patient begins to talk in a somewhat sad, empty tone of voice. She recounts plans for a party she is giving for her two-and-half-year-old child. She hopes the child will enjoy it, not dread parties as she used to when she was a child. She has been out with her fiancé and she found herself biting at him, reproaching him for his decadent past, he had been a philanderer, a wastrel. Pause. Her menstrual period is one day late and she thinks she is pregnant, but she doesn't seem to care about it. Pause. She has the feeling something is wrong inside, something repulsive is inside her, which reminds her of the feelings the man had in The Immoralist, who felt repelled by his wife's tuberculosis. Pause. "I went to a boring party and hated it [silence]. I wish you would say something, I feel empty. I got mad at my baby and hit her, then the baby became very loving [silence]. I feel remote and far away."

[4] At this point I intervene and say: "You feel remote and empty because you seem to be afraid to look at that hateful monster inside you." The patient answers: "That monster was red, actually dark red-brown, like old menstrual blood. It was a medieval fiend, like one sees in the paintings of Hieronymus Bosch. I am like that; if I were a painting, that's what I would be, full of all kinds of demons of sex, bowel movement, homosexuality, and hate. I suppose I don't want to face my hate for myself, for Bill, for my baby, and for you. I haven't really changed and I had thought I had made much progress [silence]."

[5] I intervene: "We recently uncovered a new monster: Your anger at men's penises and your disgust with your vagina. And you are running away from it by trying to escape into emptiness." The patient

replied: "You sound so sure of yourself, as though you have it all solved. Maybe I am running. I read a book about a man giving his wife cognac to get her drunk so she would be a better sexual partner and she pretended to be drunk so she could let out her real feelings. Maybe I'm like that. I'd really show you men what I could do sexually. I sometimes get the feeling that underneath this meek slave-girl exterior I present, I have a streak of grandiosity. I'd show you poor 'fuckers' how to really use a penis if I had one. Yes, when Bill was trying his damndest to satisfy me the other night, I looked at him and it flashed through my mind, who's the 'slavey' now. And that yardstick, I recall asking you once, what yardstick do you use to measure neurosis with? I hate to feel stupid and sometimes you and this analysis make me so. I could be as sharp as you, if I dared. But then I become afraid I would lose you or I'd become repulsive to you and you would desert me. I suppose I have to develop more trust in you. I can't expect Bill to take all this—but you ought to be able to. . . ."

[6] I submit this fragment of an hour to demonstrate how I worked with the patient's resistance by bringing in the content to help me. I interpreted to her she was running away into emptiness to avoid the monster of her penis envy, her hateful, internal penis and the masculine identification. This formulation helped her recognize how she tried to deny and then to project this hateful introject onto me and onto her fiancé. She could see its resistance-producing effect and was able to begin to explore it inside herself. The clarification of the content helped her to work with her hostile-depressive transference resistance.

In the first paragraph we learn of a dream reported by the patient. In the second Greenson tells us of recent analytic work, which we cannot evaluate. We are then told "if we know all this, it is obvious that the manifest content of the dream is a continuation of these themes." Perhaps so. But then Greenson proceeds to make several assumptions with different degrees of tentativeness. He asserts that "being photographed in the nude refers to problems of exposure as penisless," although he offers no previous analytic material that might possibly support such an assumption. More important, the assumption must be questioned because no associations are reported to the dream, and it is a cardinal principle of clinical psychoanalysis that we generally understand dreams only in the light of associations. This principle or guiding rule can be considered to be part of the general strategy of attempting to discover specific and individual meanings. Such meanings are context-dependent and are generally—though not always—discernible only if associations are given. Finally, and most important, as best as can be judged from the second paragraph, Greenson seems to have already established the theme for his understanding of the hour.

In the third paragraph we hear of the patient speaking with many pauses in a sad and empty tone of voice. She is apparently depressed. At this point, Greenson offers an interpretation. Essentially he appears to be saying that her feeling of remoteness and emptinesss are defensive; they represent her way of avoiding looking at the inner hateful monster. But he does not tell us the basis for his understanding that the patient was being defensive. She replies by further describing the monster of the dream and then telling of the demons that she feels inside of her. But as best as I can judge, there was no confirmation for the interpretation offered.

In paragraph five, Greenson elaborates on his interpretation; instead of working with the patient's overriding and all-pervasive hate, he pursues his own—preconceived—line of thought. He seems not to be following the patient's experience but pursuing a tendentious theme almost alien to what the patient has been talking about and based only on what are, at best, tentative stereotyped assumptions or hypotheses. The patient's reply sounds as if she feels angry, misunderstood, and even confused. She seems to be struggling hard to be a "good" patient. She admits that maybe she is running, and she seems to pick up the phallic theme. But she is upset, angry, revengeful, retaliatory—hardly insightful. Finally, as I read the hour, the session ends almost pathetically as the patient tells of how stupid the analyst and the process make her feel and of her disappointment in Greenson and how she must restrain herself because of her fear of losing him.

Greenson's sixth paragraph offers several difficulties. We find no confirmation for the interpretation offered to the patient. We are given no evidence that the patient recognized "how she tried to deny and then project this hateful introject onto me and onto her fiancé." Indeed, it is difficult to know what this statement means in clinical experiential terms. Is Greenson saying that her angry feelings to-

ward him and her fiancé were due to her projecting onto them her
hateful internal penis? If so, then we should be told something about
her fiancé. On the basis of what we have been told, we do not know
what she may have been reacting to in this hour. And if she is angry
with Greenson perhaps she has cause, for perhaps she feels misunderstood and confused.

Greenson tells us that his "clarification" helped the patient, but
we hear of no relief of immediate tension or depression; no acknowl-
edgment on the part of the patient that the analytic interpretations
were correct; confirming evidence, relevant memories, for example,
were not forthcoming. We hear of no new awarenesses; the analytic
process seems not to have been fostered in any discernible way;
there is no working-through process, not even the beginning of one
in any meaningful sense. The patient does not appear to be a true
working partner in the process, with a sense that she is learning and
making discoveries about herself. On the contrary, the hour ends
with the patient sounding disappointed and confused. She com-
plains that she feels stupid and that sometimes the analyst and the
process make her so, but she seems ready to submit to the analyst so
as not to be repulsive to him and not be deserted by him—signs, I
believe, that serious problems may exist in the analytic situation.
As I read the analytic material, it seems to be the very kind of hour
where the analyst should consider making fairly radical revisions in
his hypotheses and general approach.

On the basis of the fragment of the hour presented, one can say
that Greenson seems to be working with the patient's experience in
only a limited way. Everything points to the fact that active independent analytic work by the patient is not present, and we must
therefore wonder if it has ever been encouraged. Likewise, we do not
hear of any true "regression in the service of the ego"—free associative, disordered experiences by the patient—and we must wonder
why these are not present and if perhaps the analyst has not encouraged them. We read nothing at all of the patient going further and
deeper into the specifics of her moods, emptiness, depression, feelings to her child and her fiancé.

The patient's annoyed response to Greenson's interpretation and
her complaints about him and the process are not viewed as possibly
being reasonable and legitimate, but, if I understand Greenson,
they are seen as having no meaning other than the projection of a

hateful introject. Hence, if errors were committed by the analyst and the patient was responding to these errors, Greenson remained totally unaware of the feedback he was getting.

As I read Greenson's material there is evidence that some meanings are assumed instead of being discovered and that the assumptions are apparently based to a great extent on stereotyped ideas concerning genital conflicts. As a result, the assumed meanings have a highly intellectualized flavor, remote from the patient's experience; they do not emerge naturally from full free-associative contexts involving the depth of the patient's experience. Greenson assumes that being photographed in the nude refers to problems of exposure as penisless. No evidence is given that this formulation emerged from any free-associative context or that alternative possibilities were considered. And the analytic process reported seems not to have allowed for confirmation, refutation, or even for the establishment of any one of innumerable alternative hypotheses.

Especially striking, to my mind, is Greenson's general approach to the patient's mood of emptiness, remoteness, and of feeling far away. These experiences are treated as purely defensive, to avoid some genital conflicts. Here I must disagree sharply: I consider the feelings of emptiness and remoteness significant enough to have alerted me to inquire further, and I would have expected to find them referring to significant antecedents. These feelings are consistent with the symptoms that led the patient to seek analysis and with the bits of history we are given. Greenson (p. 30) has told us that for several years the patient had "episodes of feeling out of things, numb, 'gone,' 'like a zombie.'" We are told later (p. 185) that the mother was a warm-hearted, erratic alcoholic who at times abandoned the patient; that father deserted the family when the patient was age $1\frac{1}{2}$; and that the mother's subsequent three marriages each lasted about a year. And when the patient was 15, the mother insisted that she shift for herself. Such a history would alert many of us to listen for the family pathology, for the devastating traumatic consequences that such pathology could have on a patient. An hour such as the one reported might possibly have been an entrée into such issues because the patient spoke of many of the symptoms originally complained of. Instead, Greenson focuses on genital issues and apparently sees feelings of emptiness as being nothing but defensive. Even the original symptom, the "impulsive-obsessive idea" of having a sexual affair with a Negro (p. 30), does not necessarily indicate that genital conflicts are at the forefront. I have, for example, seen serious depersonalization in a patient who suffered early trauma and who came into analysis with sexual problems as his chief complaint. He suffered from impotency. We later discovered that anxieties about his penis were only part of extreme anxieties about his entire body.

Greenson apparently recognizes that the symptom involving a Negro had early roots. He notes (p. 31):

> The sexual desires for Negro men also served an important defensive function against strong homosexual impulses to women. These in turn were shown to be derived from deeply repressed oral sucking impulses toward the mother, which the patient had felt as a threat to her separate identity. Alongside of this conflict was an enormous primitive rage toward the mother, which was perceived as dangerous to the mother's existence and was also felt as a threat to Mrs. K.'s own existence.

I find such general, jargon-laden, stereotyped dynamic formulations almost meaningless. They give me no idea of the specific impact of specific events on a specific person, early in life.

Before closing my remarks on this case I would like to point out that many of us who have abandoned these stereotyped approaches might arrive at some very different hypotheses about this case. We would recognize the possibility that this patient's symptoms might have been connected to very early traumatic states, and Greenson does tell us enough to indicate that the patient's early experiences may indeed have been devastating.

One possibility I would have been alerted to (note that I say "alerted to"—a very tentative hypothesis) is that at some time this patient suffered from serious shocklike episodes, a possible reaction to massive trauma, overwhelming rages, separations, and extreme frustrations, for instance. I am reminded of Bowlby's (1973, pp. 54–55) fascinating summary of observations on infants under 7 months of age returning home from a hospital. They are described as "strange." They did not focus on or attend to specific features, though they craned their necks and scanned their surroundings. Their expressions were blank. They were oblivious to attempts by adults to make contact. Some infants avoided adults and "gazed" through them with a blank look.

Is it not possible that such experiences could leave residues describable later in life as feeling "numb," "gone, "like a zombie"—the very feelings that Greenson's patient speaks of ? A patient to be discussed more in detail later on, Mr. R., whose agitated, depressed, controlling mother undoubtedly had a severe postpartum reaction following his birth, could dramatize an experiential state in a form that seemed to be reactivations of early experiences. He would walk around the office, gazing and staring expressionlessly (like a zombie), looking through the analyst with no sign of recognition.

Whatever the truth about Greenson's patient, my point here is simple. It is infinitely more helpful—in the sense of giving patient and therapist more options—to consider that perhaps the patient's initial complaints and current experiences—feelings of emptiness and remoteness, feeling far away, out of things, numb, gone, and like a zombie—may perhaps represent her struggles with significant residues of archaic pathological states than to dismiss such experiences, as Greenson apparently does, as essentially nothing but defenses related to genital conflicts.

Case Report By Kovel

A vignette by Joel Kovel (1978) in a paper on metapsychology and the historical point of view also illustrates some important characteristics of what I am calling the stereotyped approach to psychoanalytic therapy.

> The patient is a 28-year-old physician, in analysis for two and one half years for chronic depression. The following is drawn from a Monday session:
> He begins by telling at length of the frantic weekend he spent with a number of girl-friends and of the difficulty he is having putting his financial affairs in order. An ex-girl-friend owes money, and he is afraid to ask for it back and ashamed of his fear. He muses about his compulsiveness with women, then directs his attention at the analyst: "I wonder what you think of all these repetitions; I feel like I'm a mess, completely out of control." He then speculates about the source

of his behavior; perhaps it's a reaction to feelings brought out last week about being sexually interested in his younger sister. At any rate, he's very glad to be back in the office and eager for the session. Next, however, he recollects that he was ashamed to tell A, one of his new girl-friends, anything about the analysis. He rationalizes this as due to her possible disapproval. Then suddenly he turns with pride to the fact that he finally went to the barber over the weekend and got his hair cut, thus overcoming a minor phobia. As he does so, however, his hand reaches up to touch his hair: "I just recalled that a bug had landed in my hair on the weekend, and as I thought that, I imagined it returned." He drops the subject to say how embarrassed he is that he makes so much more money than A. They made love this weekend and he learned afterward she didn't have any birth control: "I wonder if she'll become pregnant . . . probably not . . . she has this loose, vag- abond-type life, but she takes very good care of herself. She brought a whole set of hairbrushes down and spent hours brushing and groom- ing her hair." He turns to the analyst again. "Will I ever become like you . . . you're so successful? You must be making so much money now, why don't you see me for nothing? I want to make a lot of money too. When I was young and we were poor I wanted to become wealthy so that I could take care of my parents. . . . I want a greater closeness here, you're so distant. . . . I think I'll tell you another fantasy about my kid sister, then you can tell me I'm wrong."

At this point the analyst intervenes: "The kind of contact you want is as a dirty, messy boy who's wrong and out of control."

"The air is very stuffy in here. I'm finding it hard to breathe and I want the session to be over . . . isn't that a stain on the wall? I suppose you'll tell me to leave now . . . you do that and I'll punch you right in the nose. . . . I hate the way you control things around here. . . . I know, I want it to be that way but I hate it anyhow . . . you know, I kind of get the feeling that when I was very little my father would ask to wipe my ass after I shit . . . of course, I would refuse."

"Something of that sort is returning here now. You would wish for me to touch you that way; and when you imagined the bug in your hair and touched it with your hand, you were doing to yourself what you would forbid me to do."

"This is too much for me . . . I feel so defeated and hope- less . . . how am I ever going to figure this all out? I'm such a terrible patient. . ."

The example [Kovel tells us] is fairly representative of an analytic process in full swing—in other words, one for which some assessment can be made of the unconscious. The patient is associating fluidly, moving between past and present, transference and reality, self and other, and body and world. Enough resistance exists to provide dynamic tension and structure to the emergent fantasy, and not so much as to stifle it [1978, pp. 63–65].

A little later on Kovel elaborates (pp. 68–69):

. . . one can make a reasonable guess (allowing, to be sure, for the fact that in the real case much more corroboration would be needed) about the unconscious content of this material. It would not be hard to agree, for example, that:

a. The patient regards the analysis as something going on around the toilet bowl (he's a mess; he's afraid to talk about it; the air is stuffy; surfaces are stained).

b. He wishes the analyst (and his father) would wipe him (the intensity of the reaction denying same; his abject wish to be close to the analyst; the bug recollection and his need to touch his own hair to wipe it away again).

c. He sees himself as a woman-castrate *vis-à-vis* the analyst (and his father), and hopes to become pregnant anally by him (the evident identification with the girl-friend A through the cleanliness, the grooming, her poverty compared to him and his compared to the analyst; the concern with her pregnancy. . .).

That these truths cannot be apprehended more than intellectually (at this time, in any event) is revealed by his evident disorganization following this second interpretation. One might guess—and further acquaintance with this patient would tend to confirm—that the disorganization represents a suffusion of the self with qualities of the object. That is to say, instead of talking about the matters fecal and castrative, he becomes a messy castrate.

First of all, I must say that I have no idea why the analyst made the three formulations concerning the unconscious content. He seems not to be staying close to the patient's experience, nor can it be said that he is following the patient's emotional line. From the patient's report that he is a mess, the air is stuffy, etc., the analyst concludes that the patient regards the analysis as something going on around the toilet bowl. Perhaps so, but innumerable other interpretations of the very same material are possible, ones that are closer to what the patient may actually be experiencing at the time.

Second, the author's three formulations regarding the unconscious content are actually only very tentative hypotheses. Initially he speaks of them as "a reasonable guess"; then he says "it would not be hard to agree" with them. Finally, and with no further evidence for selecting these formulations from innumerable other possible ones, the author refers to them as "truths."

Third, the vignette demonstrates something that is typical of stereotyped approaches to psychoanalytic therapy: a striking reductionism wherein complex human experiences are reduced to clichés. I have no idea how or why the analyst equates the patient's apparent sense of disorganization with castration. Disorganization and confusion are very complicated human experiences, not at all easily reducible to anything that might legitimately be called "castration" experiences. Indeed, the words *castration* and *castration anxiety* are used so loosely in psychoanalysis as labels for so many different and unequatable experiences, that they have become, to my thinking, virtually meaningless.

Finally, and most important, there seems to be little genuine, related, empathic communication between patient and analyst. The patient does not give the impression of being an active, independent, thinking, working partner. The analyst seems to be seeing the patient as a collection of "unconscious" contents about which only the analyst has special knowledge and thereby knows the "truth." Most striking is that what sounds like the patient's legitimate confusion about the analyst's interpretations are merely interpreted, in turn, along the very same lines that seem to have confused and disorganized the patient in the first place.

Note that the patient feels defeated and hopeless directly after the analyst says something the patient clearly does not understand. But, as is typical of depressives, he blames himself for not understanding. He apparently cannot tell the analyst what he legitimately ought to be able to say, namely, that perhaps the analyst is out of touch with what is going on in him.

Similarly, when Greenson told his patient that she was running from her anger at men's penises and her disgust with her vagina

EXAMPLES FROM THE LITERATURE

when actually she was telling him of a global kind of hate, she seemed confused and reacted with anger and obvious self-depreciatory remarks: "I hate to feel stupid and sometimes you and this analysis make me so."

I have referred in my preface to my high regard for the work of Paul Diesing (1971). Diesing's interests have been in philosophy and the social sciences. His description of how a researcher studies a society shows a definite resemblance to the kind of thinking I am advocating for psychoanalysis, a kind of thinking that stands in sharp contrast to that of Greenson and Kovel. In the following remarks Diesing is describing case-study methods in the broad area of the social sciences—which includes psychoanalysis and psychotherapy, toward which Diesing is distinctly sympathetic. He writes:

> The participant observer and the clinician work their way into the system they are studying and try to become an active part of it in order to understand it from the inside. They conceptualize their knowledge in terms that the system members themselves use or could understand, though they also try to go beyond the understanding that system members have achieved. They test the objectivity of their knowledge in part by seeing whether it is intelligible and acceptable to system members, and in part by attempting to act on it and seeing whether their actions are understood and accepted in the system [p. 264]. . . .
> When the researcher's actions and responses are inappropriate from the standpoint of the subject, when they produce confusion and misunderstanding, the researcher is acting on premises that are different from those of the subject. . . .
> A clinician who is prevented from understanding his subject by inappropriate biases can still interact with him and produce changes, but he cannot explain or interpret the changes from the standpoint of the subject. Nor can he verify and correct his interpretations because of the difficulties of communication and rapport. Consequently, unless some other method of control and verification is used, his account of the changes cannot be reliable [p. 282].

Diesing's remarks support my view that case reports of the kind just given are questionable because the analyst's responses to the patient led to confusion and misunderstanding. To this I add that they are also questionable because of the self-depreciatory reactions they evoked.

Case Report By The Blancks

A case reported by Gertrude and Rubin Blanck (1974) is an excellent example of the stereotyped approach and is especially instructive because interspersed with the dialogue are comments revealing the thinking of the therapist.

The patient came for treatment because of excessive anxiety about her appearance. The therapist was a woman. In reality, according to the authors, the patient's appearance was satisfactory enough, but her overconcern with her hair, skin, and figure alerted the therapist to two levels of interrelated underlying causes for such excessive anxiety. First was the level of castration anxiety, but, in addition, it was felt that the presenting problem also encompassed a faulty body image, the elaboration of which antedated the phallic phase. The birth of a brother was felt to be crucial. Therefore, the following general hypothesis was formulated (pp. 319–320):

> "When you were a baby and compared yourself with your brother, you thought you were damaged. . . . You proceeded in your development to the point where every girl would prefer to have what a boy has. The next developmental step was hindered by earlier fears about the adequacy of your body. You are left with this doubly layered feeling of bodily inadequacy which causes continuous anxiety about your appearance."

The authors point out that the therapist's silent formulations are "hypotheses" and that the interpretation cannot be known without the patient's ongoing help and confirmation as each step toward the ultimate interpretation is taken. The authors also state that the analyst must be ready to alter or discard a hypothetical interpretation if the patient's responses fail to confirm it and lead to new hypotheses. These statements by the Blancks are certainly acceptable. Let us see whether they were followed in actual practice.

Before proceeding, however, I would point out that the analyst in this case apparently began treatment with a specific formulation, one based on a clinical theory, and on some of the initial complaints and history. She thereby of course automatically reduced her options and deprived the analytic process of its natural spontaneous unfolding.

The authors say that the therapist's hypothesis was "nearly, but not exactly, correct," and to "illustrate how the interpretation is made from the surface down to increasingly deeper levels" they reproduce some of the dialogue.

To the patient's remark that she felt she ought to see a dermatologist about her skin, the therapist replies: "You think constantly about your appearance because you are not sure that your body is always as it should be [p. 320]."

This response, according to the authors, is designed to begin a series of interpretations "which does not exclude the phallic but which is broad enough to cover feelings about the more basic issue of body image [p. 320]" preceding the phallic. But the heuristic therapist would wonder why the phallic or any other theme is being pushed when so little is known. We have absolutely no idea why the patient is seeing a dermatologist, and there is therefore no justification for immediately assuming concern on the part of the patient about her appearance. The patient might have any of a number of motives for going to a dermatologist, and only by making reasonable inquiries of the patient can one get any true idea about what may be going on. She may be going for itchiness, allergy, venereal disease, or even for a lump she fears is cancerous. In brief, there are many more possibilities here other than the one selected by the therapist, and the discovery of any of these other possible motives could lead the therapeutic work into any number of directions. If the patient reported anxiety about skin cancer, the direction of therapeutic work might proceed toward anxieties about death and aging. What is important to note here is that the therapist's selection of the issue of appearance is based on the initial formulation and is tendentiously directed along the lines of that formulation.

Patient: Sometimes I think I look better than at other times.
Therapist: You are not always certain that your body is the same.

Patient: I did not know much about my body when I was a child.
Therapist: Where was your curiosity [p. 320]?

The authors tell us that this question was asked both to encourage curiosity and to elicit historical material. Thus the therapist learned that there was no attempt to masturbate.

Patient: I always feel there is something wrong [p. 321].

The authors tell us that the therapist preferred to deal with this "classical phallic statement" slowly because more prephallic material had first to be interpreted. Again, the therapist is making an unsubstantiated assumption. I do not know why the patient's feeling that "there is something wrong" is a classical phallic statement. A patient can feel that "something is wrong" for virtually an infinite number of reasons, and the only way to get some reasonable understanding of what is going on is to inquire of the patient and get "free associations" and the full informational context. But here too, the "understanding" of the therapist is tendentiously directed by the initial stereotyped formulation.

After asking the patient if she had noticed her mother's body changing in pregnancy and receiving the compliant reply, "Well, I must have but I don't remember that,"

Therapist: But you often worry about gaining weight.
Patient: I had a dream last night. I was going on a trip abroad. You
           were the tour director. You divided us into two groups—
           experienced travelers and novices. You put all the men in
           the superior group.
Therapist: You feel I value men more?
Patient: Yes, men are always more admired.
Therapist: They have something more to be looked at.
Patient: Oh, you mean a penis [pp. 321–322].

The authors say (p. 321) that "a dream, presented following an intervention, confirms that the intervention is correct in content and timing." I know of no evidence for this statement; it is inconsistent with clinical dream theory, and I find it incomprehensible. They state further that the dream is more on the phallic than on the broader level of body image, again a statement I do not understand. We have no associations to the dream, and it has always been a cardinal principle of psychoanalytic therapy that dreams generally cannot be understood without associations.

What is striking about this case is that, although the authors speak of hypotheses and the need for confirmation, in actuality the therapist did not treat the initial formualtion as a hypothesis for which evidence may or may not be forthcoming. It was treated essentially as a frame of reference to be imposed on the patient, as a belief system into which the patient was subtly indoctrinated. Alternative possible understandings of the data were not considered; and repeated assumptions were made with minimal or no evidence but based on the initially assumed frame of reference or belief system. In addition to the assumption that the patient saw a dermatologist because she was concerned about her appearance were the further assumptions that when the patient said "there is something wrong" she was referring to something phallic and the unconfirmed assumption that prephallic material has to be interpreted before phallic material. When the patient can do little with the issue of mother's bodily changes during pregnancy, the therapist reminds her about her concern about gaining weight, implicitly assuming that any concern about weight gain must have to do with mother's body changes. Finally, when the subject arises of men always being more admired, and the therapist refers to their having something more to be looked at, the dutiful patient, by now apparently thoroughly indoctrinated into the therapist's system, comes up with the to-be-expected intellectualized cliché about a penis.

The material presented offers very little evidence that any analytic process existed which can lead to discovery, one wherein individual meanings emerge, and the patient is actually a working partner, fully experiencing what is being verbalized and able to confirm or refute interpretations offered to her. The case appears to be typical of what I have called stereotyped approaches wherein the "answers" are thought to be known from the very beginning and the task of the analysis is essentially to "interpret" the presenting material until the patient comes to recognize the "truth" of the assumed answers.

Nor do the authors comment about the patient's dream wherein the therapist is identified as "the tour director" and the patient as a "novice." We have no associations to the dream and cannot therefore say what this may have meant to the patient, but the session reported does sound as though the patient was taken on a "tour" of the initial stereotyped formulation, with the therapist directing and pointing out the sights of the belief system to the inexperienced "novice."

Case Report By Arlow

A psychoanalyst who has had considerable influence in psychoanalysis is Jacob Arlow. Much of his writing demonstrates what I am calling a stereotyped approach. Arlow, for example (1963, p. 17), writes:

> . . . a young woman secretly in love with her employer developed agoraphobia when she discovered that he was engaged to be married. She also suffered from intense claustrophobia in certain shops. This symptom could be traced to her anxiety over an impulse to steal. Both the agoraphobia and the anxiety over the temptation to steal, upon analysis, prove to have been derived from a phantasy of forcibly seizing and stealing the phallus. This phantasy had its origin during the sixth year of the patient's life, shortly after the death of her father. She had responded to his death with intense feelings of disappointment, thinking that now that he was gone she could never realize her expectation of getting the phallus-child from him. She accordingly would have to take independent and violent action on her own. The engagement of the employer was more than the rupture of a libidinal tie. It constituted a confirmation by reality of her earlier disappointment in phantasy. The employer, now lost to her forever, was bestowing his phallus upon some rival. This situation not only reactivated her furious determination to get what she wanted, it also weakened the opposition of the superego to such a wish, inasmuch as the patient felt righteously aggrieved.

In this instance the findings are reported in nonspecific, jargon-laden terms remote from clinical experience and language so that the patient's individuality is largely lost to view. No evidence is given for the findings, nor do we learn anything about the analytic process that may have generated them, although Arlow is describing how neurotic symptoms are precipitated when a patient is confronted with a situation containing elements that were supposedly present in the original traumatic situation.

What stands out in this report, in which the dynamic formulation centers exclusively around genital conflicts, phallic wishes, and the like, is the apparent abandonment of what we know about human experience. We might with some justification call it an abandonment of "common sense." Thus, the reaction of a child to the death of a parent is subtle, complex, profound, with innumerable consequences; and there are well-known typical kinds of reactions to death as well as highly individualized ones. Yet, of all of these possible reactions—known to both analysts and nonanalysts—Arlow reports only on disappointed phallic longings, an idea that seems to fit in neatly with the stereotyped theme central to his case report. Arlow does not tell us how he arrived at his findings, but one can reasonably suspect that, here too, a highly tendentious analysis was conducted, one in accordance with Arlow's position stated elsewhere in the same paper (p. 22): "Because a considerable degree of ego development is necessary for the structuring of intrapsychic conflict, the basis of symptom formation in the psychoneurosis is to be found rather late in the period of infantile sexuality." Arlow seems to use a theoretical consideration not as a hypothesis about clinical data for which evidence may or may not be forthcoming but as a reference point from which to draw conclusions about data, an approach that can easily lead to an oversimplification and even a distortion of the clinical material.

Case Report By Brenner

Charles Brenner has also had considerable influence in psychoanalysis. Brenner is not oblivious to the significance of confirmation of interpretations or analytic conjectures, and he discusses these issues at length (1976). An examination of this discussion sheds considerable light on stereotyped appoaches. One could hardly argue with much of what Brenner, in the following, has to say about the nature of theory and hypotheses:

> . . . the word "interpretation" will refer to what an analyst tells his patient about his psychic conflicts, while the word "conjecture" will be used to refer to an analyst's formulation in his own mind of what he has learned about a patient's psychic conflicts [p. 36].
>
> Conjectures, then, are the hypotheses that an analyst develops, whether consciously or unconsciously, to explain the nature and origin of the conflicts that determine what he has learned of his patient's mental functioning and mental development. They are an analyst's explanation of why a patient is the sort of person he is and why he behaves and talks as he does . . . [p. 39].
>
> Insofar as the aim of psychoanalysis is self-knowledge, all analysts agree that it is himself that each patient must learn to know, not what he has in common with the rest of mankind.
>
> It follows then that psychoanalysts, like other scientists, must have some way of putting their conjectures to the test. They must have some means of deciding whether a conjecture is valid or not, whether they have guessed correctly about a patient or whether their conjecture must be revised, expanded, or even abandoned in favor of a different conjecture [p. 41].
>
> Proof of a psychoanalytic conjecture, like proof of any hypothesis, theory, or law in natural science, means accumulation of supporting evidence [p. 42].
>
> The fact that an analyst has reached a conjecture intuitively does not guarantee its correctness. . . . Validating evidence must be sought elsewhere [p. 43].

Let us now compare Brenner's comments on hypotheses and confirmation with his actual practice. Here is a case report he offers (1976, pp. 150–152) as evidence to show that the analysis of a conflict results in the disappearance of a symptom.

> . . . a woman in her thirties was anxious while flying in an airplane. She complained particularly of the fact that, should something go wrong, she was just a passenger. There was no way she could get to

the controls and try to save the situation. Not that she could fly a plane herself. She had no experience whatever as a pilot. But the feeling of being unable even to get to the controls was somehow associated with great anxiety whenever she let herself dwell on it. Her further associations included the fact that on one occasion when she flew in a small, private plane she experienced no anxiety. She attributed this to the fact that there was at least a possibility for her "to do something" if necessary in a small plane, where she sat in the cockpit.

The nub of this patient's major conflicts was the fact that her younger sibling, her junior by four years, was a boy, while she "just a girl." She was partly furiously jealous, partly hopelessly dejected, and constantly guilty in consequence of what she unconsciously considered to be her castrated, inferior state. If one knows what the controls of an aircraft look like, it is easy to guess that for this patient, to sit at the controls of a plane with the control stick—which, incidentally, is colloquially known to pilots as the "joy stick," i.e., the penis—between her legs unconsciously gratified her wish to have a penis herself. Her conscious thought about being unable to get to the controls was understandable as the derivative or representative of two closely related unconscious ideas. The one was that if she were a man, if she had a penis, everything would be fine. She wouldn't have to be upset, because there would be no danger of anything terrible happening. The other unconscious idea was a wish to kill and castrate her brother, and, for that matter, her father as well, a wish that frightened her very much. To put things more connectedly, her symptom could be understood as follows. To fly a plane symbolized for the patient being a man with a penis. Being "just a passenger" symbolized being "just a girl," inferior and castrated. The anxiety she felt corresponded to the dangers—punishment and retributive genital injury—associated with her jealous, murderous, and castrative wishes, wishes that were stimulated whenever she had to be a passenger, while some man with that big stick between his legs flew the plane. . . . A complete accurate statement of her symptom would be that whenever she had to fly with nothing between her legs while a young man with whom she had no personal contact sat with a big stick between his legs and was the boss of the whole venture, she became anxious. When, however, she sat next to the man in charge, with something between her legs as well, she wasn't a bit frightened.

First, a comment on what Brenner has to say concerning the controls of a small plane. I consulted a friend who has been flying small planes for many years. Brenner's description of the controls of a small airplane are accurate for planes that were flown many years ago. In the past 20 years it would be most unlikely, although not totally out of the question, that any small plane in which the patient may have flown would have had controls of the type Brenner mentions. What is significant here is that Brenner gives no indication that he learned anything *from the patient* about the nature of the controls.

In general, it is hard to accept Brenner's dynamic formulations in light of what is known of the complexity of human psychological phenomena. Fears of flying and the whole issue of the need to be in control are extremely complicated, multidetermined phenomena. Brenner reduces the patient's symptom picture to a standard cliché based on his ideas about what the controls of the plane looked like— a guess that conforms with his clinical orientation, a guess for which no confirmation is given. Indeed, we have little idea of how exactly the patient experienced the plane or how she may have viewed the controls. We know only that she felt more comfortable in the small plane. Furthermore, we are told nothing about the nature of the therapeutic process; we know nothing about what the patient thought about Brenner's "guess." Brenner's presentation eliminates all other possible interpretations of the fear of flying and the need to feel in control. It is entirely possible that, by superimposing his own ideas about the controls of the plane, by not finding out what the "controls" meant to the patient, Brenner lost much significant material and held the case at the artificial level dictated by his simplistic clinical theories.

Brenner also tells us (pp. 151–152) that at the time she first told of her fear of flying, the patient was hardly conscious of jealousy of her brother, much less of being angry at him and wanting to have his penis for herself. Brenner also adds that, as analysis progressed, she became more aware of the various elements of her penis envy. Perhaps so, but because details are not given, we cannot evaluate Brenner's comments. Even the disappearance of the fear of flying, which Brenner also reports, does not necessarily confirm that the symptom was understood and correctly analyzed. Symptom disappearance is also a complicated issue. Symptoms can disappear even before treatment begins and before anything is understood (see the case of Mrs. A., for example).

I return now to Brenner's discussion of the issue of validation or confirmation in psychoanalysis (1976, pp. 43–45). He writes:

> The evidence that is most often used to validate a conjecture and that has the broadest range of possibilities for doing so is that which derives from a patient's response to a conjecture when it is put to him as an interpretation by his analyst. Even if it has not been put to him as an interpretation, however, a patient may confirm a conjecture by what he says (and does) spontaneously after the conjecture has been formulated. For example, the suicidal patient who was mentioned in the previous chapter behaved, at a certain stage of his analysis, differently on Monday and Tuesday than he did later in the week. It was my conjecture that this was so because he missed me over the weekend. Before I interpreted this to him, though, I waited a couple of weeks for confirmation of my conjecture by repetition of his behavior. Only after this was forthcoming was an interpretation of his behavior offered to him.
>
> This sort of confirmation might be described as repetition of the evidence on which the conjecture was based in the first place. It would make little difference to the course of analysis whether such a conjecture is consciously formed now or a week or two from now. In some cases evidence confirmatory of a conjecture may turn up in a patient's associations only after months or years. In one case, for example, a young man's competitive activities, vocational as well as avocational, were severely inhibited by fears of being humiliated by his opponents or competitors both verbally and physically. It was not till after this had been interpreted to him many times with many different examples, however, that the conjecture that he feared castration in particular was confirmed by a memory from late adolescence. He remembered thinking to himself at that age that he could probably be a superlatively successful student if his balls were cut off so that sexual wishes and masturbation didn't interrupt him when he wanted to study.

Let us start by considering Brenner's first important point. Noticing that a patient may behave differently on Monday and Tuesday is reasonable to observe and to call to a patient's attention. The conjecture or hypothesis that the patient behaved differently on these days because he missed his analyst is also reasonable and plausible.

But the repetition of the altered behavior does not constitute confirmation of the conjecture or the hypothesis. The repetition of altered behavior only confirms the hypothesis that the phenomenon tends to be repeated; it does not confirm the causal hypothesis implicit in Brenner's conjecture. The ancients observed repeated sunsets, but the daily repetition of this phenomenon confirmed only the hypothesis that this phenomenon tended to be repeated; it did not confirm a hypothesis that sunsets are caused by divine intervention.

What is especially important about Brenner's remarks is that his clinical hypotheses can never be subject to refutation—a state of affairs that is totally inconsistent with his statements about science and hypotheses. Most, but not all, phenomena that are of interest and that are studied tend to repeat. If the mere repetition of a given phenomenon becomes confirmation for an explanatory hypothesis about it and is even called "evidence," then every hypothesis becomes automatically confirmed by the very existence of the phenomenon the hypothesis is supposed to explain. If Brenner's ideas about the nature of confirmation are generally accepted, then we can well understand one important reason why stereotyped approaches have continued unchanged and uncorrected throughout the history of psychoanalytic therapy.

Turning to Brenner's second important point: He tells us that in some cases evidence confirmatory of a conjecture may turn up in a patient's associations only after months or years. He tells us of a case where only after repeated interpretations of fear of castration were made did confirmation emerge for this conjecture in the form of a memory from late adolescence (although the confirming memory that Brenner reports was a wish for castration, whereas the analytic material being dealt with had to do with fears of castration).

Let me begin with a simple analogy. If a patient has recurrent severe lung disease in adult life, we do not say that we have evidence for its being the common cold when we learn that the patient had frequent common colds in late adolescence. To mention only one important reason, the common cold is universal and we can therefore attribute little significance to the patient's early history. Of course, if the patient reported an early history of tuberculosis, even though the adult illness is not explained by this fact, we now have some significant, possibly relevant, information that deserves attention because tuberculosis of the lung is not universal and can recur.

By the same token, do we truly know something significant about a patient's adult pathological manifestations if we find that he expressed some castration wish or fear in late adolescence? Is it not extremely common, if not universal, to hear of adolescents, struggling with sexual stirrings and having trouble concentrating on their studies, reporting a castration wish during a moment of despair? What seems of greater significance for the whole issue of confirmation is something Brenner does not tell us. What did he do with the patient in the period—perhaps months or years—when he repeatedly interpreted the patient's castration fears? What made Brenner sure of his path? Did he, as the first discussant of the case of Mrs. A. advised, simply interpret on the basis of his clinical theory until the patient stopped resisting? If he did, it is hard to reconcile such a procedure with the ideas about science, hypotheses, and confirmation Brenner mentioned earlier.

I know of several patients who were for months hammered with interpretations that they did not understand until they finally submitted and came up with exactly the kinds of memories and associations they knew the analyst wanted to hear. I saw one young man in treatment who was desperate enough to deliberately falsify his associations to a dream because he had no other way of dealing with his former therapist, who expressed constant dissatisfaction with the course of treatment because oedipal material was not forthcoming. When the therapist heard the obvious oedipal material, his reaction, as reported by the patient, was, "Good, now we are getting somewhere." From what I knew of this therapist from other sources, I had reason to believe that the patient's report was basically accurate.

If we work and formulate constantly with concepts such as "castration anxiety," "penis envy," "Oedipus complex"—concepts characteristic of current stereotyped work—and if we take any memory, even one that occurs months or years later, as confirmatory of the original formulation, how can we fail to "confirm" our original formulations? After all, if we wait long enough, sooner or later we will almost always find something that can be made to fit one of these stereotypes. Possibly this automatic, inevitable confirmation of hypotheses points to another important reason why much of current clinical theory has remained unaltered and unchanged for so long in psychoanalytic therapy.

Case Report By Greenacre

The final vignette to be discussed is actually an analysis by Phyllis Greenacre of the painter Piet Mondrian. In the wealth of detail presented and in her great awareness of and sensitivity to the impact of early life events, Greenacre differs sharply from most psychoanalytic writers. Yet, a careful reading and rereading of the material to be discussed reveals some characteristics typical of the stereotyped approach. The following is an abstract of the ideas Greenacre presents. I have quoted and paraphrased her extensively in order that her ideas can be studied in their context.

The discussion of Mondrian is part of a paper titled "The Primal Scene and the Sense of Reality" (Greenacre, 1973) wherein Greenacre presents "some aspects of the influence of the primal scene on the development and functioning of the sense of reality. These become evident in certain circumscribed distortions of external reality and especially in the creation and persistence of specific illusions [p. 10]." Her ideas are based on her "own clinical experience, supplemented by the clinical reports of others and the findings of many colleagues who have done systematic work in studying the behavior of infants [p. 10]."

She concludes:

The primal scene and related experiences have pervasive effects on a child's later life and character, especially in shaping the manifestations of both sexual and aggressive drives. The effects are powerful in the first months of life when the infant's separation from the mother is scant and the primal scene is apt to be a most intimate and repetitive experience.

Disturbances in the sense of reality are more specific and differentiated during the second year when rapid maturational changes produce drastic shifts in the infant's contact with the outer world, resulting in disturbances and contradictions in his perceptions. The primal scene may then be an overwhelming experience in its strangeness, arousing infantile reactions of loneliness, alienation, or of feeling overwhelmed, accompanied by changes in the state of consciousness. Under other, less severely bewildering conditions, it excites acute and primitive jealousy to the point of infantile rage.

Defense by primitive denial is then set in motion. . . . Together with the defense of isolation, denial forms the basis of tenacious walls of containment which both support and restrict the developing character of neurosis [pp. 39–40].

Greenacre (p. 26) speaks of denial so strong that it forms "walls of defense" which may take on various forms. "But the wall, in whatever form, is built to restrain wildness, to hold in check impulses felt as though of murderous rage or nearly uncontrollable sexual impulses. These, probably generally, are more explicitly expressed in masturbation fantasies, which are in turn feared [p. 34]."

"The life and work of Piet Mondrian," according to Greenacre, "present another form of the wall, modified in an extraordinary way in accord with the demands of this talented artist." Greenacre's "facts" pertinent to her study come from different sources, including the painter's own writings and his art.

Mondrian became an artist at age 14 "and from then on pursued his course with a single-minded devotion to the goal of purifying his vision, to free it from all subjectivity of emotion. He started out as a realist. . . . But he passionately hated motion of any kind and found people in action the most disturbing of all." He therefore stopped painting them. He loved flowers, but they had to be painted singly, not in relation to one another. Trees he painted at first singly and stately, but later "they appeared with twisted and tortured limbs, as though arrested in a state of agonized motion [p. 34]." Even the ever-changing sea and sky suggested more motion than he could tolerate.

Greenacre (p. 35) tells us that Mondrian

stated that he saw with realist eyes past beauty or (ordinary) reality of man, and that pure reality must be painted without the infiltration of *any* subjective feelings or conceptions. Since particular form and natural color evoke subjectivity, he felt he must reduce his pictures to the elements of form and primary color alone. Ultimately he felt that the only really constant relationship is expressed in the right angle; that the two fundamental forces of nature are expressed in the horizontal and the vertical meeting in the perfect right angle. . . . He was

clearly eradicating the family circle and any of the comforting round-
ed forms of life and human contact. It is not hard to see that he must
have felt the danger of an overwhelming force of aggression in himself
and the need of strong containing walls both in life and in his
painting.

Mondrian began to paint brick walls, but later the small right
angle of the joinings, which at first only stood out like little crosses,
became prominent in his paintings. Next, the crosses became rectangles of different size and distribution, "each enclosing its own
primary color." Mondrian

is said to have spent hours arranging and rearranging these to form a
pattern which would have absolute balance. . . . This search for per-
fection in both expression and strong containment of the primordial
forces progressed through various stages until it reached the composi-
tions of infinitely precise rectangular form, for which the painter
became famous in his later years [p. 35]. . . .

His paintings seemed to reflect, to an unusual degree, what was
going on in his own attempt to live. There was an increasing effort to
extricate himself from particular personal relationships and to live in
a perfectly balanced cosmic harmony. . . . He insistently fled from
motion and emotion as though these were the devils of darkness. . . .

Mondrian was a rebel in a life-long struggle with his father, who is
described as a sententious tyrant, a Calvinist schoolmaster who wished
his son to become a teacher. . . . [Mondrian] was an amiable young
man, markedly shy with women. His appearance was arresting partly
because of his large luminous eyes which were prominent in photo-
graphs and in self-portraits. He was then obsessionally worried about
possible blindness. . . [p. 36].

There were two breakthroughs of wildness in behavior. On one
occasion he leaped into the sea from a high overhanging cliff. The
other eruption, which was repeated several times, was his destroying, by shooting, of self-portraits that displeased him.

He was generally an ascetic, though he knew many women and
had compulsive infatuations which never lasted. He was fond of
dancing and "when he was approaching sixty and had begun to take

dancing lessons, he would pick out the prettiest girl on the dance floor, but was as stiff as a ramrod, attempting only vertical and horizontal movements [p. 38]." He apparently favored the Charleston which, in contrast to erotic dances, he considered a "sporting dance" because the partners did not touch each other and spent so much time and energy doing and keeping track of the steps that they could have no time for thoughts of sex.

Although Greenacre's speculations or hypotheses seem reasonable enough, alternative interpretations of the data are also possible. Perhaps, as Greenacre (p. 35) writes, "It is not hard to see that he must have felt the danger of an overwhelming force of aggression in himself and the need of strong containing walls both in life and in his painting." But it is equally possible that he may have had a great fear of dissolution and disorganization, the possible consequence of massive trauma, experiences that are not at all the same as an "overwhelming force of aggression."

But let me turn to the last paragraph of Greenacre's discussion to see how she attempts to bring her facts and hypotheses into line with her original basic primal-scene hypothesis. She writes [pp. 38–39]:

> Obviously, this is the story of a talented man who had from childhood struggled against both sexual and aggressive drives. Nor is this strange when one considers that probably from his earliest years he suffered from extreme stimulation. For he was the oldest of five children born to the sternest of Calvinistic fathers, who was a headmaster in the school. The children came in about ten years and there was every chance that this oldest child had multiple primal scene experiences as well as awareness of the birth of the younger siblings, certainly a situation which inevitably would compound oedipal jealousy, and sibling jealousy and envy. His symptoms themselves bespoke the extremest sensitization to movement and noise; his infantile anger was expressed in his wish to keep all objects, whether animate or inanimate, separated from each other. Not even flowers should be seen with intertwined stems. He seemed to have taken into his body the multiple and unorganized as well as rhythmic motion around him, and to have attempted to convert it into a cosmic rhythm which would be perfect and eternal, and to project this in his painting. His fascination with dancing with his whole body in a state of stiff erectness

proclaimed, unknown to him, the displacement of genitality to the total body self. He was ultimately unable to live according to the art form he had created, in which motion and emotion would be walled safely into rectangles. But he had only a brief period of freedom before he died.

Without qualifying her remarks Greenacre writes that Mondrian's "dancing with his whole body in a state of stiff erectness proclaimed, unknown to him, the displacement of genitality to the total body self." How can Greenacre know this? The only way whereby we could get even some tentative evidence for such an assertion would be if some analytic process existed, or if we knew something about Mondrian's experience while dancing, or if there was some good evidence from other related and relevant case material on the artist. But none of these conditions exist, at least as far as we know. Greenacre is here merely attributing arbitrary stereotyped meanings to externally observed phenomena, losing thereby the essence of clinical psychoanalysis, which deals with inner subjective experience, the thoughts, fantasies, and feelings of a particular person. Dancing in a stiff, erect position can have innumerable meanings; indeed the different meanings can change over time.

But more important, what connection is there between extreme stimulation of a primal-scene nature and being the oldest of five children born to a stern Calvinist father whose children were born within about 10 years? Why do such family conditions make for any more stimulation of a primal-scene nature than other family constellations? On this issue Greenacre is silent.

Greenacre has taken an interesting set of data—Mondrian's special artistic style—and collapsed it into a stereotyped, familiar formula. In truth, Greenacre knew very little about Mondrian's inner life or has told us very little. We know virtually nothing about his early experiences. His mother is not even mentioned. We understand little if anything about his fear of blindness, something one should be very curious about in this man. What Mondrian tried to do in his paintings, at the level of "observable" or "manifest" phenomena, was undoubtedly accurately portrayed by Greenacre, for instance, his attempt to free his paintings of emotion and subjectivity, his apparent intolerance of motion. But these phenomena are consistent with many personal meanings and could have had their origins in innumerable and very different infantile circumstances. And the data given us in no way justify any exclusive focusing on primal-scene trauma as the primary or sole cause. Alternative explanations are possible, and one can quite reasonably suggest that primal-scene trauma may not have been significant at all in Mondrian's case and that perhaps other traumata were, but we know nothing of these from the data at hand.

What is especially interesting is that Greenacre is quite aware of the full range of infantile traumata. Indeed, in this very paper, she speaks of early significant traumata in addition to that of witnessing the primal scene:

> those which have involved estrangement from or loss of one parent or the other very early; and those which are associated with overwhelming violence to the infant's own body. Among the latter I would include operations, whether with or without anesthetic, febrile illnesses with deliria, and even the attacks on the infant's body through the use of repeated enemas [p. 26].

I most certainly agree with Greenacre on these issues, and I would add a further very significant trauma: rearing by grossly disturbed—alcoholic, psychotic, depressed—parents. Nor is this list exhaustive. What is significant here is that all of these traumatic states can conceivably lead to massive and overwhelming frustration, rage, and anger—massive stimulation—with consequent severe complex pathological consequences: problems in reality testing, learning, body imagery, object relations. Any of these traumata can conceivably leave a residue of massive anxiety, a feeling of tenuousness about oneself and the world, an overwhelming feeling of helplessness, hopelessness, loneliness, alienation, confusion, a sense of depersonalization and derealization, and a feeling of not being alive (as with Mrs. A., for example). All of these types of traumata can apparently lay the foundation for severe sexual disturbances of many kinds. Finally, and especially important in the case of Mondrian where visual issues are so prominent, there is good reason to believe that visual and perceptual pathology may occur in many states of high anxiety and overwhelming panic, whatever the initiating cause. Edvard Munch's famous painting, "The Scream," gives eloquent testimony to perceptual distortions of oneself and the outer world in states of extreme pain, anguish, and total panic.

Greenacre may be right about Mondrian and the significance of primal-scene trauma in his life. She may also be correct about the significance she attributes to primal-scene trauma in general. But she adduces virtually no meaningful evidence from her study of Piet Mondrian to support her basic theme.

I think the only correct position about Mondrian one can take on the basis of the material Greenacre presents is that, as analysts, we are certainly interested in his unique painting style, but we do not know enough about the man's personal history and inner life to say what the deeply personal meanings, motivations, and historical determinants of this style might be.

3 General Characteristics of Stereotyped Approaches

Before listing some of the general characteristics of stereotyped approaches, I must emphasize once again that I see Freudian therapy as a spectrum of processes. When I characterize the stereotyped approaches I am attempting to characterize one broad segment of the spectrum. No given treatment process or case report can demonstrate all of the characteristics to be mentioned, just as no given treatment process or case report can reveal all of the characteristics of the heuristic approaches to be discussed later. It should be mentioned that a given treatment process may reveal characteristics of different parts of the spectrum of processes. To state my point somewhat differently: I am fully aware that the "purely stereotyped" analyst no more exists than does the "purely heuristic" analyst. The basic purpose of the following list of characteristics is to facilitate discussion, merely part of an effort to understand and specify the different approaches subsumed under the name of Freudian.

Finally, and of great importance, as I emphasized in the introduction to this book, there is a fundamental difference between *psychoanalytic clinical theory* and a *theory of the psychoanalytic therapeutic process*. The latter is the focus of this work, and the characteristics to be discussed all refer to the psychoanalytic process. Because of his role as founder of psychoanalysis, Freud's clinical theories have formed the basis for most stereotyped approaches. I therefore discuss the characteristics of the stereotyped psychoanalytic process in the context of Freud's "classical" clinical theories. But any psychoanalytic clinical theory can become the basis for stereotyped processes. *The principal characteristics of stereotyped psychoanalytic processes are the same regardless of the clinical theory on which they are based.*

(1) Typically, and of fundamental importance, those who work in a stereotyped manner believe that they understand the case almost completely from the outset. Large-scale formulations are made very early. The primary aim is to fit the case into the clinical theory that forms the basis for the early formulations. Meanings are in large part assumed rather than discovered.

(2) The psychoanalytic process is viewed as an attempt to get the patient to understand the initial formulation. To carry this out, although the patient is asked to "free associate," data presented by the patient are all too often selectively filtered for whatever may fit the formulation, or else the data are merely forced or collapsed into the formulation. A tendentious approach is taken, and alternative possible interpretations of the presenting data are neglected and may not even be recognized. The "analysis" or therapeutic process is often reduced to a process of subtle indoctrination.

(3) The patient's failure to understand the analyst or to accept what he says is viewed as resistance. This resistance, in turn, tends to be understood and interpreted along the lines of the very formulation the patient did not understand in the first place. Or else resistance is understood or interpreted in terms of still another formulation that is questionable in itself and if offered to the patient would probably also not be understood (see the case report of the first discussant of the case of Mrs. A.). Most important is the fact that the patient's objections to an interpretation tend not to be seen as having any intrinsic legitimacy.

(4) There is a striking tendency for the stereotyped therapist to believe that he possesses an understanding of the "truth"; that he has a privileged awareness of the nature of the patient's "deep unconscious." Tolerance of uncertainty and ambiguity is not a hallmark of his work. He tends to present formulations dogmatically. Although he will often say that interpretations are little more than hypotheses and that the clinical theory is likewise only a body of general hypotheses, in actual practice, interpretations are all too often treated as facts and clinical theory is all too often treated as unequivocal truth, as scientifically established clinical law.

(5) The issue of evidence is of little significance. The awareness or understanding of the need for constraints on thinking, of check-points to substantiate ideas is minimal. All too often, to demon-strate a given thesis, one questionable, unsubstantiated assumption is merely added to other equally questionable and unsubstantiated assumptions.

(6) The stereotyped worker tends to think (and write), not in terms of the patient's experience, but in highly intellectualized jar-gon, in clichés based on supposedly "true" clinical theory. I refer here to the endlessly repeated "castration anxiety," "Oedipus com-plex," "sadomasochism," "sibling rivalry," "homosexuality," "penis envy," "primal-scene trauma," and the like—all concepts deriving directly from the clinical theories of Freud. Furthermore, those who work with Freud's clinical theories in a stereotyped process tend to view case material almost solely from the standpoint of later stages of development. Preverbal experiences and environmental factors such as early infantile or later childhood trauma from illnesses or from parental personality are seen as significant only insofar as they have influenced oedipal development.

The tendency to think in clichés is associated with a reduc-tionism: simplistic, limited, cliché-ridden meanings are attributed to highly complex phenomena, which may actually have multiple meanings that change over time.

Also associated with the dominance of clichés is a looseness and nonspecificity of thinking. Clinical theoretical terms are used in so many different ways and in so many disparate contexts that they tend to lose meaning. For example, the term, "castration anxiety" is employed to refer to so many different kinds of experiences that it is hard to know what it signifies. (Some colleagues insisted on seeing the extreme anxiety of Mrs. A. as "castration anxiety.")

Clinical theory as it is used in stereotyped work has an im-poverishing effect on the treatment situation. Inasmuch as the pri-mary focus is a limited body of (supposedly) established clinical theory, individual experiences are viewed essentially as exemplify-ing this theory. The full richness and vividness of individual experi-ences are lost; the specific complicated pattern of events that deter-mine individual meanings is not discovered.

(7) The patient has a minimal role in establishing the truth of what may be going on or in what may have happened to him. Gener-

ally the patient is not viewed as an equal working partner, capable of confirming, revising, or refuting suggested interpretations, capable of evaluating what he hears, and fully capable of arriving at insights independently—indeed, often more capable than the analyst at arriving at insights. Because of the failure to view the patient as a working partner, it is impossible to know from reports of stereotyped work what the analysis or therapeutic process may actually have meant to the patient. The "true" meaning may have no relationship at all to the jargon-laden formulations presented about the case.

(8) Although often thought of as "classical" and Freudian, stereotyped approaches all too often abandon some of the basic tenets of Freudian thinking. Formulations are made about dreams, for example, even in the absence of associations.

(9) Built into stereotyped approaches are innumerable circular, self-confirming hypotheses in which refutation has no place. There is generally no true place for any process leading to discovery. As a result, stereotyped approaches have not progressed very far in many years. Stereotyped workers find only the known and the familiar. Their case reports endlessly repeat the same basic themes, with only minor elaborations and variations.

As a result of the repetitive practice of stereotyped approaches with their intrinsic circular reasoning wherein the existing clinical theory stemming from Freud is automatically and of necessity constantly being "reconfirmed," a body of clinical theory has been built up that is deemed to be "classical" and characteristically "Freudian." But it is very difficult to evaluate the validity of this theory because the processes used to support it have been so faulty.

Heinz Kohut's psychology of the self, one of the most stimulating and controversial developments of the past decade, has challenged "classical" psychoanalytic thinking. In an attempt to ascertain whether Kohut was proposing changes in psychoanalytic clinical theory or in the theory of the psychoanalytic process, I am confining my discussion to his 1979 paper, "The Two Analyses of Mr. Z," because it is there that one gets the clearest picture of Kohut vis-à-vis the analytic process. This paper is particularly interesting and instructive because in it Kohut tells us how he changed course in

midstream—a most unusual procedure for any experienced analyst
to adopt. Kohut writes (p. 5):

> The theme that was most conspicuous during the first year of the
> analysis was that of a regressive mother transference, particularly as
> it was associated with the patient's narcissism, i.e. as we then saw it,
> with his unrealistic, deluded grandiosity and his demands that the
> psychoanalytic situation should reinstate the position of exclusive
> control, of being admired and catered to by a doting mother who—a
> reconstruction with which I confronted the patient many times—had,
> in the absence of siblings who would have constituted preoedipal
> rivals and, during a crucial period of his childhood, in the absence of a
> father who would have been the oedipal rival, devoted her total atten-
> tion to the patient. For a long time the patient opposed these in-
> terpretations with intense resistances. He blew up in rages against
> me, time after time—indeed the picture he presented during the first
> year and a half of the analysis was dominated by his rage. These
> attacks arose either in response to my interpretations concerning his
> narcissistic demands and his arrogant feelings of 'entitlement' or be-
> cause of such unavoidable frustrations as weekend interruptions, oc-
> casional irregularities in the schedule, or, especially, my vacations. In
> the last-mentioned instances, it might be added, the patient also re-
> acted with depression accompanied by hypochondriacal preoccupa-
> tions and fleeting suicidal thoughts. After about a year and a half, he
> rather abruptly became much calmer and his insistent assertion that
> his anger was justified because I did not understand him lessened
> conspicuously. When I remarked approvingly on the change and said
> that the working through of his narcissistic delusions was now bear-
> ing fruit, the patient rejected this explanation, but in a friendly and
> calm manner. . . .
>
> The centre of the analytic stage was from then on occupied, on the
> one hand, by transference phenomena and memories concerning his,
> as I then saw it, pathogenic conflicts in the area of infantile sexuality
> and aggression—his Oedipus complex, his castration anxiety, his
> childhood masturbation, his fantasy of the phallic woman, and, es-
> pecially, his preoccupation with the primal scene—and, on the other
> hand, by his revelation that, beginning at the age of 11, he had been
> involved in a homosexual relationship. . . .

Kohut proceeds to set forth his "classical" understanding of the
case and continues (pp. 6–7),

In my interpretative-reconstructive attempts I moved in two directions: I tried, more or less successfully, to address myself to the elements of pregenital fixation as they related to the infantile sexual ties
to his pre-oedipal mother; and, increasingly, but with scant success, I
tried to discern and to interpret to him the motivations for his clinging to pregenital drive aims—or even regressing to them—namely,
that the fear of taking a competitive stance *vis-à-vis* the father had
forced him to return to the earlier development level, or, at any rate,
that castration anxiety prevented him from making the decisive for-
ward move.

All in all, my approach to Mr. Z's psychopathology as it was mobilized in the analysis can be said to have been fully in tune with the
classical theories of psychoanalysis. His masochism, in particular, I
explained as sexualization of his guilt about the pre-oedipal posses-
sion of his mother and about his unconscious oedipal rivalry.

[A little further on, Kohut tells us:]

I pointed out his tendency to retreat from competitiveness and male
assertiveness either to the old preoedipal attachment to his mother or
to a defensively taken submissive and passive homosexual attitude
toward the father.

The logical cohesiveness of these reconstructions seemed impecca-
ble, and in view of the fact that they were entirely in line with the
precepts about the unfolding of an analysand's conflicts and about the
ultimate resolution of these conflicts brought about in a well-con-
ducted analysis—precepts that were then firmly established in me as
almost unquestioned inner guidelines in conducting my therapeutic
work . . . [p. 9].

I can still remember the slightly ironical tone of my voice, meant to
assist him in overcoming his childish grandiosity . . . [p. 14].

As a result of a changed clinical orientation and the second analysis of Mr. Z, Kohut understood what his earlier interpretations
meant to the patient:

. . . my theoretical convictions, the convictions of a classical analyst
who saw the material that the patient presented in terms of infantile

drives and of conflicts about them, and of agencies of a mental appa-
ratus either clashing or co-operating with each other, had become for
the patient a replica of the mother's hidden psychosis, of a distorted
outlook on the world to which he had adjusted in childhood, which he
had accepted as reality—an attitude of compli. nce and acceptance
that he had now reinstated with regard to me and to the seemingly
unshakable convictions that I held. . . .

Within the analytic setting, the patient complied with my convictions by presenting me with oedipal issues [p. 16].

Kohut's statement that his early interpretations had become for
the patient a replica of his mother's hidden psychosis is very nicely
stated and, to me, extremely convincing. I have known of several
similar situations. They represent one form of the outcome mentioned earlier where the meaning to a patient of a stereotyped analysis has little to do with the analyst's interpretations. Also, as I
have noted earlier, I have known of several cases where oedipal
issues were presented by the patient, as in Kohut's case, because the
analysands recognized that these were the issues of interest to the
analyst.

Turning to the earlier part of his essay, where Kohut speaks of
working as a "classical" analyst during the first analysis of Mr. Z, I
would say he was working as a stereotyped analyst.

Many changes occurred in the second analysis of Mr. Z and, obviously, for the better. But the fundamental question is, what has
really changed? Kohut's analytic process? The emphasis on a "new"
clinical theoretical entity, "the self," or the recognition of the significance of the pathology of a patient's mother does not mean that
the *psychoanalytic therapeutic process* has necessarily changed. We
can be as convinced, unquestioning, insistent, ironic, and as provoking of a patient to the point of rage—as Kohut concedes he was in
the first analysis of Mr. Z—whether we are interpreting issues concerning "the self" and an unempathic mother or issues concerning
the Oedipus complex and castration anxiety. And we can see a patient as "resistant" if he does not accept an interpretation no matter
what that interpretation may refer to.

Crucial here is what Kohut would have done if the patient objected to an interpretation about his mother's having been psychotic
and unempathic. Would he have maintained absolute, unquestion-

ing confidence in his point of view and insisted on it, even though
the patient became repeatedly enraged and protested that he wasn't
being understood, as happened in the first analysis? Would he have
viewed the patient's objections as manifestations of resistance?

Returning to my previous distinction between psychoanalytic
clinical theory and a theory of the psychoanalytic process, I have
said that *any* clinical theory can form the basis of a stereotyped
process. It can be the "classical" clinical theoretical ideas of Oedipus
complex, castration anxiety, and penis envy, or the "newer" clinical
theoretical ideas concerning the self, narcissism, and the unempathic mother. My question, therefore, can be stated as follows:
Have Kohut and his colleagues moved from a typical stereotyped
stance toward a heuristic approach—an approach where genuine
discovery is at the forefront—or *have they merely given us some new
stereotypes?* Kohut and his colleagues speak much of empathy, and
that, I think, is fine, even though one can apparently still practice a
rigid, stereotyped form of therapy, as in the first analysis of Mr. Z,
while writing about the importance of empathy (see Kohut, 1959).
But I do not see where they have yet dealt in any fundamental way
with the difficult issue of the *psychoanalytic therapeutic process*, the
issues of hypotheses and evidence. Perhaps these deficiencies will be
corrected in time. To judge by one of Kohut's later summarizing
statements (see Kohut & Wolf, 1978), he considered his theory still
very much in the formative stage. Until these issues are dealt with
and progress toward their resolution is made, we are entitled to be
very cautious about accepting any of the theories that Kohut has set
forth, just as we are entitled to be questioning of "classical" clinical
theory.

Although many analysts do not proceed along stereotyped lines,
the general impression conveyed by the literature is that the stereotyped approach to the psychoanalytic process *is* psychoanalysis—
"classical" psychoanalytic therapeutic process. Indeed, those favorably inclined to psychoanalysis, as well as critics of psychoanalysis,
equate the two. Two examples from the literature will illustrate my
point regarding the confusion of psychoanalysis and the stereotyped
approach. The first is from Aaron Beck (1976, pp. 315–316), who is
comparing psychoanalysis with cognitive therapy.

A patient who had a fear of heights was told by his analyst, "Your fear of going to the top of a building is based on your fear of getting to the top of your profession. You are afraid—on an unconscious level—that if you reach the top, you will be castrated. As a child, you were afraid that if you beat out your father, he would cut off your penis. Now any success has the same meaning."

In a subsequent discussion with me, the patient reported having had the following thoughts following his analyst's interpretation: "I'm not really afraid of going to the top of the building. I'm afraid of having my penis cut off. . . . That's pretty foolish." This line of reasoning convinced him there was no objective danger. He was then motivated to experiment with taking an elevator to the top of high buildings. Whenever he felt anxiety during these "experiments," he repeated to himself, "I don't have to be afraid. I just have this hang-up about being castrated."

Beck, justifiably, has questions about the accuracy of the interpretation given to the patient, but points out that "the potency of psychoanalytic probing and interpretations of unconscious meanings lies in their persuasive attack on the conscious beliefs." Beck is questioning what is characteristic of what I am calling the stereotyped approach; the heuristic worker, to be discussed later on, would tend not to make such interpretations.

Beck, pointing to some of the differences between cognitive therapy and psychoanalysis, notes (pp. 316–317) that "the cognitive therapist does not look for hidden meanings in the patient's thoughts, whereas the psychoanalyst deals with them as symbolic transformations of unconscious fantasies." Here I would say that he is roughly but not exactly on target, but that he is definitely not on target when he speaks of "psychoanalysis" in the following remarks (pp. 316–317).

In contrast to psychoanalysis, cognitive therapy deals with what is immediately derivable from conscious experience. . . . By staying close to the patient's conscious ideas, the cognitive therapist has certain advantages over the analyst. First, since the discussions center around concepts that are essentially within the patient's awareness, the therapist's inferences, connections, and generalizations are read-

ily *comprehensible* to the patient. Consequently, the patient is able to
fit the formulations directly to conscious experiences or to reshape the
formulations to fit the data. Therapist and patient actively collabo-
rate to work out the formulation that "feels right" to the patient and
discard the ill-fitting formulations. The "superficial" formulations of
the cognitive therapist, in contrast to the "deep" interpretations of the
analyst, may be continually tested, rejected, or refined by the patient
in his experiences outside therapy. The analyst's interpretations of
unconscious processes, on the other hand, do not allow for invalidation
by the patient. In fact, the patient's rejection of an interpretation is
regarded as a sign of "resistance."

Almost all of Beck's comments are true, but only for the stereotyped approaches to Freudian therapy or analysis; they do not apply
to a heuristic approach.

I suspect that adequate specification of the different types of processes now being practiced by Freudian analysts may reveal that,
although important differences exist between so-called Freudian
and non-Freudian therapies, there may well be important common
denominators to all types of effective therapies regardless of the
names under which they are subsumed.

Now let me quote from one who is favorably inclined toward
analysis and who is attempting to understand its nature. In an
article titled "Testing an Interpretation within a Session," John
Wisdom (1967, p. 46) asks:

How does one assess whether a patient's responses confirm or refute
an interpretation or clinical hypothesis? That is the basic methodological problem. Take a situation in which the patient waxes in-
dignant about the traffic he encountered on his way to visit a married
woman he had designs upon; bad as it is, he remarks, perhaps it used
to be more dangerous in the days of horses because even today, he
says, he saw a horse snap at a man trying to control it. The meaning
that would most probably be ascribed to this little scene with the
horse by analysts is that it represents hostility from the patient's
father or from the analyst. Further, the danger occurs in a context of
possible adultery. So the analyst gives the Oedipus interpretation,
and receives the reply from the patient that he has nothing against

his father but has against his boss, who is loud and sharp tongued; still his bark is worse than his bite. This response provides a new disguised version of the interpretation: a man instead of a horse and biting replaced by barking. But emphasis has to be put on the disguise: in other words the response has itself to be interpreted before we can consider whether it confirms or refutes the interpretation being tested. And this may look like some sort of circular process, because it would hardly seem reasonable to test an interpretation by another one whose truth is just as much open to question.

The problem here is perhaps the most basic scientific or methodological problem in the entire subject.

Wisdom's example, which forms the basis of a thoughtful discussion, represents the stereotyped approach. The heuristic worker would not think of an oedipal interpretation as a primary possibility, although, by the same token, he would not rule it out. He would set up a process of investigation, a process leading to discovery to find out what meaning should be ascribed to the scene with the horse. And the result might have little to do with standard oedipal interpretations.

PART TWO

A HEURISTIC APPROACH TO PSYCHOANALYTIC THERAPY

4 Psychoanalytic Therapy as Heuristic Process

What I am calling the heuristic approach to psychoanalytic therapy stands in sharp contrast to the stereotyped approaches that have so far been the focus of our attention.

I must again emphasize that I am not suggesting a new form or even any significant modification of psychoanalytic therapy. I am attempting to describe and conceptualize one segment of the spectrum of Freudian approaches, one that many therapists use quite naturally, even though such terms as *heuristics* or *working models* may be totally unfamiliar to them.

To organize thinking and discussion about a heuristic approach, I believe it helpful to ask some of the kinds of questions generally asked in other scientific disciplines: What are the phenomena of interest to psychoanalysis? What specific problem or area of inquiry is selected for study? What are the goals? What criteria do we have that meaningful results have been obtained, that goals have been reached, or that progress toward the goals is being made? And finally, what is the nature of the procedures used for study?

What, then, is the nature of the phenomena of interest to psychoanalysis? To put it in its broadest terms I would say that psychoanalysis is interested in the inner emotional world of subjective experiential states—thoughts, fantasies, feelings—and the private world of personal meanings and motivations. I would say too that psychoanalysis is broadly concerned with the unconscious processes that go on in every person. Here we can legitimately introduce the clinical theoretical term *unconscious processes* much as physics is defined as the study of energy, also a theoretical term. Inasmuch as "unconscious processes" have become accepted by the general scientific community as being scientifically useful it is legitimate to use the term to define the nature of a discipline.

Second, what is our specific problem or area of inquiry for study? The answer for the practicing heuristic clinician is the individual case, an answer deserving elaboration. Clinically, psychoanalytic therapy attempts to understand one unique individual. As a result of genetic endowment, family influence, and particular life history, we find at any given moment a particular person at a particular moment who is constantly changing over time in many ways, although important characteristics persist. We have no known way to replicate the precise phenomenon under study. The analyst attempts to understand highly personal, individual meanings and motivations. Approaches to a patient based on probabilistic assumptions must therefore be used with great caution.

To illustrate this last point, many probabilistic statements can be made about a population. For example, one may be able to say that five out of every 100 in a given population will probably die in a certain year. But what can be said about a population does not necessarily apply to the individual. Thus, we cannot designate the five individuals who will probably die that year. Probabilistic approaches may be useful when the number of variables is known and the probabilities are high. Thus, an internist may reasonably prescribe a broad-based antibiotic for an infection without knowing the specific organism involved, because the number of known pathogens is relatively small and it is probable that the broad-based medication prescribed will be effective. The number of variables represented by the individual, however, is not small. On the contrary, the informational complexity is astonishingly large. Indeed, the amount of information transmitted by the genetic code and the amount present in the human organism at any moment as a result of learning and experience is so astronomically large that the number I would have to put down, according to informed estimates, would be virtually incomprehensible.

Returning to psychoanalysis, we may be informed that frequently in a dream or as part of a symptom a snake may represent a penis. We cannot be given probabilistic statements about such occurrences, and even if it could be said (based perhaps on some study) that the snake represents the penis in more than three-quarters of the cases examined, we have no way of knowing off hand if the case that we are studying falls within or outside of this figure.

Turning now to the third issue, what are our specific goals? The heuristic therapist replies that his goal is to *initiate and foster an analytic process, beginning with whatever the patient brings up.* The fundamental rule of psychoanalysis is to ask patients to tell whatever they experience without censoring, and this rule guides our process. The patient determines the issues to be dealt with, whatever they may be—marital problems that came up the day before, a sexual problem that came up the night before, a problem at work, or some unexplained anxiety, fear, feeling of depression, and so forth.

I emphasize that we have no specific content in mind as our goal when we practice heuristically. We cannot even say that we are seeking to understand or alleviate a presenting symptom. True, we can say that it is our hope that eventually a symptom will be understood and alleviated, but we do not have the understanding and alleviation of a symptom at the *forefront* of our thinking as goals to be attained. Indeed, a symptom presented on initial history may not come up for analysis for years, if ever. In disciplines related to psychoanalysis— behavioral or biofeedback therapy—for example, a presenting symptom would be the immediate addressable problem and the alleviation of it would be an explicit and perhaps even the principal goal.

Fourth, in answer to the question of our criteria that goals have been achieved, meaningful results have been obtained, or that progress is being made, I suggest, as a reply, the attainment of an optimal process, or, more specifically, "good hours."[1] I use the term hour broadly. It can correspond to a temporal hour, or it can be part of an hour, or even a group of related temporal hours that deal meaningfully with an issue. The good hour is one wherein patient, therapist, as well as competent observers would agree that something important happened, something "true," "real" or meaningful, both cognitively and affectively. Often, these are dramatic hours, but they need not be. Good hours are especially important because

---

[1]Ernst Kris (1951) also wrote of the "good" analytic hours, but he gave no clinical examples and only a limited description of it.

so many of our sessions are murky, uncertain, confused, and it is often very difficult to know what has happened. The good hour is akin to a successful experiment which has given clear-cut, valid, unambiguous results. Thus, a good hour presents a small-scale, relatively successful situation permitting of relatively rigorous examination. We can therefore profitably ask what did patient and therapist do to reach or generate the particular hour? I have informally studied such hours almost from the beginning of my career and am thoroughly convinced of their usefulness. ("Bad hours," where matters progress disastrously, are also of great help. Here one can profitably ask what went wrong to make for the unhappy consequences.)

The good hour is actually an observable *cross section of the optimal process at a particular moment.* It is a "marker" of the presence of an optimal process. The presence (or absence) of good hours enables us to make an ongoing evaluation of the state of the process. These hours serve as a gauge or indicator to "measure" the development of the process. The characteristics of the optimal process and the good hour will be clearer when I deal with them, later, in the context of illustrative case material.

In the general domain, then, of the phenomena of interest to psychoanalysis—the inner emotional life of thought, fantasy, and feeling—we deal clinically with one area, the individual case. Our goal is to set up an optimal therapeutic process which begins with whatever the patient brings up. That we have attained this goal or made progress toward it is evidenced by the presence of this optimal process and the good hours, which are actually markers of this process.

The fifth question, what is the nature of the procedures used in attaining the goals mentioned—the optimal process and the good hours—I try to answer in the following chapters where I discuss heuristic strategies and working models.

In line with my claim at the beginning of this chapter that what I am describing is not a new form of therapy, I would like to call attention to the consistency of what I have herein outlined with Freud's (1913, p. 130) well-known comments regarding the analytic process:

> The analyst is certainly able to do a great deal, but he cannot determine beforehand exactly what results he will effect. He sets in motion

a process, that of the resolving of existing repressions. He can supervise this process, further it, remove obstacles in its way, and he can
undoubtedly vitiate much of it. But on the whole, once begun, it goes
its own way and does not allow either the direction it takes or the
order in which it picks up its points to be prescribed for it.

5 The Concept of Heuristic Strategies

If, then, our analytic goal is to set in motion a process that leads to good hours, how do we go about achieving this goal? Our approach will be through heuristic strategies. When I speak of strategies I refer to plans that guide activity toward some goal and are implemented by specific procedures. Strategies are used in all walks of life, although we may not be aware that we are using them. Specifying strategies is useful for teaching; we can present the strategies that have served us best for any given purpose. More important, specifying strategies is scientifically useful in that specification can help us understand exactly what we are doing. If desired goals are not attained, the problem may lie in the use of faulty strategies.

Two categories of strategies are available to us—algorithmic and heuristic. Algorithmic strategies are plans for prescribed step-by-step procedures, which, if slavishly followed, guarantee solution; *they inevitably lead to the desired goal.* We use such strategies when the number of variables is small and complexity is comparatively not great. To prepare food according to a recipe is to use an algorithm. If one follows the prescribed steps, one attains the desired result. Algorithmic methods are used to solve algebraic problems. Cardiopulmonary resuscitation is performed algorithmically. If one follows several basic procedures and several very important subprocedures automatically, one will (assuming that the patient is intrinsically potentially resuscitatable) achieve the desired goal.

But because so many aspects of our lives are complex, uncertain, and unpredictable, algorithmic strategies are not always adequate. Heuristic strategies are used instead. Heuristic strategies are rules of thumb, or guidelines *that may or may not be successful* in attaining a desired goal. Webster (1957) defines heuristic as "helping to discover or learn." Thus, one can think of heuristic strategies as serving the process that leads to discovery or learning. Boden, a highly regarded writer on philosophy, psychology, and artificial intelligence, writes (1977, p. 347): "A heuristic is a method that directs thinking along the paths most likely to lead to the goal, less promising avenues being left unexplored."

If, for example, our goal is to keep up with the latest developments in the field of psychiatry and psychoanalysis, we develop rules of thumb to help us decide what to read in our field because we find it impossible to read all of the existing literature. We may, by reading only certain authors or certain journals, miss important material, an inevitable consequence of the uncertainty implicit in the use of heuristics. Indeed, because the most important aspects of life are complex, they are conducted heuristically. Heuristic strategies guide the rearing of children with the goal that they have emotionally healthy lives; no strategies exist that automatically guarantee success in this area. Interpersonal relationships (which may have various goals) are all conducted by heuristic strategies. Fortunately, we can revise our heuristic strategies depending on the success or failure in attaining our desired goals.

To convey some sense of the contrast between algorithmic and heuristic strategies and also to convey how heuristics become necessary as complexity increases, let me offer a trivial problem. Suppose we are asked to find all of the four-letter words ending with ENY. Inasmuch as there are only 26 letters in the alphabet, the problem is very simple; we can employ an algorithm: we need only combine each letter of the alphabet in turn with the letters ENY, check against a good dictionary, and the correct answer emerges. Using this algorithm, we get the word DENY. Actually, even in this simple case, we could have used a heuristic strategy. We might have combined only consonants with ENY, a strategy based on our experience that it is unlikely that a word would begin with two vowels. Recall Boden's definition of heuristic. Using a consonant and combining it with ENY is a path most likely to lead to the goal; using a vowel before ENY is a less promising avenue toward the goal and is better left unexplored.

But now suppose we are asked to find all legitimate five-letter words ending in ENY. Here, too, we can employ an algorithm: try letters A through Z for the first letter, and in each case A through Z for the second, a total of 26 times 26 or 676 possibilities. Then, check against a good dictionary and we will invariably get the right answer. When I first tried this problem, I used a heuristic strategy. I used common consonant combinations such as SL and TR. No legitimate words emerged. Then I tried common vowels preceding the letters ENY, such as E, and then I simply ran down the alphabet for all consonants. I came up with TEENY and WEENY. I then tried the algorithmic method. I wrote out the 676 possible five-letter words ending in ENY. I still found only TEENY and WEENY. So, my heuristic strategies seemed to have worked in this case. Even with this very simple problem we can appreciate the definition of heuristic given by Simon, a leading researcher in the field of artificial intelligence, who writes (1979, p. 152): "We use the term heuristic to denote any principle or device that contributes to the reduction in the average search to solution."

If we are asked to find six- and seven-letter combinations of words ending in ENY, the number of possible combinations goes up markedly, and it becomes increasingly cumbersome to employ an algorithmic method.

Thus far, we are still dealing with extremely simple situations where the number of variables is comparatively small. A nontrivial system of great complexity which has been studied extensively in recent years is the game of chess. It has been estimated that there are 10^{120} different possible sequences of moves from the beginning of a standard chess game; and even the fastest computers would require an astronomical amount of time to scan all of the possible sequences of moves and their consequences before deciding what to do. To play a winning game, human beings generally employ special heuristic strategies which select what are likely to be the best moves from the astronomical number of possible ones. These strategies guide the moves in the local, immediate situation at any moment. (To work out heuristic chess-playing computer programs, much time is spent interviewing good chess players to find out the nature of their individual strategies. They are asked to do the equivalent of "free association" as they play, thus revealing their strategies and general thinking.)

Because of the vastness, complexity, unpredictability, and multi-determined nature of the phenomena we confront in psychoanalysis, as well as the unbelievable amount of what is unknown and not easily knowable at any given moment, algorithms are of little use in psychoanalysis.[1] There is simply *no prescribed procedure* that can guarantee us success. Heuristic strategies must be used, and the idea of heuristics is actually implicit in much of our literature, although it has yet to be fully and systematically studied. For example, the suggestion that we interpret defenses before we interpret what is being defended against is a heuristic strategy, a guideline, a general rule of thumb. Similarly, the fundamental technical rule of free association is a heuristic strategy.

Freud understood the idea of heuristic strategies and how they contrast with algorithms, although he never used these terms. He beautifully captures the idea in the following statement (1913, p. 123):

In what follows I shall endeavour to collect together for the use of practising analysts some of the rules for the beginning of the treatment. Among them there are some which may seem to be petty details, as, indeed, they are. Their justification is that they are simply rules of the game which acquire their importance from their relation to the general plan of the game. I think I am well-advised, however, to call these rules 'recommendations' and not to claim any unconditional acceptance for them. The extraordinary diversity of the psychical constellations concerned, the plasticity of all mental processes and the wealth of determining factors oppose any mechanization of the technique; and they bring it about that a course of action that is as a rule justified may at times prove ineffective, whilst one that is usually mistaken may once in a while lead to the desired end. These circumstances, however, do not prevent us from laying down a procedure for the physician which is effective on the average.

---

[1]Milton I. Klein (personal communication) has pointed out that, in contrast to psychoanalytic therapy, behavior modification therapy is fundamentally algorithmic.

In distinct contrast to the heuristic approaches I am advocating, stereotyped workers tend to use an algorithmic approach. For them a good analysis is a rote procedure wherein the presenting material is understood and interpreted mechanically in terms of an existing clinical theory, and the goal is to get the patient to accept the interpretations offered, as well as the clinical theory on which the interpretations are based. If the patient refuses to accept the analyst's understandings, interpretations, or clinical theory, his refusals are viewed as manifestations of resistance, although the patient may be making genuine efforts to correct the analyst's errors. The stereotyped therapist then attempts to "analyze" (to get rid of) these resistances so that the process can proceed smoothly algorithmically—mechanically—to the goal the therapist envisages.

One important point about heuristic strategies deserves to be emphasized, and that is that we focus on strategies used in an immediate situation. The analyst or therapist must act at a given moment within an existing context. The strategies must guide him to do the optimal thing at a particular moment, optimal in the sense that it is the best thing to do to foster the analytic process. Specifically, the heuristic strategies should guide the analyst's response when a patient asks a question, is unable to talk, comes late, misses a session, or tells of being extremely anxious, upset, depressed, angry for no apparent reason, or tells a dream.

In regard to dreams, Freud (1923, p. 109) suggested several possible strategies in dealing with the immediate situation of a presented dream (though he called them "technical procedures): "proceed chronologically", he advised, pick out an element for work such as "the piece which shows the greatest clarity or sensory intensity"; ask the dreamer about the events of the previous day which may be associated in his mind with the dream; allow the dreamer "to decide with which associations to the dream he shall begin." When Freud then adds, "I cannot lay it down that one or the other of these techniques is preferable or in general yields better results," he once again captures an essential aspect of heuristic strategies.

Patients, too, employ strategies. Whenever we communicate with others we are following some strategy, even though we may not be fully aware of it. We ordinarily try to be as logical as possible and not say anything bizarre or offensive. This strategy however is not useful for psychoanalytic therapy. Implicit in the fundamental rule of psychoanalysis is a totally different strategy: We want patients *not* to censor, *not* to be concerned with sounding bizarre or offensive. The strategies that a patient can use require specification and will be discussed later.

The heuristic approach is basically pragmatic and empirical. The strategies I am suggesting are included because they seem to work. All strategies, both algorithmic and heuristic, must be do-able in order to be useful. I do not think it very helpful to advise a therapist to "analyze resistances." I do think it helpful to delineate strategies that point to practicable, do-able procedures whereby resistances can be detected and analyzed. Nor do I think it helpful to tell a therapist to "use his unconscious," a recommendation probably deriving from Freud's effort to describe his technique (1912, pp. 115–116):

> To put it in a formula: he [the doctor] must turn his own unconscious like a receptive organ towards the transmitting unconscious of the patient. He must adjust himself to the patient as a telephone receiver is adjusted to the transmitting microphone. . . .
> . . . if the doctor is to be in a position to use his unconscious in this way as an instrument in the analysis, he must himself fulfil one psychological condition to a high degree. He may not tolerate any resistances in himself which hold back from his consciousness what has been perceived by his unconscious;. . .

It is difficult to understand how we can turn our "unconscious" toward the "unconscious" of the patient; I know of no direct voluntary way to activate the "unconscious" so that it can be "used" to understand presenting material. It would certainly be more helpful to specify the achievable, operational procedures that lead to the activation of relevant unconscious processes in the therapist and allow him to understand presenting material, which is what I attempt to do in subsequent chapters in this book. It is hardly accurate to say that a tennis player thinks of using his hand and eye coordination when he plays. There is no direct command or instruction available to voluntarily activate this reflex response. It is much more accurate to say that the good tennis player thinks of keeping his eye on the ball; as a result, hand and eye coordination are automatically activated. Tennis instructors shout to novices: "Keep your eye on the ball!" not "Use the hand-eye coordination reflex!" The first instruction—or strategy—in contrast to the second, is meaningful, practicable, do-able.

The most important reason for adopting a heuristic approach is that it is most effective in reducing the ambiguity and uncertainty, the enormous complexity of the phenomena with which the psychotherapist works.

Complexity and The Reduction of Uncertainty

When a patient tells us that he is "upset," we know very little. The reported feeling is complex, ambiguous. We do not know if he is angry, anxious, depressed, or any combination of these or other states; and, if he is anxious, we do not know the nature of the anxiety, how it is experienced, the nature of the accompanying ideation, and so on. Uncertainty, complexity, and ambiguity are reduced by relevant information.

I noted earlier in the example given of moving from a four-letter word to a five-letter one, and then to a six-letter word, all ending in ENY that complexity can easily build up appreciably. By the same token, we can generally sharply reduce complex, uncertain, and ambiguous situations through the generation of relevant information. If a man tells us that he is in love, we really know little about his state. He could be in love with a man, a woman, a child, an activity, a cause, or with many other things. If it is a woman, we do not know if it is a sexual love or a nonsexual one, or some combination of the two. It can be seen how rapidly, we can markedly expand the branching tree of possibilities, and how impossible it is to say that we understand something when a person tells us only that he is in love. But suppose we get some relevant input. Suppose the man tells us that, at the given moment under scrutiny, he is in love with a woman; further information will be needed to reduce this uncertainty, but at least we know that at this moment he is consciously not speaking of love for a man, a child, a thing, an activity, or a cause.

In brief, the fundamental purpose of the heuristic strategies used in psychoanalytic therapy is to generate and organize relevant information input. Good heuristic strategies reduce uncertainty, complexity, and ambiguity and increase the possibility of understanding something about the individual under consideration. They reduce the search necessary for understanding.

Some of the ideas just expressed are familiar in other branches of medicine. Blois (1980, p. 193), for example, in an excellent article writes:

> Whereas nearly everything is possible at the beginning of a patient's visit, the field of possibilities then becomes progressively restricted. As more information is obtained the possibilities are reduced until only a relatively small number of potential disorders remain. The cognitive universe, in which further fact finding and inference takes place and in which a decision must finally be made, becomes smaller, more detailed, and more specific. More important, a sense of structure emerges. The alternatives not only become fewer, but they are sharpened, and relations among them appear. . . .
>
> The number of things that can be truthfully said about any object in the world is unimaginably large, and the only way in which we can speak usefully of things is to confine ourselves to matters that are relevant. By "relevant" I mean connected to the topic or purpose with which we are engaged at a given moment. It is only through this selection of relevant attributes that we succeed in communicating at all.

Blois also points out (p. 195) that when a patient is first seen "almost all the facts that could be stated about a patient would be irrelevant to the problem of finding out what is wrong. It is the physician's task to select from this unimaginably large number of indifferent and neutral facts the ones that happen to be relevant."

Blois says that when we first see a patient, we are in effect facing the world in all of its complexity. He then adds (p. 195):

> How does the physician deal with this complexity . . .? Many distinguished physicians have taught that history taking is the most critical step in the entire diagnostic process, and that this phase is the one that separates the exceptional physician from less able ones. From the viewpoint of information theory, this idea seems quite plausible. Consider the manner in which we might go about measuring the

difference between the diagnostic worth of a fact that is volunteered by a patient and a fact that is elicited in response to a question. In one standard compilation of diseases, 3262 diseases and "medical conditions" are listed, with each defined in terms of clinical and laboratory attributes. In our studies of this compilation, the term "nosebleed" (or its synonyms) was found to occur in the description of 27 different diseases. If a new patient whom we were seeing reported "nosebleed," our attention would be drawn to these 27 diseases, and not to the 3235 in which "nosebleed" is not considered to be a characteristic. If on the other hand, we routinely asked all patients whether they had "nosebleed," most replies would be negative; this approach would enable us to reject only 27 diseases instead of 3235. The "diagnostic" or "selection" power of a positive response is thus more than 100 times greater than a negative one for this attribute. And when patients volunteer facts, they are almost always stated in an affirmative sense. Patients do not report the symptoms that they do not have. The amount of information obtained from a random inquiry about symptoms (yielding mostly negative responses) will therefore be very small. If, in contrast, the patient is encouraged to volunteer affirmative (positive) symptoms, the information value is clearly much greater. Every practitioner knows this approach and practices it instinctively, although it is not widely recognized that this practice rests on a firm theoretical basis. By beginning in this way (with the "chief complaint") the physician equipped with both common sense and medical knowledge is provided with a means for exploiting relevance. This is the physician's method for dealing with the unimaginably complex.

Blois focuses on the initial interview or interviews, but his remarks can be applied to any and every psychoanalytic session. Each session is an "initial" interview in the sense that we do not know what has happened to the patient in the interval between sessions, and also in the sense that we do not know what is important to the patient at the moment of entering our office.

The "diagnostic" or "selective" power of the positive responses that Blois refers to can be applied to what we call "spontaneous free association" in psychoanalytic therapy. I have no doubt that, in contrast to the 100-fold power noted in the case of a patient who spontaneously reports a nosebleed, spontaneous free association has even greater power in appropriate situations because we deal with complexity of a much greater order of magnitude. Freud's faith in "free association" can now be amply buttressed by contemporary information theory. Encouraging a patient to talk freely without censoring is an excellent heuristic strategy. It maximizes the input of relevant information and cuts down on the search for a solution.

I think that the overwhelming complexity, uncertainty, and ambiguity of our data in psychoanalytic therapy is a fundamental problem, both from the cognitive and emotional standpoints. It is very difficult to tolerate the uncertainty and complexity of our daily work. All of us have a great need to master situations, to know, to understand, to order and organize situations—and rapidly too. Clinical practice markedly enhances this pressure. Patients want answers and quick relief, and often in clinical practice important judgments have to be made on the basis of comparatively little data.

Stereotyped approaches with their preconceived assumptions based on existing clinical theory seem to offer a rapid ordering and organization of the data, quick understanding. They therefore have enormous appeal, especially to the beginning clinician. But this ordering, organization, and understanding of stereotyped approaches can be false because the order and organization they impose is external to the patient. They do not reduce complexity by a natural, creative process of generalization and learning. They do not find the intrinsic order and organization potentially discoverable within natural phenomena. In actuality, stereotyped approaches generally eliminate complexity; they tend to filter out what does not fit existing clinical theory. And in their most extreme forms, stereotyped approaches take the rich, vivid, multifaceted, and intricate tapestry of human experience and reduce it to a handful of simplistic clichés which are mistakenly claimed to represent the "deep unconscious."

6 The Concept of Working Models

The nature of human memory has been of central importance in psychoanalysis. A concept of memory is implicit in the idea that the past influences the present—one of the basic assumptions of psychoanalytic thinking. Self and object representations, familiar concepts in psychoanalysis, are actually concepts about memory organizations. In recent years human memory has been studied intensively in the fields of cognitive psychology and artificial intelligence (see, for example, Abelson, 1981; Lindsay & Norman 1977; Loftus & Loftus, 1976; Neisser, 1976). It has become clear that human memory is not static; it appears to be involved in highly dynamic structured systems variously labeled maps, models, representations, knowledge structures, schemata, or scripts. I have used some of these terms in discussing aspects of learning, psychopathology, the analytic process, and so on (Peterfreund, 1971, 1976; Peterfreund & Franceschini, 1973).

In a discussion of perception, Neisser, a leading cognitive psychologist, comes close to my thinking when he defines (1976, p. 54) the term *schema* as:

> that portion of the entire perceptual cycle which is internal to the perceiver, modifiable by experience, and somehow specific to what is being perceived. The schema accepts information as it becomes available at sensory surfaces and is changed by that information; it directs

movements and exploratory activities that make more information available, by which it is further modified.

From the biological point of view, a schema is a part of the nervous system. It is some active array of physiological structures and processes: not a center in the brain, but an entire system that includes receptors and afferents and feed-forward units and efferents.

For some years Bowlby, who has been thinking along similar lines, has made extensive use of the term *working model* (see for example, 1969, pp. 48–49, 80–83, 267; 1973, pp. 203–209) to imply something more than a static map or representation. He notes (1969, p. 82) that these working models are "none other than the 'internal worlds' of traditional psychoanalytic theory seen in a new perspective." Bowlby and I share many ideas on these issues, and I have adopted his term *working model.*

The information that constitutes the different working models emerges from the information selected and organized by the organism over time. As Bowlby says (1969, p. 80): "Selection is unavoidable, partly because the environment is so enormously complex, partly because our sense organs provide us with information about only a limited aspect of it, and partly because, to be usable, a map needs to concentrate on those aspects of the environment that are most relevant to the achievement of set-goals." One can conceptualize learning as the emergence of working models. The models develop throughout life and are originally based on innate givens—inborn genetic programs. Thus, any working model at any given moment represents both phylogenetic evolutionary development and ontogenetic learning.

At the present time working models are not exact, rigorously definable concepts. The systems that constitute working models can be conceptualized in information and information-processing terms and in terms of stored programs. Biologically, they are parts of the nervous system, as Neisser describes the similar systems he calls schemata. When working models are activated, most of the processes take place without accompanying awareness, as is probably the case for most activity in the central nervous system. But *specific processes are associated with awareness,* including various cognitive and emotional experiences: images, sensations, feelings, fantasies, thoughts. Thus, whatever we experience (any phenomenon of awareness or consciousness) is only part of the activity of the entire working model associated with that experience. When, therefore, I suggest, as I do later on, that the therapist interpret input with working models of early development, I am suggesting a do-able, operational procedure. One can voluntarily pay attention to or activate knowledge and memories of early experience (phenomena of awareness). As a result, relevant working models associated with that experience and processes not associated with consciousness are also automatically activated.

The experiences of awareness or consciousness that accompany the activity of working models may even take the form of relatively "pure" sensorimotor phenomena unaccompanied by experiences we usually think of as cognitive. For example, I am a fairly competent typist, but I cannot offhand say exactly where the letter P or E is on the keyboard; I can nonetheless easily type my name. To reconstruct the keyboard in the absence of a typewriter, I would first have to allow my fingers to move to the correct positions and then observe where they went. The activation of my working model related to typing is primarily associated with sensorimotor experience with minimal visual imagery. Similarly, if one asks a good tennis player how he swings his racket on the backhand, he may have to check his body sensations as he actually goes through the motions of swinging the racket before he can give an accurate answer. Whether the working model is associated with cognitive, emotional, sensorimotor, or visual experiences is of importance for clinical psychoanalytic therapy. Experiences associated with retrieval of information related to the first years of life may take only sensorimotor form, unaccompanied by visual imagery or words, as in the case of Mr. R, referred to earlier (and to be discussed more in detail later).

Working models of one's physical body and psychological self, of the environment, and of other people are essential in all phases of normal activity. Different models are active in different ways when one walks, plays, reads, writes, converses, or has sexual intercourse. Working models make prediction, calculation, and adaptive behavior possible. Such models attain their highest level of sophistication in man, but are undoubtedly present in some form in lower animal forms, as Bowlby (1969) points out. Lower animal forms probably develop models of terrain, the location of important, safe, or dangerous objects. Dogs, for instance, probably develop working models of their environment based on smell.

All working models are changed by the very information received. They must be constantly updated, adapted, readapted, checked and rechecked for consistency—both for internal consistency as well as for consistency with other models. Such processes are basic aspects of learning and are apparently in large part associated with the phenomena we call "consciousness" or "awareness." At times, updating requires only small modifications of the existing working models; at other times, extensive modifications are necessary at all hierarchical levels. The serious illness or death of an important person, for example, may require such vast modifications. What psychoanalysis has long referred to as "working through" can be viewed, in large part, as a learning process, as an updating, a readapting, a checking for consistency of working models. Dreaming, incidentally, may in part represent some such updating process. Finally, it should be noted that normal adaptive learning often requires that a model not be merely updated but discarded, and a radically new one substituted—an idea familiar enough from the history of science.

One can say that as a result of the activity of existing working models, information is highlighted; information is selected for different purposes. The working models activated when one plays tennis, for example, allow information to be selected or highlighted from the external world that differs from that which is selected or highlighted when one plays golf. A tennis player notes the position and movement of his opponent, a consideration that has little meaning for a golfer; and a highly advanced tennis player is more exact and specific in his perceptions than a novice. The working models of the tennis player will thus differ considerably from the working models of the golfer. Likewise, a child's world differs from that of an adult's, partly because his rudimentary models allow different selections to be made from the outside world. A paranoid delusional patient with fixed, unchangeable models may select highly limited input from the outer world. Finally, it should be emphasized that, by virtue of their specific selective activities, working models implicitly act as filters of information. Thus, a man seeking a homosexual partner will tend not to select and process information related to what the heterosexual world would call an attractive woman. Information referring to her is filtered out.

I have mentioned the relationship of working models to learning. The complicated nature of this relationship deserves emphasis. One cannot begin to learn how to hit a tennis ball well, for example, without some initially acquired working model and associated, readily available, sensorimotor representations—however rudimentary—of what constitutes a good swing. After one acquires this model and sensorimotor representations—obtainable from observing others, let us say—one then tries to "model" one's actual bodily motions on the basis of this initially acquired inner representation. But even this description is a gross oversimplification of the actual processes. There is generally a "dialogue" between the initially acquired working model with its associated sensorimotor experiential representation and the bodily movements actually performed. Error-correcting feedback modifies our actual performance, and this in turn leads to modification and updating of our originally acquired inner models and associated experiential representations. As a result, we may succeed in "fine tuning" our model, its associated sensorimotor experience, and our actual performance. Models, associated sensorimotor experience, and actual performance all become adapted to actual capabilities, age, bodily build, and so forth. We can then use both the results of actual performance as well as our models and their associated experiential representations to evaluate and correct future performance—a process that has important implications for psychoanalytic therapy.

To anticipate what I later discuss in detail, I believe that what is commonly called resistance can be defined in terms of the mismatch between our model of an optimal therapeutic process and what we are confronting in actuality. We "error correct" or reduce this mismatch by interpretation, attempting thereby to make the actual process closer to the optimal. Our model of the optimal process is acquired initially from multiple sources, but it too must constantly be corrected, updated, or "fine tuned" by experience.

Programs and stored information, which constitute the working models, can be activated so that an approximation of an original experience can be reexperienced. We can see a house and later retrieve the appropriate information that enables us to get a mental image of the house originally seen. Different aspects of the house can be highlighted by different programs associated with the working model. One program can be used to highlight architectural style, another to highlight the nature of the surrounding terrain.

From childhood to adulthood, we understand the world through our constantly changing working models. We each interpret existing information in our own way, selecting and processing it to arrive at our particular view of the world, our individual "reality." It is through these interpretations that information attains meaning—both generally accepted denotative and connotative meanings, as well as the personal meanings of special interest to psychoanalysis.

It also deserves to be emphasized that our working models enable us to rearrange the world we know, imagine new combinations and possibilities, imagine how things would appear under different circumstances, calculate the possible consequences of action to be taken. As Bowlby (1969, p. 81) says: "if the model is to be of use in novel situations, it must be extended imaginatively to cover potential realities as well as experienced ones." In brief, our working models allow us to experience a miniature stage or platform to predict, evaluate, and test. Here indeed is one of the most advanced attributes of the human mind. And it is of great interest that working models with many of the capabilities mentioned are apparently present by what Piaget calls the sixth stage of the sensorimotor period (at about 18 months of age), before there is any adequate language system.

One important implication of the idea of working models deserves emphasis at this time, an especially relevant one for the psychoanalytic process.

We cannot approach any event as totally neutral, unbiased observers, free of the learning of the past, and there is no point in pretending that we can. (It is indeed fortunate that this is so, for current informational input would result in chaos if models of past learning and experience did not exist.) To speak of "observations" in psychoanalysis or in any other discipline as though they were "pure" and "unbiased" is simply nonsense. In actuality the analyst is always selecting from the vast amount of input potentially available to him, guided by the models and strategies available to him. If we think of working models as being associated with theories about a given domain—a legitimate point of view—then we can say that all observations are actually theory-laden.

We are all "biased" observers, and the question is not whether we are biased, but what are the optimal "biases." Which ones allow us to understand more about the inner life of a patient; and which ones permit us to assess a patient's emotional state more rapidly? It is one type of "bias" to select and organize data only through unchanging and unmodifiable models based on existing clinical theoretical ideas, as in stereotyped clinical work. It is quite another "bias" to select and organize data using a wide range of heuristic strategies coupled with working models that encompass the broadest possible range of human experience, models that are constantly modified, corrected, and updated. The former approach can perhaps be described as tendentious. The following remarks by Neisser (1976, p. 43) are relevant in this context:

> Perception does not merely serve to confirm preexisting assumptions, but to provide organisms with new information. . . . Although a perceiver always has at least some (more or less specific) anticipations before he begins to pick up information about a given object, they can be corrected as well as sharpened in the course of looking.
>   . . . perception is directed by expectations but not controlled by them; it involves the pickup of real information.[1]

The systems that we talk about—whether we call them schemata, working models, or representational models—refer to memory structures, as I have already noted. The way in which information is stored in the central nervous system is therefore of crucial importance and has many implications for psychoanalysis (see Bowlby, 1980, chap. 4; Peterfreund & Franceschini, 1973).

The cognitive psychologists (see, for example, Lindsay & Norman, 1977), speak of two classes of information in memory. First is "episodic" type of storage where information is stored in terms of the sequences of events actually experienced, including temporospatial relations between events. Obviously, a life history is represented in

---

[1]Emanuel Rice (personal communication) pointed out that Neisser is speaking of relatively normal cognitive behavior. In many pathological situations, in a paranoid patient, for example, it can be said that perception is directed and also controlled by expectations.

a direct way in this type of storage. Second is "semantic" storage where the information represents definitions and generalized propositions about the world derived from a variety of sources—personal experiences and/or learned from others. For example, we may learn from many experiences with dogs that they bark. The general proposition "Dogs bark" is stored semantically. But the specific events upon which the generalization is based is stored episodically, if it is stored at all. (We have to recognize the possibility that such information may be erased or be unavailable; there may be little need for it once the general propositions have been derived and stored). Likewise with the idea, "I am an ugly creature"—a general statement that is stored semantically, in contrast to the innumerable detailed events (overheard remarks from others, perhaps), stored episodically, from which this generalization is derived.

Recognizing these different types of information storages is important for two reasons. First, access may differ greatly. It is generally much easier to gain access to the semantic type of storage than the episodic type—something that we see daily in clinical practice. Patients can tell us many general things about themselves or about others, but find it much more difficult to give specific details of past or even of recent events from which the generalizations derive. Second, as Bowlby emphasizes, storage of information related to images of parents and of the self is almost certain to be of both the semantic and episodic type, with potential for conflict. As Bowlby writes (1980, p. 62):

> Whereas memories of behaviour engaged in and of words spoken on each particular occasion will be stored episodically, the generalizations about mother, father, and self enshrined in what I am terming working models or representational models will be stored semantically (in either analogical, propositional or some combined format). Given these distinct types of storage a fertile ground exists for the genesis of conflict. For information stored semantically need not always be consistent with what is stored episodically; and it might be that in some individuals information in one store is greatly at variance with that in the other.
>
> My reason for calling attention to the different types of storage and the consequent opportunities for cognitive and emotional conflict is that during therapeutic work it is not uncommon to uncover gross

inconsistencies between the generalizations a patient makes about his parents and what is implied by some of the episodes he recalls of how they actually behaved and what they said on particular occasions. . . . Similarly, it is not unusual to uncover gross inconsistencies between the generalized judgements a patient makes about himself and the picture we build up of how he commonly thinks, feels and behaves on particular occasions.

7 Working Models in Communication Processes and in Psychoanalytic Therapy

In the previous chapter I described working models as dynamic systems based on memory, emerging from learning and experience, and updated or reorganized in turn by new learning and experience. I emphasized that working models are present and activated in every experience and all activities. In this chapter I focus on working models—"knowledge of the world" as they are often called in cognitive psychology and in artificial intelligence—in connection with communication processes and psychoanalytic therapy. Psychoanalytic therapy is also a communication process, albeit a unique one, and we can therefore expect it to share characteristics of communication processes in general.

Linguists and information scientists have devoted a great deal of attention to the development of adequate semantic theories. They are, in effect, attempting to answer the question of how meaning is conveyed. But the problems faced by any semantic theory are truly formidable. Words can have many meanings, and these will vary according to context. As Lindsay and Norman (1977, p. 274) write, "context is the overall environment in which experiences are embedded." The word *ball*, for example, may mean very different things, depending on context. Likewise, the phrase *mind your business* is difficult to interpret in the absence of context. It can be a reproach equivalent to "Mind your own business and stop meddling in mine," or it can be an exhortation, as indeed it was when it appeared as a legend on one of the earliest American coins, the

Fugio cent. The latter meaning is understandable enough when one recognizes the work ethic and general social context at the time this coin was minted.

It has become increasingly clear that any semantic theory must take into account inferential processes—complex cognitive processes based on models of different aspects of the world. For example, when we hear of *dilated pupils,* we do not think of students because our model of the world tells us that the pupils of the eye dilate and students do not.

Proverbs are understandable only if adequate world models and complex cognitive processes are available. We wonder about possible psychopathology if, for example, an adult gives a very concrete or literal response when asked to give the meaning of "When the cat's away the mice will play." A more abstract or general response, such as "There is a tendency for one to take advantage when authority or threatening figures are absent," requires a rather elaborate working model of the world. One must view the concrete aspects of the proverb as but an instance of a larger generalization—to arrive at which requires elaborate processing of information.

We can often make sense of ambiguous or poorly constructed sentences only because we share models of the world with the communicants. Suppose we were to hear the following: "I read a book on Christmas, on the subway, on a horse." The most reasonable interpretation of this awkward sentence is that the speaker read a book about a horse during Christmas while in the subway. Syntactic rules and definitions based on the most elaborate of dictionaries could not have led to this interpretation. Interpretations other than the one mentioned are not likely, though not altogether out of the question: From what we know about the world, it is not likely that the speaker read about the subway during Christmas while sitting on a horse, and even less likely that he read a book about Christmas while sitting on a horse in the subway.

It is most interesting to see how ambiguous ordinary, everyday language is and how necessary it is to invoke the activities I am talking about. For example, the advertisement "an old movie house" is ambiguous, but is more likely to mean a movie house that shows old films; it is not likely that one would advertise the fact that the theatre is an old one. And the sign that I once saw advertising "unfinished furniture headquarters" most likely referred to a head-quarters for unfinished furniture. It would be reasonable to assume that the sign was not advertising the fact that the furniture head-quarters was unfinished.

Winograd, a leading worker in artificial intelligence, emphasizes how knowledge affects our understanding of language (1972, p. 33):

> If we say "The city councilmen refused the demonstrators a permit because they feared violence," the pronoun "they" will have a differ-ent interpretation than if we said "The city councilmen refused the demonstrators a permit because they advocated revolution." We un-derstand this because of our sophisticated knowledge of councilmen, demonstrators, and politics—no set of syntactic or semantic rules could interpret this pronoun reference without using knowledge of the world. Of course a semantic theory does not include a theory of politi-cal power groups, but it must explain the ways in which this kind of knowledge can interact with linguistic knowledge in interpreting a sentence.

The examples so far have been of comparatively simple situa-tions. When we consider more elaborate linguistic phenomena, ex-planatory conceptualizations become more and more difficult and complex. It becomes increasingly evident that "Language is a pro-cess of communication between people, and is inextricably en-meshed in the knowledge that these people have about the world" (Winograd, 1972, p. 26).

Consider, for example, the following brief imaginary interchange. John says, "Hello, David; I hope you are feeling better." To which David replies, "Thank you, I am much better." Implicit in John's remark is a model of David, including his current state of health. Also implicit is a model of the world in which it is deemed appropri-ate for friends to discuss some issues of health. David's reply up-dates John's model of him. Suppose John then says, "And how is your son; he is probably interested in colleges now?" To which David replies, "Oh yes, he is doing well and has been visiting colleges to find one of interest." Here too, many models are implicit. John has a model of David's family, and a model of the world in which colleges have a place. David's reply once again updates John's models. Note, too, that David and John share similar or related models and can therefore process and interpret information in a similar way to arrive at similar meanings. One can say that as John and David converse they activate or evoke in each other relatively similar models. Communication could not take place in the absence of such models.

Now imagine the following interchange: John says, "Hello, David; I hope you are feeling better." To which David replies, "I am David all right, but I have not been ill." And when John asks, "And how is your son; he is probably interested in colleges now?" David replies, "I have no son." Communication between John and David is obviously in trouble. Something is radically wrong with John's models of David and his family, and mere updating of them may not suffice. Extensive modifications may be in order and perhaps relatively new models substituted.

Thus far the examples mentioned have been everyday illustrations of human discourse, essentially "cognitive" in nature. When we deal with such "cognitive" examples we can communicate meanings fairly accurately, provided, as already emphasized, that the communicants have had similar experiences and have therefore developed similar working models.

When we deal with emotionally dominated contexts the limitations and ambiguity of language per se become more evident; communication is less accurate, and the importance of working models becomes even more evident. It is especially, I believe, when we deal with the full range of human emotional contexts that we can recognize that communication is possible largely because of the evocative power of language. Language activates the appropriate working models in the receiver, and this activation is associated with emotional experiences, thus permitting utterances to be understood. For example, the terms *love* and *hate* can refer to many different subjective psychological experiences with a host of associated images and fantasies. We must therefore use many modifiers and metaphors to portray the unique qualities of the specific subjective experiences that may be covered by these broad terms. To be truly understood, we must evoke similar experiences in the receiver; we must activate in the receiver the appropriate and relevant working models. One can say that empathy, the ability to experience what another person experiences, bridges the gap between words and experiences.

In psychoanalytic therapy, we certainly deal with the full range of human discourse—cognitive and emotional.[1] But, and most impor-tant, psychoanalytic therapy is not the same as ordinary discourse. We can think of it as a unique extension of human communication. We "understand" and arrive at "meanings" both in everyday commu-nication and in analytic therapy, but the "understandings" and the "meanings" are not always the same. Thus, for instance, if in every-day discourse we were asked, "Are you a Jew?" we would understand the term in its usual denotative sense to mean one whose religion is Judaism, or in a well-known connotative sense to mean one who drives a hard bargain. It would never occur to us to think that the person might be asking, "Are you one who rots and dies?" Yet in one analytic case (see Peterfreund & Franceschini, 1973) the evidence was convincing that the term *Jew* did have this unusual, highly personal connotative meaning, what we psychoanalysts usually un-derstand as an "unconscious meaning."

As I have repeatedly stressed, it is necessary for psychoanalysis to begin to specify how it arrives at such personal meanings, how it understands "the unconscious"—the hallmark of psychoanalytic work. Psychoanalytic therapy is a communication process, and both ordinary communication and psychoanalytic therapy are based on complex models of the world, but obviously the models and/or the strategies for their use must differ in important ways. One basic aim of this book is to focus on the models used in psychoanalytic therapy and the optimal strategies for their use.

I turn now to a brief sketch of some of the specific working models the therapist uses in the psychoanalytic therapeutic process. Dis-tinctions between models are not sharp or clear. I fully recognize that in describing the models I am oversimplifying highly complex issues—unavoidable in a work such as this.

---

[1] I use the terms "cognitive" and "emotional," but loosely and only for conve-nience. Actually I find it very difficult to distinguish between cognitive and emo-tional elements in any life experience, and in an information-processing frame of reference the distinction becomes unnecessary. Different experiences—whether we call them cognitive or emotional—are associated with the different ways that infor-mation may be processed.

The first working model the therapist employs is a general one of "knowledge of the world," of people and things in our culture and times, normal expectable, cognitive and emotional relationships. This general working model includes information related to how one deals with the animate world, with family, friends, associates. It includes such things as the average expectable reactions of a person to being hurt, and the expectable range of reactions of a person to the death of a beloved. The model also includes information related to the inanimate world, enabling us, for example, to evaluate the probability of crossing a street safely when we notice a car coming our way. In general, this working model includes all of the attributes that psychoanalysis has long called the "object world."

Second, the analyst uses a working model of his own personal history, character traits, idiosyncracies, abilities, typical reaction patterns, moods, and experiences; a model of his own body and its functions. Here we have all of the relatively stable aspects—cognitive and emotional—of what psychoanalysis has long spoken of as the "self," in this instance, the analyst's self.

Third is a working model of cognitive and emotional experience in infant and child development. The therapist has at his command an idea of how an infant possibly experiences and reacts to traumatic events—illnesses, accidents, massive frustrations, separations; how a child may experience sexual feelings toward a parent or peer; and fantasy elaborations of all of these experiences. This model includes various levels of primitive ideation. Contemporary research on infancy and childhood can enhance this model considerably.

Fourth, the analyst has a working model of the analytic process: how it evolves; what it feels like to free-associate and to speak of illogical, "crazy," embarrassing, and painful feelings and fantasies; what it feels like to talk very directly about the therapist.

Fifth, the analyst uses a working model representing the distillation of all previous learning and clinical experience, including innumerable observations and generalizations. Such a model might include generalizations about the clustering of character traits, for example, and the association of certain symptoms and character traits with specific infantile experiences.

Sixth, based on the patient's history and on innumerable observations and discoveries during the therapeutic process, the analyst develops a specific model of the patient, including characteristic modes of thinking, feeling, and reacting, the meaning of significant phenomena, etc.—a "flesh and blood" model of a total experiencing human being.

Seventh, in contrast to the working models so far described, which are actually models of experience, one can think of two groups of working models that form metamodels, theoretical models based on the previously mentioned models. The first of the two is more closely related to clinical experience than the second, and I will refer to it as a *clinical theoretical metamodel*. In line with the distinction between clinical theory and a theory of the therapeutic process, made in the introduction to this book, we can say that this metamodel includes, first, *clinical theories*. Such concepts as conflict, repression, defense, the Oedipus complex, unconscious processes, self- and object representations, latent and manifest content of dreams, and so on have their place in this metamodel. Second, this metamodel includes concepts related to a *theory of the process*. Such concepts as resistance, transference, therapeutic alliance, working through, free-association, interpretation, and so on therefore also have their place in this metamodel.

Eighth is the second metamodel, also a group of models based on the previously mentioned models. It can include elaborate information and information-processing and systems models, neurophysiological models, genetic, chemical, and hormonal models, and so on. As indicated, the concepts in this metamodel are more removed from clinical experience than the first metamodel, although they can be related to clinical experience.

The metamodels, especially the first one which includes both clinical theories and a theory of the process, have their concrete experiential representations in the other working models. Thus, to work properly an analyst cannot merely employ the idea "Oedipus complex." He must use *what it feels like in terms of the actual experiences* of a child. He must have available activatable representations of the range of a child's feelings toward either parent. These representations may be related to the second working model (concerning the analyst himself), and to the third working model of infantile and childhood experiences. Similarly, it is almost useless to think of schizophrenia in terms of world-destruction fears and restitutional fantasies unless one can also capture something of the actual experiences to which such words refer.

In brief, I cannot emphasize too strongly that for the heuristic worker all of the working models, except the metamodels mentioned, are *broad-based models of human experience*. They are based on the full richness, strength, depth, vividness, subtlety, and complexity of thought, fantasy, feeling, and sensation, including all levels or states of "raw gut" emotionality.

PART THREE

CASE ILLUSTRATIONS OF THE HEURISTIC APPROACH

INTRODUCTION

In order to demonstrate strategies and working models, I now present several case illustrations from different times in my career, although when I recorded some of the illustrative material I had not yet acquired the language of "heuristic strategies" and "working models." I use my own cases simply because I know them best.

If the presentations are not always as detailed as might be wished for, I should explain that I generally do not take notes during a session, but usually write up good illustrative material after the hour. Often, when I detect especially interesting material emerging, I may take simple reminder notes of one or two words to help me in reconstructing the session, especially if I am trying to capture the patient's exact words. It would certainly have been better had I systematically tape-recorded the sessions.

It is impossible to capture even a fraction of the processes that go on in any one hour. Some of the hours to be presented may therefore seem to be vague and sketchy. A given "good" hour can illustrate only a few processes. I hope that the description of many "good" hours will help to convey the full richness and complexity of what actually took place in the sessions.

8 Case of Mrs. C.

Mrs. C. came to me very early in my career. Her case demonstrates some of the conditions that can lead to stereotyped approaches. It also demonstrates some of the problems that can result when models are limited.

Very early in the analysis, Mrs. C., in a state of great agitation, told me of her lifelong snake phobia. She began to sob hysterically. She was afraid there was a snake in the office, that I was the snake, and that I was going to harm and attack her. She left the couch and walked around the room in panic. I must confess that she made me rather anxious. Although I knew from the initial interview that this depressed and anxious daughter of alcoholic parents was seriously ill, the stormy nature of the early sessions took me by surprise. I was taken aback by the chaos, the extreme turmoil, and the somewhat odd way in which the snake material emerged. Too much had happened too soon. The experience for the patient was very direct and immediate; she actually seemed to believe that there was a snake in the office.

In an effort to bring the situation under control and deal with my own anxiety, I began in a somewhat intellectualized way to try to figure out what was going on. My thinking went approximately as follows: According to standard psychoanalytic teachings, the snake is a symbol for the penis. It was not unreasonable to think that a young woman in analysis with a young male analyst would be overwhelmed by sexual fantasies, feelings, and fears. It seemed plausible to conclude that I was dealing with a typical male-female sexual transference, problems with their roots in the Oedipus complex. Fortunately, I had already learned that when I think in this way, it is a sure sign that I am in trouble. I was approaching the case material in a typical stereotyped way. It may be true statistically that for a given population the snake represents a penis, but I had no evidence at all that Mrs. C. was part of the statistic. So far, I had no idea what the snake meant to my patient, and I had not yet established an analytic process to enable me to find out.

I was able, after my initial personal difficulties, to calm Mrs. C. down, to listen freely, and to begin to find out what the snake fear meant to her. To do this, it was necessary for her to free associate and to allow disordered experiences—experiences of a lower order of organization than those that usually occur—to take place. She had to capture all of the component details and attributes of her experiences regarding snakes, as confused, chaotic, and frightening as these might be. She had to allow the input of relevant information to reduce the uncertainty about the meaning of her fears. The snake was indeed being used as a stimulus for associations, much as one would use a dream element in analysis. This analytic work led to the discovery that the patient experienced a snake as a vicious, destructive, cold, unrelated, and unresponsive animal that can suddenly destroy, with no concern for what it is doing and utterly impervious to reason. Snakes were untouchable animals that could get inside a person, coil up and destroy from the inside. As analytic work continued, the picture simplified and the innumerable possible meanings of the snake fear were reduced. It became quite clear to me and to the patient almost simultaneously (it was hardly necessary for me to interpret much) that the snake was the mother whom she feared, her archaic image of her destructive mother, a very disturbed, paranoid woman who had been institutionalized several times for alcoholism. The patient had been given frequent violent enemas (the snake coiled inside?), and she always consciously fantasied that her mother would not have done these horrible things if she had been a boy and had a penis. She fantasied having a penis which in some way could extrude the enema tube. The patient also had pathological images of her own body: she was afraid, for example, that she could be turned inside out. It seemed quite possible that this particular anxiety may have had its roots in the enema experiences; she may have experienced the violent intrusions into her body and the explosive extrusions of the enema water as in some way exploding her from inside and extruding her innards, thus, in effect, turning her inside out.

More specifically, then, the transference was modeled on a deeply disturbed mother-child relationship, and it was this relationship that was at the forefront of the analysis for a long time. Her wishes to have a penis emerged with striking clarity in the analysis in the context of the realities that molded them and gave them specific and unique meaning. Later on in the analysis, direct genital feelings toward me emerged, modeled on open incestuous feelings toward her father. But no snake symbolism accompanied this development.

To review my approach to the patient's behavior: I had temporarily resisted the analytic process. Because of my own anxiety, I began to work in a typical stereotyped fashion, starting with large-scale formulations based on standard "dynamics." I was also doing what many of our patients tend to do, namely, I was looking for quick intellectual answers instead of tolerating confusing emerging experiences and allowing the "answers" to emerge from the analytic process, that is, from extensive, detailed, relevant information input. The "answer" that emerged concerning the meanings of the snake fear surprised me, but it was very convincing, and, of great importance, it was an "answer" that the patient and I arrived at almost simultaneously. Since then I have had other patients for whom snake fears had similar meanings.

Another fragment of an hour from the same patient illustrates the way meaningful associative connections—visual scenes, images, and so on—can emerge spontaneously when we are in good contact with the patient's inner world and can allow the activation of a full flesh-and-blood working model of the patient's life.

One day the patient, who was taking a mathematics course at the time, told me of her difficulty with abstract mathematical concepts. I was able to get her to elaborate on her experiences, and she told me how distant from and unrelated to the abstract symbols she felt. "They are dead; they have no meaning," she said. "They give you nothing. What good are they? They are lifeless; they really stand for nothing. It is like being in a room with dead people." As she spoke, I was listening carefully while also attending to what I knew of her early experiences and past history and, quite spontaneously, I had

an inner visual image of this patient walking into her home and
finding her mother drunk and stuporous on the floor. I began to
experience some of the feelings that the patient might have had at
such times. These were scenes that I knew she had experienced on
many occasions, but they had not recently come up in the analysis. I
reflected on what to say and on how to use my associative connections, but it was unnecessary for me to say anything because she
immediately began to speak of these very same scenes. She told of
walking in on her drunken "dead" mother, of doing things for her
when she was drunk, but with no feeling, "getting nothing from it.
There was no meaning, no point to it at all. Mother was nothing
more than a dead symbol of a mother." She told of going through her
teens on her intellect, doing the right things out of intellectual
knowledge of what one is supposed to do, but with no sense of connection to things around her and no feeling of inner relatedness. She
acted as if she felt that the world of people represented only a "world
of dead symbols."

That I was able to "predict" correctly Mrs. C.'s associations was
an indication of the accuracy of my working model of her and of the
fact that I was in good contact with her at the time. Actually, we are
constantly making such "predictions" in all human communica-
tions. For example, we are constantly automatically anticipating
the end of a sentence when we listen to someone speak. Such antic-
ipations allow us to fill in gaps or detect slips of the tongue, and the
like.

Unfortunately, although I did well with Mrs. C. in many ways, I
also erred very seriously. The patient had been referred by her husband's therapist who took the attitude that Mrs. C. was sicker than
her husband. Although I was supervised on this case by an out-
standing heuristic clinician, we both erred in focusing exclusively
on the patient's dramatic early traumatic history. We too, I regret to
say, saw the patient as sicker than the husband. We failed to see
that some of Mrs. C.'s sexual "difficulties" were determined not only
by her early pathological history but were responses to the husband's current immature behavior. We were working with a limited
model of psychopathology and with a limited model of the patient's
current life.

The patient stopped treatment after about eight years with mixed
feelings about both me and analysis, reactions I obviously did not

understand at the time. She came back several years later, in deep despair that her marriage wasn't working out and believing that she had somehow failed to go "deep enough" in her first analysis to overcome her marital problems. She resumed analysis for this reason. Her husband's role in their difficulties quickly became clear to her. This was a shattering experience not only because of what it revealed about the marriage, but what it revealed about her treatment. In no uncertain terms, she confronted me with my failures and the failures of her earlier treatment. I did what little I could. I apologized and helped her deal with her feelings toward her husband as well as toward myself.

A case of this kind can humble even the most complacent of analysts and constitutes an excellent example of how one can hurt a patient, even if inadvertently. A silent, unconscious "conspiracy" on the part of three analysts resulted in my failure to invoke a complete model of the patient's current life. But I do think it fair to say that I had fostered an analytic attitude and a degree of trust that allowed her to return to me, resume the analytic process, and give me an opportunity to correct my errors.

9 Case of Mrs. D.

Mrs. D. was what any psychoanalyst would call a "fine" analytic patient. She was a gifted, expressive young woman with unusual access to her inner life. Her case illustrates the use of the "good" hour to understand the analytic process. It was with this patient, who I treated rather early in my career, that I first began to observe, as best as I could, what goes on in such hours.

Some of the hours that I shall be presenting may seem vague and sketchy, and many hardly satisfy me when I review what I have written. As I mentioned earlier, a given "good" hour can illustrate only a few processes, and it is only when we examine many such hours that we capture the full richness and complexity of what actually takes place in our sessions.

One day near the end of her first year of analysis, Mrs. D. was telling me how uncomfortable she had felt at a party recently given by her divorced father. She had had great doubts about going to it, but finally went. She struggled during most of the hour to capture the full quality of what was disturbing her; I can present only a few fragments of that struggle.

Her father had invited her, along with many other young people, including young women of about her age. He paid little attention to her; she had no special function at the party, even though she was the only member of his family who was present. She felt lost; she did not know most of the other people—arty and bohemian types and not the kind with whom she is generally most comfortable. The noise and excitement were confusing; visually, things seemed blurry. Her father was very busy greeting everyone boisterously, each with a loud "Hello, how are you? Good to see you," and "Come on, let's dance." He went from guest to guest, greeting everyone in essentially the same way and responding to each in the same manner—including the patient. She found herself standing in the corner, alone, lonely, somewhat bewildered, and wanting to leave.

After some time I told Mrs. D. that I thought she had felt that her father had no real or full relationships to other people. Her reply was, "Your words are like glue. When you say something so correctly, there is little more for me to say. If my father decided to take pictures, he wouldn't care who was in front of the camera as long as someone was there whose picture he could take. And my husband is no different." She then went on to talk of her beginning awareness of her husband's deep emotional disturbance. Her father was an extremely narcissistic, hypomanic, impulsive, and infantile person, but a brilliant businessman. The patient had been married only a short time when her husband became increasingly withdrawn from her, depressed, unrelated, and hostile. In public and when she first knew him, he appeared to be friendly, open, concerned, and involved with people. However, in his work he made little distinction among the people with whom he was associated. Though she had previously described behavior of her husband which seemed to me to indicate that he was disturbed, it was only slowly and as a result of hours of the kind just described that the patient began to be *aware* of his disturbance.

Note what happened here. The patient provided a stimulus for analytic work; she described a situation that was distressing to her and spontaneously began to associate to it. She attempted to capture the detailed qualities of her experience, how she felt, to what she was reacting, and so on. The patient had to allow seemingly unrelated, somewhat disordered mental contents of a lower order of organization to enter the analytic situation. Clinically, the patient had to partially abandon or efface her present self in order to capture or reexperience the event being analyzed. This was stressful and painful for her; she was near tears as she spoke. She was simultaneously observing her experiences and carefully searching for the best possible words to describe them.

In the broadest terms, I believe we can say that the patient had allowed the activation of memories related to the event under analysis; there was a relatively random search through a segment of memory, a vast input of relevant information. The activation of these memories led her to reexperience the event with the associated feelings of loneliness, confusion, blurred visual images, and so on. Clinically, the patient was paying a great deal of careful attention to the event that had upset her. To an unusual degree, she was able to focus carefully and in depth on a segment of her recent life.

Complex processes allowed Mrs. D. to detect and sort out her inner experiences, to compare and relate them, to match them against inner word representations in order to find the exact words to express the inner phenomena. As a result of this activity, she became increasingly aware of the depth and variety of her inner experiences. One can be quite sure that in these activities there are an enormous number of feedback relationships, trial-and-error activities, and constant "error" corrections. Genuine free association is, I believe, characterized by groping and searching, in contrast to slick and empty talk. Constant "error" correction takes place as one focuses on experiences and tries to find ways to describe them, while simultaneously maintaining vigilance for new and seemingly unrelated experiences.

At the beginning of the hour, I was somewhat preoccupied and not able to pay careful attention to Mrs. D. Phrases such as "Oedipus complex" and "sibling rivalry" came to mind. These were, in fact, quick and easy intellectualized ways to organize the patient's material—analytic clichés which might have had some remote relevance. Actually, in this context, they indicated my temporary inability to make adequate contact with the situation and my anxiety upon recognizing that I was not following the patient well enough—another example of how, early in my career, I tended to fall back on stereotyped approaches to handle personal difficulties that were temporarily interfering with my ability to work. Fortunately, however, for most of the hour, I was able to make adequate contact with the patient and with the situation being analyzed. I was able to "empathize" with her; quite spontaneously, I found myself partially experiencing what she was experiencing. I entered her world and experienced a visual scene in which I "went to the party" in her place. In the year of analytic work, my working models of this patient and of her father had been built up, models of their relationships, characteristic responses, and so on. I was listening and experiencing with these models activated. I could therefore survey the scene experientially and attempt to experience what he might be experiencing as he went around greeting everyone in the same raucous way. I could also attempt to experience what his daughter might experience on being greeted in this way. Clinically, I had to identify temporarily with both the father and the patient. As these activities were carried out, there was an automatic or spontaneous adding or filling in of the scene with multiple images and feelings generated from many sources, including the working models based on my personal experiences as well as my experiences as clinician. And I was constantly observing and evaluating my experiences: my responses to the patient, my responses to the father, my experiences while temporarily identified with the patient, my experiences while temporarily identified with the father, and so on. I then sorted out, compared, and matched these experiences, discarding some tentative ideas and retaining others as the hour progressed. In brief, I was stepping into and out of the scene, gathering some data when I was in the scene, evaluating and making some inferences when I stepped out of the scene, and at times returning to the scene in a particular way to test some tentative inferences. Finally, as the patient continued to speak, I began to experience the father's detachment, not only from the patient, but from all of the guests he seemed to be greeting in such a friendly manner. His responses were in fact basically empty ones. My awareness about the father emerged suddenly. It was the kind of insight frequently referred to as the "Aha" reaction. I like the phrase "coalescing with conviction" because it conveys the idea that a disparate and confused picture seems to simplify and one has an inner conviction that one has caught the essence of things, the unifying principle in what seem to be disparate phenomena. But such "flashes of insight" generally come about only after one has tolerated much uncertainty, tolerated the input of considerable relevant information from many sources, only after much work, and only after many ideas are discarded and innumerable selections are made.

Before saying anything to the patient, I reflected on and evaluated my reactions for a few moments. I decided that they were fairly "normal," relatively free of my own distortions and difficulties. Mrs. D.'s responses to my interpretive remarks indicated that I had caught the essence of her experiences; the idea about her father, which had organized the material for me, served also to "glue" or to coalesce the experiences she was trying to describe. The experience had become simplified and more understandable for her, clear enough so that it was not necessary for her to refine or correct my remarks. Mrs. D. immediately confirmed my remarks with the picture-taking example. The insightful understanding served as a stimulus for further associations, and she went on to tell about her husband. This was the beginning of the working-through process; the analytic understanding was being generalized; it was automatically being applied to new areas and to different relationships. I might add that Mrs. D. was usually very circumspect in her replies to my interpretations. She did not agree to or confirm my remarks very readily, as will be seen shortly. I had to be extremely accurate in what I said to her, and she did not hesitate to tell me when she felt that I had fallen short.

I wish to emphasize three clinical factors about this vignette. First, without any deliberate effort on my part I was not acting as her father did. I was relating to her fully in the context of the analytic situation, and I was treating her as an individual. Implicitly I was offering her the opportunity for a "corrective emotional experience." I use this expression, and will continue to do so, with full recognition that it has had a long and controversial history in psychoanalytic therapy. But it does express what I am trying to say, and what I mean by it will, I hope, be clear if it is recognized that I do not at all refer to anything like the deliberate acting of a role (Alexander et al., 1946). I was treating the patient professionally, as a person, in the context of what she was talking about, and I have little doubt that this made a difference, as I think will be even clearer later on.

In brief, we are never truly "neutral" observers and interpreters. In every word and comment we implicitly convey something of our life experience, our standards and beliefs, something of what we feel about the patient as a human being. How could it be otherwise?

Second, my interpretive remarks were presented only as a very tentative hypothesis. I happened in this instance to be accurate. Usually we are not so accurate, and good analytic patients generally find that they have to correct our comments. But they will do so only if the analyst permits and implicitly invites this type of error-correcting feedback.

Third, when the ideas of Oedipus complex and sibling rivalry occurred to me, I was much too remote from the clinical material. I was temporarily "resisting" the analytic process. I was using meta-models and clinical generalizations, a level much too abstract to enable one to understand the specific observables in a given case. I had to make more immediate contact with the clinical material and find the simpler generalizations embodied therein. I had to enter the patient's world, allow a degree of disorder, and permit different levels of thought, feeling, and imagery, as well as find generalizations among them.

About my own mental activity, one thing deserves to be mentioned. Certainly, extremely complex processes were taking place, as I have indicated, including rapid information retrieval. The terms *evenly hovering attention* or *evenly suspended attention* (Freud, 1912) are useful descriptive expressions, but they tell us little about the underlying processes. I believe that these terms can be said to refer to an experience resulting from very rapid information retrieval and highly complex processing, including the rapid testing of many hypotheses. The analyst is very active in his supposedly "passive" listening state; but it is a special kind of activity.

Finally, I always find it instructive to ask: "What other way might there have been to approach a given hour?" I certainly cannot say that the interpretive remark I made to Mrs. D. was the only correct one. Many other possibly accurate remarks undoubtedly could have been made about different aspects of the situation. The one I made was generated out of the particular relationship I had with this patient. Another analyst would undoubtedly have found other, equally accurate, interpretations.

It is also instructive to ask, "How far could I have taken the situation had I continued with the ideas of "sibling rivalry" and "Oedipus complex"? The answer: Very far. I could easily have built up elaborate formulations, very plausible ones, according to traditional teaching. Many clinicians advise that we always focus on the ever-present transference. Certainly, clinicians recognize the importance of sibling rivalry: this patient had a younger sibling, and rivalry did exist. Using the well-known idea of displacement, I could easily have formulated the following: When the patient was upset with her father, it was in truth only a displacement; she was actually upset with me, since it was I who greet all of my patients—her "siblings"—in essentially the same way. Although such formulations at the beginning of a case are popular in psychoanalytic therapy, they have long lost any meaningfulness for me. Such formulations are generally useless because they do not emerge from a process leading to discovery, from the generation and organization of new and relevant information. The formulations are also dangerous to use because they give one a false sense of understanding what is going on, in contrast to recognizing the true uncertainty and complexity of clinical situations when initially encountered.

Later in the analysis, Mrs. D.'s failure to give "average expectable" emotional responses enabled me to further the analytic process and provided some insight into the nature of her defenses.

One day Mrs. D. came in to tell me how excited she was that her divorced mother was to be remarried. She could hardly wait to tell her friends. She had found out the news quite accidentally while making a casual call to her sister. The mother was going to sell their house and move to another state.

I was struck by the patient's response. It was hardly one that I would have expected from her or from most people. Mrs. D. was not told directly about the mother's marriage; and without her being consulted, the house that she had lived in and loved was to be sold. The family was now to be completely broken up. And, finally, I knew that the patient did not like the man the mother was going to marry. Mrs. D.'s reactions were indeed puzzling. Sorrow, anger, or some other form of emotional upset would certainly have been more appropriate than delighted excitement.

My first attempt to explore the matter brought forth the response that it was "really great" that her mother was going to be remarried. But when I confronted the patient with the total inappropriateness of her responses, the situation became much clearer. I discovered that, before coming into the analytic session, the patient had called her mother and had spoken to her like a good, dutiful daughter. The mother had told the patient that she would be married on Christmas; and Mrs. D. replied that it was "a fine time, a wonderful time to be married." The mother's reply was, "How sweet of you."

Actually, the patient was deeply upset about the marriage. She had already begun to think of ways to keep the house in the family.

And Christmas was an unbelievably bad time for the mother to be remarried. It was the only time the children and their divorced parents customarily got together; it was the only time that they were a family.

Mrs. D., I further learned, had been aware of her true feelings and experiences when she spoke to her friends and was able to tell them how upset she was. But the analytic session followed the call to the mother. During the hour, she spoke to me as though it were necessary for her to continue to act like the dutiful sweet daughter.

While Mrs. D. was reporting her initial reactions, I was filling in the scene with relevant information, average expectable responses based on working models of reasonable human responses, as well as with the characteristic responses of the patient based on my model of her that had been built up over time. This filling-in process usually takes place automatically and spontaneously and will be rather extensive if the analyst is in full contact with the situation and not defending himself in some way. Because Mrs. D.'s responses did not match the experiences that I was using as a "standard," I thought the patient was defending herself. My working model predicted a range of reasonable human responses: I was alerted by the mismatch between the patient's actual reactions and the predicted ones.

In Mrs. D.'s case, it was possible to make a relatively successful reconstruction illustrating a basic aspect of the analytic process, one that is generally present but not often so clearly detectable. I am referring to the analyst's constant attempt to find the best match between the input information and some standard of reference. An insightful "Aha" experience, the kind of thing that I've referred to as "coalescing with conviction," emerges when one finds a good match based on a great deal of information.

The hour I am describing took place in the seventh year of analysis. It brought to the fore a constellation of distressing feelings that had repeatedly come up in the analysis but had thus far eluded genuine understanding. I had many ideas about these experiences, but nothing had really "jelled." I see two sets of circumstances that, combined, would explain the emergence with such clarity of the constellation of experiences during the session I am describing. First, the patient had recently been deeply disappointed by the man she loved and felt would want to marry her. His "dumping" her was quite sudden and totally inexplicable. She had been extremely upset for several months and was therefore more involved in the analysis than she had ever been. During this period she felt that she was living only to come to the analytic sessions.

The second set of circumstances requires that we turn the calendar back by a week or so. Before the session I have been describing I had made some interpretive remarks which she felt were quite bad. She felt that I had been misunderstanding her for several days, and that I had used words that had no meaning to her and that did not capture the essence of her experience. Because of its relevance to the hour I have been reporting, I must describe what I said to the patient that she felt was so inaccurate.

For several sessions, she had been speaking about her mother, how tense, anxious, and impatient she was, how she could explode and fall apart when the patient attempted to express different moods and feelings or complain about various things. I tried to relate this to the transference. I said that she was "guarded" in her relationship to me, and suggested that she was afraid that I might become irritated and explode the way her mother did. The word *guarded* infuriated the patient. "When you use words like guarded, I lose all sense of myself and of you," she exclaimed. Then, with great turmoil and anguish, she spelled out the constellation of experiences she had been attempting to delineate for many months. In order to convey the essence of the session I give the patient's words as though I were quoting them exactly; actually, I can only paraphrase what she said because I wrote up the session sometime after it occurred.

> There is a great part of me that doesn't feel your presence. Part of me isn't aware of your existence. In part I don't know who I am, where I am, or where you are located in space. I have no inner sense of you, no inner sense of contact with you, no feeling of warmth between us; I feel disoriented in relationship to you. It is not a question of "guardedness"; I am not guarding myself from anything; I can't find you; I don't know where you are; I don't know how to reach you; I don't know how to make contact with you. I feel helplessly blind, and I wondered if there was a time in my life when I actually was blind and no one was aware of it.

Mrs. D. became increasingly upset as the hour went on and then said:

When you use the word *guarded,* it becomes something that I must
reach; I must work to get to it, and all by myself; it is a frantic life-
and-death feeling, and I must be able to do it, I must, I must, I must! I
must be able to reach you and the words that you set up. The word
guarded is not my inner experience; it is an outside view of how I
appear; and when you use it, you show no awareness of what is going
on inside of me. When you use words like that, you push me into an
abyss, an endless abyss; and I don't know where I am, where you are,
and how to reach you. And for me, it is life and death. I must use all of
my strength to reach you, and I have to do it on my own; there is no
one to help me, no one, no one, no one touching me or reaching out to
me. And I don't know how long I can go on; I don't know how long I can
keep going.

As I listened, I was struck by the patient's frantic, agitated, highly emotional reaching out, the life-and-death quality, the untouched, blind, and disoriented feelings. It was obvious that she was
absolutely desperately trying to make contact with me, trying to
make contact with the word *guarded* that I had used, desperately
trying to have me understand.

I felt at a loss; I could see no way to reach her, in an analytic
sense, through understanding. I did not understand the specific
meaning of these experiences; and I did not know what I could say
about them that would be meaningful and helpful. I had heard elements of these experiences for a very long time, and I found them to
be rather confusing. I felt, too, that if I did not understand her in
this hour, I might never understand her, because it was unlikely
that I would get another hour as rich in imagery and feeling. As I
listened from within her world of experience I also searched through
my store of memories, feelings, and impressions about this patient
based on multiple working models. I recalled the traumatic events
in her early life—a tonsillectomy, a celiac syndrome followed by
many enemas, an accident resulting in loss of consciousness, and, of
great importance, a serious strabimus, on which much analytic
work had already been done. I compared and matched the experiences being reported against the kinds of experiences that might
have been present at the times of these events. Nothing matched
well. I wondered about the relation of the eye problem to the experiences being reported, but the match was adequate only in some
respects. In general, it was poor. Perhaps a feeling of disorientation

might be part of a strabismus in early life, with double images and
resulting confusion? But feelings of blind, desperate groping and of
not knowing where one was did not match anything that I could
imagine to be the experience of a child with strabismus. I knew a
great deal about the mother, for instance, her inability to touch and
fondle the patient (who was an unwanted baby); but still, nothing
gave me a true sense of conviction, an experience to indicate that a
good matching had been achieved. I could only sense from the dif-
fuseness, primitiveness, and totality of the experiences being reported that they had to do with very early periods in her life.

The hour finally ended. I was disappointed that I had not understood what was going on; something was eluding me; nothing had
really fallen into place. As the patient walked out of the office, the
chain of my associations went from her mother, who had been unable to touch and fondle the patient, to thoughts of how the patient
had been fed early in her life. It suddenly came to me that if the
patient had been fed with a propped-up bottle, the experiences she
was reporting might have had their origin in the bottle's falling and
being unavailable. It seemed to me quite natural that an infant
would react with blind, helpless, and agitated groping, with a sense
of life-and-death desperation, and with a feeling of being all alone
and making no contact with anyone—just as the patient described
her current state in the analytic situation. The idea came to me as a
deep, insightful experience, a coalescing with deep conviction, and a
sense of relief that I had, perhaps, begun to understand something,
and that perhaps a genuine discovery was taking place. The match
between the experiences reported and scenes that I could imagine
seemed good in its details and specifics. Quite suddenly, after many
months, things had become simpler. I did not think that the patient
had ever told me anything about her early feeding experiences; but
feeding with a propped-up bottle fit the psychology of the mother; it
fit everything that I knew about her and about such people in general. I had filled in reasonable and specific possibilities concerning the
mother's behavior because I had a reasonably good working model of
her.

Next day Mrs. D. continued with the general theme of the previous hour, and it was quite appropriate for me to share with her my
hypothesis, my reconstruction. She was able to confirm it completely. She had, as I had known for some time, been raised on a

very rigid schedule. Neither parent came to comfort her when she cried desperately at night. She was fed by a bottle that was propped up near her face. This was a well-known family story. A younger sister was fed in the same way, and the patient had distinct recollections of frequently "sneaking" her hands into her sister's crib to help her get the bottle back when it fell. I suggested to Mrs. D. that her mother was probably too impatient and tense to stay with her during feeding. This also proved to be accurate. She recalled that her mother would prop up the bottle for her sister and then vacuum the house—proud of how much she had been able to accomplish, although she could not hear the sister's cries while vacuuming. There was every reason to believe that the patient's early experiences were basically no different.

Mrs. D. was pleased and surprised that I surmised a probable truth about her early life which she had never told me. Derivatives of the early experiences were worked through, e.g., their close relationship to the current difficulties with the man who was disappointing her; she experienced him as "teasing" her, holding out the promise of a loving and tender relationship and then, suddenly and inexplicably, withdrawing, leaving her feeling helpless, confused, desperate, alone, and empty. During the session, after the one in which I told her of my reconstruction, she reported that when she came into the office she had the sense of seeing me in a much sharper way. It is interesting to note that Mrs. D. apparently felt helplessly blind when left alone as an infant, desperately trying to locate a lost bottle, but was able to see me in a sharper way after a session in which she felt understood and not abandoned.

Her extreme reaction to my previously having misunderstood her now also became clearer. When I used words such as *guarded,* I was not reaching the depth of her experience at the moment. I was not making accurate and complete contact with her. The patient experienced me as though I were her unrelated mother; and she experienced my words as though they were the bottle that had eluded her; desperately and frantically, with a life-and-death feeling, it was necessary for her to find out what I meant and to make contact with me as she had frantically to do with the lost bottle on innumerable occasions. My accurate reconstruction evoked in Mrs. D. a deep sense of warmth toward me; she experienced me as reaching out to her and attempting to make contact with her. And indeed I was; I was trying to make contact with her through understanding, within the bounds of an analyst-patient relationship. The hour illustrates the idea that reconstructions have meanings that go well beyond the obvious intellectual content.

This clinical example illustrates the idea that every piece of good analytic work may implicitly and automatically carry with it a corrective emotional experience—new experiences, new information that makes the updating of working models possible. Indeed, it may well be that the possibility for this corrective emotional experience makes the specific analytic work possible. In other words, in this case, the patient would not have worked so hard to make herself understood and the reconstruction would not have been possible if she had not felt that somewhere I truly wanted to help and understand her. Or, to state the matter in a different way, patients generally will not tell the analyst of painful and difficult experiences if they expect the analyst to behave in a traumatizing way, as other important figures may have done in the past.

The case also illustrates the kind of constant error-correction that, I believe, is characteristic of the analytic process. Indeed, it is the constant correction of errors that, in great part, allows the process to move on. My use of the word *guarded* was not a "bad" error, if indeed it can be called an error. What I was attempting to convey by using the word proved subsequently to be fairly accurate, although within a somewhat different emotional context. I was, however, wrong to use to word at this specific time and within the specific emotional context of the hour in question. Initially, I missed the full depth of her chaos, confusion, and disorganization. But, my very misunderstanding served, in part, to bring out the frantic reaction that made the reconstruction possible. My error was in part responsible for the good analytic work because it magnified the very experiences that I had misunderstood. This magnification made my subsequent understanding possible. In the hour and in relationship to me, the patient was living out the very experiences that she was talking about. Finally, it was necessary for me to shift focus, to allow myself to be corrected. If I had not allowed this, I would have been resisting the analytic process.

Again we can see that the analyst's evenly hovering or suspended attention is not a passive, drifting thing. I had to allow a free memory search and the input of a vast amount of relevant information without immediately focusing on any one element to the exclusion of others and without immediately discarding any element. The information had to be sorted, grouped, and patterned. A trial-and-error process was set up, with constant testing of tentative hypotheses as I attempted to match the input information against various "standards" and rate the matchings for best fit. When I grouped the information primarily around the feeling of blindness and tried to match it against the "standard" of how a strabismic child might experience the world, the match was poor but not absolutely zero. Therefore, I did not discard it completely, but I resumed my search for a better match. The more detailed the information input and memory search, the more detailed the "standards" of comparison, and the closer the matchings, the greater is one's sense of conviction that things have coalesced and simplified.

I think the sense of relief I experienced came from many sources. For one thing, a great deal of effort is required to carry out the analyst's activities; one must tolerate considerable stress, confusion, and disorder. In a sense, the analyst is proceeding in an unnatural direction—away from the order and organization, the known and the familiar we prefer. The analyst must allow temporary disorder and disorganization; he must keep in mind a vast number of variables and their positions and relationships to each other; he must set up innumerable hypotheses and allow himself to abandon them if necessary. Relief comes when things have simplified, when he has found a new explanation, generalization, or pattern, a new order or new level of hierarchical organization for the information at hand. In this case, I could now view all of the seemingly confused and unrelated experiences involved in the particular constellation being analyzed as elements of a larger pattern: repeated traumatic feeding experiences.

Another vignette concerning this patient further illustrates some of the issues I am dealing with. One day, after speaking emotionally of severe traumatic aspects of her early life, Mrs. D. had the feeling that I was cold, aloof, and distant, that everything she had been saying was chaotic, and that this chaos affected me so that I was bewildered and helpless and did not know what to do. I interpreted to the patient that I thought she felt that her mother was cold, aloof, confused, and had been bewildered and paralyzed by her when she was an infant. My comments were meaningful and helpful to her.

Again, my interpretation emerged from a matching of input against several models. But I would like to emphasize one point. My comments were basically accurate in a classical analytic sense. The patient was living out something in the transference that was related to the emotional content of the hour. I was implicitly saying to her, "You are reacting to me as though I were your mother, as though I am confused, bewildered, and paralyzed by you, just as you experienced your mother." I was showing the patient where the distortions of today's reactions came from. But I was also providing her with a corrective emotional experience—new experiences, new information, which allowed change and reorganization of working models to take place. The very accuracy of my interpretation indicated that I was neither cold, aloof, confused, bewildered nor paralyzed by her. I was "all there" and in control of the situation.

On more than one occasion Mrs. D. told me that whenever I said something to her, she would breathe a sigh of relief as she checked off to see if I was intact, organized, under control, not confused, not afraid to talk, not getting irritable, and not angry. These responses were probably related to her relationship to both of her parents. They were multidetermined, as such reactions usually are.

Every considerate, tactful, empathic word I ever uttered to Mrs. D. seemed to have been meaningful at many different levels. They provided direct human experiences—specific information—to correct and change the existing pathological working models of close, adult, parental figures, as well as related working models of herself. This information made possible a revision of models at innumerable hierarchical levels, a revision in the direction of healthier and more stable models of herself and others—what classical analysts call self- and object representations.

One final vignette about this patient: One day, Mrs. D. returned from a holiday spent with her divorced parents. She was upset, depressed, and disappointed. They had gone through the motions of having a "jolly good time," but the patient felt that it was all pretense and meaningless. As she spoke, I said that she seemed to be holding back from crying—an obvious enough interpretation. Anyone who has ever cried would have had little trouble inferring as much from the huskiness and nasal quality of her voice, and so on. She agreed with my comment, and then spoke of her attempts to maintain a "hard-wall" attitude. She couldn't see the point of crying; it did no good. She then spoke of her hopelessness and loneliness. And she did allow herself to cry. She expressed her resentment toward her parents and especially how upset she was at the cold behavior of her father.

In this hour I was doing much more than conveying to the patient some intellectual knowledge about her inner state. I was not silent and cold. I was implicitly permitting her to cry, and my comments indicated that I was ready to listen to her, that she had someone to cry to, that I did not look down on someone who cries, and it was therefore not necessary for her to continue with the "hard-wall" attitude. None of this was deliberately thought out in advance on my part. From an analytic standpoint, the hour was not at all unusual; it was standard, everyday analytic work. I was not acting any sort of role; I was reacting quite spontaneously. But, in doing so, I was behaving more maturely than either of her parents. Her mother felt that all feelings and emotions must be controlled; and her father always gave logical reasons why one need never cry, regardless of the circumstances.

Again, implicit in my interpretive comments, was the possibility for a corrective emotional experience for the patient. My remarks reflected innumerable working models of my own. Quite obviously, I believe that crying is a basic human reaction, observable in every child, and that it has a most important role in mature, adult life. And I have always found that it is a good sign when previously inhibited patients finally allow themselves to cry. Thus, my remarks reflected my image of her, my attitude about the expression of emotions, and my tolerance of her feelings. If I had been intolerant or impatient with her tears or if I had been basically unsympathetic, I would not have made the comments that I did in the manner that I made them; and her "hard-wall" attitude would have continued.

10

Case of Mr. E.

The following sessions from one patient's analysis occurred when I had already had a number of years of experience as a psycho-analyst.[1]

In the first of the sessions to be reported, Mr. E., a 36-year-old married attorney, spoke of the enormous pressure he was feeling. His mother had died a few weeks before; his son was extremely ill and hospitalization was required; professional problems were enormous—an important case was in progress; and financial demands and difficulties were becoming increasingly serious.

He reported feeling explosive, torn apart; there were "demands, demands, demands" from all sides. At one point he broke into tears. He wondered if he could go on; he could tolerate it no longer and wondered if the tension could kill him. He rasped at me, angrily demanding that I do something. Because I had not seen the man for a few days, I could hardly get my bearings. I therefore asked him why he could not go on and talk further about his feelings and such things as the specific nature of his bodily experiences, and what had happened over the weekend to upset him so. He responded by expressing fear that if he talked, he might get out of control, become disorganized, not be able to work, telephone, or carry out his respon-

---

[1]When I asked the patient for permission to use some of the clinical material for publication, he asked that he be allowed to review the clinical details written about him. He reported that these were accurate.

sibilities in his office. He added that he was also afraid to talk because he might go wild and even do physical damage to my office.

I pointed out that such fears were in no way commensurate with the actualities and that it is almost always helpful to talk about them. More important, I pointed out that, true, he was having enormous and unusual reality difficulties, but that these had apparently evoked something that seemed very early, global, frightening, and primitive, and as yet we had no idea what that was.

Inasmuch as Mr. E. seemed paralyzed by anxiety and could hardly verbalize, I plunged into an identification with him: I allowed the activation of my mental image or working model of him and began to describe how he might be experiencing the world. I said that he had been talking for some time about a world that he seemed to experience as vulturish: picking, pulling, burdening, and tearing at him, and at the same time oblivious of him. As I spoke I was essentially free-associating myself, while identified with him; I was using a working model that had been built up from many sessions. My remarks were not thought out in advance, and I even used some Yiddish expressions which were part of his emotional language. The patient agreed, in general, with my description of how he seemed to be experiencing the world. I was apparently approximately on target.

But equally important, I was searching my memories based on my working model of this patient in an attempt to see in what way I could connect present adult experiences with his early infantile experiences. I was also using my understanding of how an infant or child might experience traumatic events. I knew that Mr. E. had had eczema at an early age. Had today's "real" events evoked residues of early infantile experiences connected with the eczema? I felt uncertain here; the match was not very good. I also considered the possibility that early experiences related to enemas might have been activated because I thought that the explosiveness, tension, and delayed anger matched reasonably well with how a child might experience repeated enemas. Because the fit seemed reasonably good, I suggested this possibility to the patient: that archaic feelings and experiences related to early enemas had possibly been reactivated by his current difficulties. My comments came at the end of the hour, and the session ended inconclusively.

I wish to call attention to the complexity of the activity that was going on in me. I was attempting to capture exactly what his current emotional world was like, what he was experiencing; and I was also searching through experiences based on models of his early life as well as models of infantile and childhood experience in general. Thus, elaborate search and matching sequences were taking place. Different hypotheses were being formulated and tested, with evaluations of the degree of match in each instance.

The next day Mr. E., most uncharacteristically, thanked me for the previous hour, said he had felt very much relieved after the session, and that I had given him much to think about. One financial burden turned out to be not as bad as he had originally feared, but it was the session that had helped him the most. He felt that I had handled him well; I had responded to him. I did not seem to be afraid of him or to fear his losing control. Since the last session, he had become aware for the first time that when someone asks him to do something and/or brings up a problem, he automatically asks, "What can I do?"; he doesn't evaluate what can be done. And exactly this sort of situation had arisen between the sessions, except that this time he was aware of what was happening. He had been told of the need a member of his family had for help, and had found himself automatically assuming the burden and then getting extremely angry. He realized that he takes on burdens almost automatically, with minimal awareness; and only later do violent feelings arise, at times accompanied by anal itching.

In his calmer state during this session, he could describe more clearly the nature of his bodily feelings. He felt drained, emptied, as if everything was taken from him. He felt that "it was all happening to me; there was no control." He then added, "It is like a vacuum cleaner, sucking everything out."

At this point, I said that these experiences might well be very close to how a child experiences an enema. Mr. E. then recalled that at age 6 he had had a prolapsed rectum. This historical information was completely new and unexpected. His mother and an uncle got him into the bathroom, bent him over the bathtub and by pushing his leg back and forth enabled the protruding tissue to slip back into place. "Frightening as hell!" was my response. He said that it certainly was; and being "scared to death" was what he remembered most vividly.

I pointed out that the expertness with which his mother and uncle handled the situation suggested that perhaps the problem was a recurrent one which they had learned how to handle. Mr. E. agreed that it had probably happened before and wondered why. He noted that even now his father constantly worries about the balance between how much food is taken in and the amount of feces that goes out. He then recalled being on his mother's lap and how the enema "bone," covered with Vaseline, would be slipped into his anus. "It was almost pleasant," he said. I said, "You had to let it happen, hardly aware that it was taking place, and only later in such a situation would you begin to feel a violent, explosive feeling and then everything emptying." I said, too, that while on his mother's lap, his legs and arms could easily be held tightly as the enema water was put it; in other words, everything was out of his control; it was all happening to him. The patient was struck by the apparent close relationship between how he might have experienced the recurrent enemas and how he was experiencing current events. He added the recollection of having been made to hold his buttocks together to keep the enema water from coming out before getting to the toilet.

Mr. E. went on to say that now, as an adult, he really has no understanding either of how to set limits on demands that he makes of himself or how to limit the demands that he allows others to make or assumes that they are making. He described a typical incident. While he and his wife were out walking, she admired something in a store window. He experienced her remark almost as a demand and now felt he had to find a way to buy it for her.

The patient left the hour with what seemed like a sincere expression of thanks. In subsequent hours Mr. E. spoke of increasing awareness of his natural tendency to let things happen and then to experience deep, violent, resentful feelings. For example, he tended to allow workmen to do things in his house without first getting a detailed estimate. He would then feel violently angry if it turned out that he had been taken advantage of.

I have described these two sessions in order to illustrate a number of points. First, there was much emotional expression and immediate relief of anxiety and tension. Mr. E. said he felt better as the result of the work of the first hour. The fact that I responded and did not remain silent was of enormous importance to him, and, in itself, was partly responsible for the reduction of his anxiety. I had listened to him, a very important issue for this man. I had detected the depth of his panic and had responded to it. And I gave him a meaningful way to begin to cope with his disruptive state. In brief, he had someone to help him, someone in control, not overwhelmed as he felt himself to be, and who did not seem to be afraid of him. I implicitly tempered his fear of his own impulses by reacting calmly, not diverting him, but actually encouraging him to go on with the experiences he was reporting—a corrective emotional experience.

Second, I worked with several models. I worked with a model of everyday human experience as well as with the experiences he was reporting. The match indicated that something was wrong, unusual, maladaptive. One could argue that some of the patient's problems, such as his financial ones, might have been self-created, that he had the need constantly to create a stressful outer world situation so that he could then reexperience a painful, yet pleasurably violent, hurting, and tension-laden world—in many ways, a very familiar world for him. This hypothesis had truth, I believe, but such motivations did not seem to be at the forefront at the time. He was reacting to too many problems that could hardly have been self-created, and his reactions were the product of his entire past history.

When he insisted that I do something, I knew that I had to respond in some way. I could capture his panic and paralysis as I saw his face when he came into the office, heard his voice, and listened to him tell of his explosiveness and helplessness. I could identify with him at the moment and feel what he was experiencing, a process that is certainly a part of anything generally called "empathizing." Comparing these experiences with normal models, with this patient's functioning at other times, and with experiences of other deeply troubled and anxious patients, I knew I certainly could not remain silent.

In identifying with the patient's state, I attempted to verbalize what might be going on, something that he could not do because of his temporary emotional paralysis. I was, in effect, using myself as a model or substitute for the patient during his temporary emotionally paralyzed state. I used general complex models of early infantile experiences to interpret the information available. I was thereby led to the understanding that some very early, frightening, archaic state had probably been reactivated. Specific comparisons, including my model of the patient's early life, led me to the hypothesis concerning the enema experiences. My initial comments were only partly accurate. I was only roughly correct in the first hour.

Third, in the second session, the patient was able to return to the previous day's material and continue the analytic work on his own, bringing in a more precise description of his inner state. To correct, refine, and make an interpretation more precise is part of the therapeutic alliance, a hallmark of good analytic work.

Fourth, totally new and highly specific information emerged in response to the enema interpretation: the history of the prolapsed rectum. The patient also gave new details about his early enema history.[2]

Fifth, the patient's awareness concerning his current life situation was enlarged as a result of the analytic work He became aware of how he "lets things happen" to him almost unknowingly, and then finds himself inexplicably enraged and explosive. The patient achieved this awareness on his own, outside of the analytic sessions—another indication of a good analytic situation.[3]

Sixth, working through was evident in many ways; the patient was generalizing the awarenesses that had been attained.

Finally, the hours were not intellectualized ones, either on the patient's side or on mine. The material that came out was neither cliché-ridden nor predictable. The hours dealt with specifics, with the patient's "gut" emotions. The connections that I made between past and present were neither "pasted together" nor fitted together on the basis of clinical theoretical stereotypes. The links between the present and the past were based on the patient's experiences.

I wish to stress that the events of the two hours do not prove the enema hypothesis; they only provide evidence for it. In subsequent hours different character traits were dealt with that added further evidence for the hypothesis that repeated enema experiences were probably of great importance in Mr. E.'s early life.

---

[2]Pediatricians have informed me that prolapse of the rectum is not uncommon when a child is caught in a vicious enema-constipation cycle.

[3]Experienced clinicians may wonder about the seductive aspects of the "letting it happen," probably related to the pleasurable aspects of the "bone" penetrating his anus. This issue was not at the forefront during these hours; it came up subsequently.

Here is a third hour from Mr. E.'s analysis. One day the patient, who had recently been made a partner in a law firm, told of finding himself angry and "festering" at his office. He made rhythmic motions with his hands over his abdomen, his fingers extending out toward his legs to indicate that his anger had "pseudopods like an amoeba" and spread out over his entire body, building up to such a point that he could barely control himself. He was distressed to find how nasty, sarcastic, and denunciatory he had been in the office. He was upset with me for not helping him more; he felt that I was failing him.

He then told me that he had reviewed a document prepared by one of the young associate attorneys of the firm and was appalled at what he thought was inadequate research and defective logic. He spoke to another partner about the document, but this partner brushed aside his objections, saying only that one of the senior partners had reviewed the material and had not objected to it. The patient wondered why he became so angry, why he could not talk simply and rationally, and why he found himself beginning to get nasty and sarcastic. He wondered if rivalry with the other partner was involved. He was bothered by the fact that young lawyers in the firm seemed to prefer to go to other partners for advice and guidance, avoiding the patient.

I was puzzled by what had troubled Mr. E. and could offer no suggestion other than that he attempt to capture his full experiences at the time of the incident with the partner. When he did so, he found that the partner's appeal to authority was the factor that seemed to bother him most. Especially distressing was the brushing aside of his logical, rational arguments. The patient then recalled that when he was a young associate lawyer, he went to one of the senior partners in the firm to help resolve a dispute that he was having with a fellow associate lawyer, Dave, about the preparation of a brief. To his astonishment, the senior partner had responded, "Well, you know that Dave went to Harvard Law School and you didn't." At this point I reminded Mr. E. that when he spoke to the partner in the current incident, his logic and rationality had been brushed aside, as it had been in the earlier incident, and I suggested that he became so enraged because he felt obliterated. I was once again working from within my model of this patient, attempting to capture the level or state of experience that had been evoked. In my temporary identification with him, I felt obliterated, and this feeling motivated my comments. Even as I spoke, I had the definite visual image of a helplessly paralyzed man standing speechless. Mr. E. agreed immediately that the word *obliterated* caught his feeling exactly and then said, "You know, it almost feels like a catatonic must feel [Mr. E. had extensive legal experience representing institutionalized psychiatric patients]. "I was standing there, my anger was mounting, but I was speechless. I didn't know what to say. I didn't know what to say that would make a difference." My working model was obviously reasonably accurate. The experiential output, the image of a paralyzed man, in a sense predicted his response.

Finally, I wish to point out that as a result of these hours, my working model of Mr. E. was markedly enhanced; it was updated. And so was Mr. E.'s working model of himself. In this particular instance, radical modifications of the models were not necessary, nor did existing models have to be discarded.

In the heuristic therapeutic situation we study the individual. Success in achieving the goal of establishing an analytic process is marked by the presence of good hours. In any one good hour only a few characteristics typical of such hours can be demonstrated. However, if we review several such hours, of the kind reported in the cases of Mrs. C., Mrs. D., and Mr. E., we get a more complete picture of these hours. Here is a summary of the characteristics that have been found (many of these can be subsumed under what psychoanalysts have long called *working through*):

(a).–There is much emotional expression, usually associated with immediate relief of tension and anxiety.
(b).–The patient acquires new awarenesses about current life situations.
(c).–Links are established between the present and the past.
(d).–Memories arising for the first time confirm the links suggested between the present and the past.
(e).–The patient participates actively in the process and provides error-correcting feedback.
(f).–The patient experiences and verbalizes archaic, primitive, and disordered states.
(g).–The patient actively "relives" or revives details of the past and does not just recall generalizations about the past.

(h).–The patient feels understood. In general, there is a greater sense of trust and an enrichment or deepening of the patient-analyst relationship.

(i).–Corrective emotional experiences take place.

(j).–New generalizations, explanations, or patterns for the information emerge.

11 Case of Mr. F.

At times we get what seems to be a good hour: convincing evidence emerges for an important explanatory hypothesis, yet the process fails. When we examine the apparent good hour closely we see that important characteristics of such hours were actually not present.

Mr. F., whom I treated only a few years ago, was a young man in his mid-twenties. He was referred by a mutual acquaintance who described him as exceptionally brilliant. When Mr. F. called, his speech revealed that he was obviously very well educated, but he stuttered so severely that he could hardly give his name. Here is a description of the first long consultation.

Mr. F. was thin, rather tall, youthful looking, and had a very pleasant manner. He wore an elegantly tailored, European cut, pin-striped suit and carried an attaché case. He already held a position in a major corporation, one that required his conducting big "wheeler-dealer" types of business transactions. In both dress and behavior, this patient seemed to be well beyond his years. He told me, first, that he had been depressed for several months; he was constantly tired and had a sleep disturbance. Second, his asthma had returned, after his not having had an attack for years. Third, his stuttering had worsened. This condition had been present since age 7 and had come and gone over the years. Then too, there seemed to be some exacerbation of an old eczematous condition. Fourth, he was upset because a big business deal that he had been pushing at the corporation had fallen through.

I also learned that Mr. F. had been in New York City for only 3 years. He had been born in the suburbs of Chicago of Jewish parents, his father's family having been annihilated by the Nazis. Father survived only because he had been in one of the Central-European armies. Father was extremely bright but never successful. A cabinetmaker by trade, he did little for himself until about the last year of his life when he learned to advertise and promote himself a bit. He died, when the patient was age 17, of a coronary thrombosis, apparently his third episode. The father's death came just before Mr. F. learned that he had been accepted at one of the leading universities in the United States. On the day before he died, Mr. F. had sprayed the house with an insecticide. Only later did he learn that this particular spray could be toxic. He subsequently felt responsible for his father's death.

His first year at college was extremely difficult. He felt confused and stuttered a great deal. He saw one of his advisors frequently for personal help, and he found out later that the school authorities had been concerned about his psychological state. He majored in several technical subjects, sacrificing everything for his classwork, including his interest in music and athletics.

After graduation, he took a job with a major corporation and apparently rose very rapidly. He was indeed a very aggressive young man in a very great hurry. Success constantly preoccupied him. All his thoughts had to do with how to climb as rapidly as possible, how to keep from being held back by the bureaucrats around him, those of higher as well as of lower rank, who he felt were intellectually inferior to him and only got in his way and interfered with his more efficient ways of doing things. He felt that because the corporation mishandled the situation when it did not follow his advice, the big business deal had fallen through. Had it succeeded, it would have led to his becoming a high-salaried chief executive.

A complicating factor was that 2 years prior to seeing me, he had been injured in an automobile accident and had had a horrible hospital experience. Although his physical condition had improved considerably, he was left with some residual orthopedic problems.

He had many friends, and he tried to lead a normal social life, but he found himself constantly preoccupied with business matters. His sexual life and experiences were limited. His secretary, several years older than he, was extremely helpful to him at work and had also helped him while he was hospitalized. His first sexual experience was with her, at her suggestion. His sexual attitudes were, he told me, still mid-Victorian, and he was only beginning to learn something about women.

On the basis of this initial interview, there was much to indicate possible grandiose ideation. I checked to see if he fit some well-known clinical types. Thus, I wondered if he had true manic episodes. But, although he spoke of feeling that he could conquer all of New York City, that he felt there was no limit to his power, and he hoped to make enough money to be able to retire within a few years, he had not been subject to true manic episodes as far as I could tell.

He was calmer when seen again 3 days later, expressing many questions about seeing a psychiatrist and wondering about his need to see one. By the end of the initial consultations, I learned much of his need to set up challenges to be conquered. I learned, too, that he had suffered from enuresis until age 12. He had been placed on cortisone between ages 11 and 16 for his asthma. The side effects were serious; he became fat and effeminate looking, with large breasts. He spoke, too, of wondering if he was perhaps a "battered child" (he stuttered as he said this). He had not been an aggressive child, had avoided battles, but had been active and mischievous. His father, a tense, angry, and irritable man, would get upset at the patient's antics and sometimes smash him so hard that he flew across the room. Mother, incidentally, had had a "nervous breakdown" after father's death. She apparently became depressed and kept to herself for some years.

In the first weeks of treatment, I found Mr. F. flooded with anxiety; he ran hither and yon trying to arrange bigger and better positions for himself, being interviewed here, interviewed there, trying one scheme and then another. He was totally intolerant of any situation wherein he was not in full control and where he could not make things happen at his own pace. The corporation, for example, had plans to develop his talents that would allow him to climb slowly up the inner hierarchy. Too slow for my patient, much too slow! One could say that I observed the patient's anxiety; but the issue was much more complicated than anything conveyed by the mere word "observed." I was trying to match his behavior against working models of reasonable behavior, and the mismatch led me to judge that great anxiety was present. And another basic strategy was operative here which I have already repeatedly mentioned, but which I wish to emphasize at this time. I refer to identification with the patient, entering his world of experience. I was able to capture in myself Mr. F.'s frenzy and hecticness, the impulsiveness, the trying one scheme after another, and the feeling, to use the patient's words, of "jumping off a diving board in all directions without knowing where one is going." This identification gave me a sense of the quality of the patient's anxiety, how primitive it actually was. In effect, I used myself as a model, automatically allowing the emergence of new feelings and thoughts—new information—about the phenomena I was experiencing while identified with the patient.

Obviously, I could have asked Mr. F. directly or indirectly: "Let's stop for awhile, reflect; let's take a look at your anxiety; what is the nature of the experience; what do you think of, imagine, or fantasy when you are so anxious; what is happening to your body?" Many patients can deal directly with such questions, and answers to them can be crucial in giving us some understanding of what the anxieties are all about. But I could not do this very well with Mr. F. He was all action, hardly introspective. Indeed, the world of emotions was quite alien to him. He was struck by how driven he was and had come into treatment wondering about it, a good sign, but the "answer" to this problem, he felt, was to change the nature of his work, or change jobs, or take some other kind of action. As a matter of fact, during this very hectic period, he often thought of dropping treatment when he felt momentarily better after hitting upon a new scheme for a job possibility. His new schemes generally did not work out too well, and, as soon as they failed, he was once again depressed and upset.

I had to work quickly with Mr. F. Rather early, I was struck by the life-and-death quality of everything that was going on. His drivenness, his urge to be successful at a very young age, his extreme impatience, and the need to be in control of everything—all struck me as attributes of a man racing against time, racing against death. This idea emerged as I observed my own reactions while identified with the patient. I was using myself as a model (Diesing, 1971). He had already given me indications that he felt he might die of a coronary like his father, but even that statement did not capture the full extent of the panic I was seeing. Without knowing for sure the full quality of the anxiety as he experienced it, and working mainly with how I felt about his panic, I began to search for possible origins, using my existing working models of the patient and models of infantile and child development and experience. I was, in effect, attempting to organize the chaos in front of me, but organize it from within the patient's life history. In contrast to other cases where I could not get close to anything reasonable for several years, my search did not last long. I went almost directly to the very early asthma experiences.

Let me pause here. One basic strategy is to scan for significant signs. Mr. F.'s having asthma when an infant was a significant sign. When such signs are detected, we are alerted, our attention is focused, and specific expectations are evoked. One might say that the information about his having asthma was now "flagged" in memory as something significant. It had to be important, I felt, especially because it was chronic, started when the patient was an infant, and required potent medications later on which produced many serious side effects.

But the label "asthma" is not quite the same as the experience. So I tried to capture for myself how an infant or a child might experience repeated asthmatic attacks. I mobilized whatever stored information about experiences concerning asthma I had, including working models of early infantile experience. I have had only a few patients with significant asthmatic histories, and, as I recall, they did not have asthma as infants. I might add too that, when I started with this patient, I knew little about asthma in infancy and, initially, made no attempt to find out more; I tried to learn from the patient. I have had no personal experiences in any way related to asthma, although a few years ago, I did go into a mild shocklike state after having been stung by a wasp. I could easily recall the mounting anxiety accompanying the sudden feeling of labored breathing. And I was an adult, medically trained, knew what had happened, and what emergency actions had to be taken. How would a child or an infant having extreme difficulty in breathing feel? Panic, total terror, a feeling of being out of control, unable to grasp what was happening to him or what is taking place?

I felt that I might have been on the right track in thinking about the significance of the early asthma history, but note that I was making something of a leap, from current anxieties bordering on panic, which seemed to have a life-and-death, out-of-control quality, to an early asthmatic history which, I hypothesized, may have had very similar experiential attributes. I certainly would have preferred a slower development of the analysis, preferred having an introspective patient capable of fully capturing and delineating his inner state. But I had to work with the patient as he was, and quickly too. Within a few weeks after the first telephone call, and, I may add, there were many missed sessions as he ran around for a variety of reasons, the following session took place.

The hour began with the issue of being in control at the forefront. Much was happening at work: interviews, possible job changes. Mr. F. had come to the tentative decision not to play the corporate game, to try to avoid the bureaucratic hierarchy, and to find some position of his own where he could go at his own pace. He was much calmer, less frenzied, his stuttering had diminished. I took this opportunity to suggest that perhaps his recent frenzy, anxiety, need to feel in control, and overwhelming need to be successful might have been related to his early experiences with asthma. This was, of course, a very open-ended interpretation. But I was probing, attempting to open some doors, hoping too that I might thereby make the patient more introspective, more aware of himself and of the possible relationships of past to present. His reply was an immediate and emphatic "No!" He told me in no uncertain terms that I was all wrong! He had learned not to let asthma get the better of him. As a youngster, he used to push himself to school, force himself to go on no matter how ill he had been the night before and even though he may have had little sleep. I said that maybe what he was saying was exactly the point, and perhaps what we were seeing now was the adult version of his way of handling asthma when he was young. I said that, for a very young child, asthmatic attacks must be a horrifying and frightening experience. My last remark struck him; he could see the "logic" of what I said. He then told the following.

His asthma started when he was an infant; his condition was worse at night. He tended to awaken suddenly, unable to breathe, and he would then vomit so much that "bile" would come up. When he had an attack he would usually be alone. He went to sleep regularly with a pot next to him into which he could vomit. He was a very active child, always doing things, always on the move, but he was afraid that he would end up as an invalid. Indeed, there was a home for the disabled near his house, and he found himself very sympathetic to those who were in wheelchairs. He had fantasies of being able to do something to help these people when he was older. He was on steroids from age 11 to 16, (as I already knew). These medications were given despite their serious side effects. They succeeded in controlling the asthma. At age 16, after going off steroids, he had one of the worst asthmatic attacks of his life. Later, in his teens, other medications were prescribed.

The patient spontaneously reported two recurrent dreams from childhood which took place on the nights that he was free of asthmatic attacks. In the first, a lion or some other big animal attacked him. In the second, he would be going down a staircase and when about 10 steps from the bottom, he would jump over the bannister and land feet first. There was also some feeling of falling in the second dream. He now said that he recalled vividly his fear of dying during an asthmatic attack. Indeed, typically, he would scream, "I am dying, I am dying," until the doctor came in the middle of the night and reassured him.

I have checked Mr. F.'s history with a specialist in the field, who informed me that it is a very typical and believable picture. The patient arranged for me to get copies of his medical records. They confirmed in every detail the medical facts he told me. I learned, in addition, that his tonsils and adenoids had been removed at age 2.

I think one can reasonably say, on the basis of the material presented, that there was much to support the hypothesis of a relationship between asthma and anxieties about death and about being in control. To put the issue simply, apparently the old anxieties about the lion ready to attack in the night were still alive in the adult.

Mr. F., I regret to say, was not the best of analytic cases. Far from it! What I have presented may seem reasonably good and perhaps a bit dramatic, but even the hour I presented, which seemed to support the asthmatic hypothesis, was only a fair hour. Some of the criteria I mentioned earlier for a good hour were present. For example, links were suggested between past and present, and memories supporting these links arose for the first time. There was a significant input of new and relevant information; uncertainty was reduced. Error-correcting feedback by the patient was present to some extent. There was perhaps some new awareness of current life situations, perhaps a greater recognition of his need to have everything under control. But other things that one likes to see in a good hour were not present. I do not think that the hours gave any significant relief of anxiety and tension; there was very little meaningful emotional expression, the kind that gives genuine relief. Certainly, there was no active, detailed, vivid recall or "reliving" of the past, only relatively unemotional memories of it. And there was no working through in the sense of any generalizations of the insights of the hour, no elaboration of patterns of experience related to the asthma. Indeed, in the very next hour, little about the asthmatic history was taken up for further work. "Asthma was the answer," said the patient, and with that comment everything discussed in the previous hour was pushed away. I vividly recall how dismayed I was by this session; for me, the patient's attitude was a very poor prognostic sign.

Shortly after the sessions just discussed, Mr. F. became involved in setting up a very complex business organization and worked in a frenzy to the point of exhaustion, almost 24 hours each day, with the hope of becoming a millionaire by his next birthday and also of possibly establishing a business empire. For months, the treatment sessions were filled with the stresses of his venture. His business did prove to be quite successful in a remarkably brief period of time, but not as rapidly as Mr. F. wished. He then ended treatment fairly abruptly.

Actually, I think Mr. F. derived little benefit from the treatment situation. His case provides a good example of the difference between what we think we understand and what we can do with that understanding. I found no way to get this man to look at himself, to try to understand what had happened to him, to find out what his inner life was all about, and why he was so driven. In brief, I could not develop an ongoing analytic process. Although when he entered treatment Mr. F. wondered about his life, wondered why he was driven, tense, and depressed, his solution for internal problems was merely to try to change the external world. His life approach is perhaps understandable in view of his history.

I have often wondered what analytic therapy could offer a patient such as this and what could possibly have been done to establish a meaningful analytic process.

12 Case of Mr. G.

Here are extracts from three consecutive sessions of ordinary, decent, everyday analytic work. The case is recent. The sessions as a whole illustrate "good" hours.

A successful young architect came in on a Monday morning wondering if it was necessary for him to continue therapy. Rather vaguely, Mr. G. told of some problems with his pregnant wife on the previous day: she felt he did not pay sufficient attention to her. He had tried to relax in their small apartment by doing some professional work and also by spending some time on his hobby, chess.

On Wednesday, he informed me that his wife had been quite depressed on the previous Monday evening and even spoke of having suicidal thoughts. She too was an architect, but had left the profession in order to develop her interest in painting. She was upset on Monday about her pregnancy, fearing that the infant would interfere with her career. The patient spoke very casually about his wife's depression and suicidal thoughts, and said that she seemed to feel better on Tuesday morning. He then turned to business problems that had been present for some time.

I immediately sensed a mismatch in his casual attitude to his wife's depression and suicidal thoughts. I said that I would expect any husband to have stronger responses to such events and that he, of all people, must have had, because his sister had committed suicide (a horribly traumatic event in the life of his family). I said that it was striking how he kept himself unknowing about his wife's suicidal thoughts. He hadn't even found out what she meant and how serious she was. (In this regard, it should be mentioned that when his sister died he was quite upset that no one took her suicidal threats seriously.) In effect, I was telling Mr. G. that some defenses were operative because the expectable range of experiences seemed not to be present.

At the next session, Friday, Mr. G. told me that it was indeed true that he had not taken his wife's depression seriously. He realized this now. He then went back to Sunday's events, about which he had told me comparatively little. He described how depressed his wife actually had been on Sunday and how hard it is to live with a depressed woman. He had to turn to work and to his hobby to get away from her moods. "I want her to be the mother of my child, but not a depressed mother," he said. He told of admiring her for giving up her career to do what she really wanted to do. He then added his hope that things would eventually turn out well.

Rather firmly, I then said that he had a notable tendency to "slide away" from any situation that might disturb him or bring out strong or frightening feelings. I added that on Monday morning he had told me little about his wife's Sunday depression and certainly he reported having little reaction to her. Yet, on that Monday he had come in wondering if he should continue treatment. I said that his wife's mood on Sunday had obviously affected him because he had to wall himself off from her by working and playing chess by himself—remaining in the room with his wife physically but not emotionally. I used the expression "slide away" because I got a visual image of this man coming close to but not quite touching an event.

Mr. G. replied quickly and with some animation, "You know, you just gave a perfect description of my father. He always turned away from any emotional problem, from any strong feeling; and it is a very natural thing for me to do the same, to 'mute' everything difficult by turning away and becoming preoccupied with other things, just as my father did." It was near the end of the session, and the patient added, "But let me tell you before I leave, when I married my wife, I knew that she was different—thoughtful, introspective, and that she had troubles. But she was interesting. She was not the typical well-scrubbed girl." "Not the 4H type," I said. "Not at all," replied Mr. G., "Not the 4H, bright-eyed American girl. I knew that she was troubled, quite troubled. And I was too, at that time." Mr. G.

was referring to his own confused and emotionally troubled years in school when he first met his wife.

I should say that I knew that the patient's father had had two coronary episodes when the patient was very young, and it was always necessary for the family to be very careful not to upset the father in any way. When I described the patient's way of dealing with his wife's emotional difficulties, I was speaking from within my model of the patient; I was not thinking about the father, although I have no doubt that my knowledge of the father and the general family atmosphere was actively in the background. The patient's responses pleased and surprised me. They indicated that I was on target in an unexpected way. I had caught something of great importance in his life and personality. I did not, indeed I could not, predict the specificity of his response. The therapeutic work was all to the good; it immediately enlarged the scope of the therapeutic process for some time, and it enhanced the working alliance.

In the following week, Mr. G. not only spoke of how valuable the hours had been, but he went on to elaborate on his early relationships to his wife, what had gone on between them when they married, and how much his wife and his mother were alike.

Note that I was matching and comparing input against working models of normal expectable responses, as well as models of the patient built up over time. Note, too, the information concerning suicide in the family. As I said in connection with Mr. F., such significant information can be said to be "flagged" in memory and is therefore easily retrievable. Suicide was especially important at the beginning of treatment because Mr. G. was very mistrustful of me and of all psychiatrists. He felt that his sister's psychiatrist had mishandled her case and was in part responsible for her suicide.

Note, too, the way my interpretation received support. The all-important error-correcting feedback was in operation. My interpretive remarks were an attempt to say something about the patient's personality. He agreed with me almost completely and added highly relevant information about his father, an issue that I had previously not fully understood. He also corrected my comments somewhat when he told of tending to "mute" emotional responses, an especially meaningful and expressive term for this patient, who was also a competent musician.

PART FOUR

STRATEGIES USED IN THE THERAPEUTIC PROCESS

INTRODUCTION

The strategies to be described in the following chapters are all designed to guide both patient and therapist in dealing with some immediate situation; they are designed to help both patient and therapist to understand what is at the forefront at a given moment. Whether the event under consideration happened 20 years ago or the day before, the significance of that event can be discovered only with whatever memories are available at the current moment of inquiry. And whether the event under consideration had its roots in one or a dozen determinants, the significance of that event can be discovered only with whatever memories are available at the current moment of inquiry.

The concept of multideterminism, referring as it does to the multicausal nature of the events with which we are concerned, has been one of the most important concepts in psychoanalysis. Indeed, for me it was an especially important idea because it was the multidetermined nature of our phenomena that led me to an information-processing model. But multideterminism does not mean that at any given moment it is quite acceptable to take up any of the possible determining causes of the event being analyzed. Human psychology suggests the idea that at any given moment only one or a few of the determining factors for any phenomenon is dominant, at the forefront, more discernible, "hotter," and more available for discovery. At least this seems to be the finding of many heuristic workers. And, when a patient is angry, tense, anxious, depressed, reports a bizarre thought or fantasy about the therapist, or reports a dream, it is the task of the therapeutic process to find out what is the most pressing, most urgent, most "highlighted" determinant at the given moment. This task is pivotal in psychoanalytic therapy. (Contrast this activity with that of the stereotyped worker who falls back on his preconceived formulations and selects from the moment at hand whatever fits his formulations). To state the matter simply, if a patient reveals a depressed mood at a given moment, and if patient and analyst accept this as the focus for work, the task is to find out the nature of the discoverable determinants or meanings at this time. At another time, the very same manifest phenomena may have altogether different, discoverable determinants or meanings.

Any clinical example may require the use of multiple strategies, just as it may require invoking multiple working models. And, as with the working models, the strategies are not sharply or clearly differentiated. They overlap and interrelate, a reflection of the multifaceted nature of the phenomena that we observe. The strategies can be used sequentially in different ways; often we go from one strategy to another so rapidly that it seems as though different strategies are being used simultaneously.

I emphasize in these strategies the essentially achievable or practicable operations or, at least, potentially achievable ones. As a result of such operations, unconscious processes are activated. I cannot emphasize this point too much because, all too often, it is misunderstood. As I said earlier in this book, we cannot *use* "the unconscious" in any direct or immediate way. Indeed, we cannot do so by the very definition of the term. We know ourselves only through the phenomena of consciousness: thoughts, fantasies, images, feelings. The idea of "unconscious processes" is an absolutely necessary one, but "unconscious processes" is a hypothetical term about which one can speak in a chemical, electrical, or informational framework. It does not refer to any concrete experiential phenomena. We can say that we can carry out achievable, conscious operations according to the strategies to be discussed; as a result, unconscious processes are activated and, causally related to these, new conscious experiences emerge. (For an extended discussion of these ideas see Peterfreund, 1980).

It must be emphasized that the strategies to be described actually represent astonishingly complex processes. Any attempt to simulate them in an artificial information-processing system, such as a computer, would reveal how extraordinarily complex they actually are and how vast are the information stores employed at any given time—information based on phylogenetic history and on ontogenetic learning. Indeed, many of the strategies to be discussed are little more than overall plans which I hope will someday be elaborated on and made more specific. But even such overall plans are very useful to guide one's work. Detailed procedures can always be filled in and altered or adapted to the specific circumstances of the treatment situation.

It seems to me that formal research methods could make a significant contribution to our understanding of the strategies that therapists use. Videotaped recordings of a session could systematically be presented to a group of analysts who could then subsequently be interviewed for their thinking.

They could be asked what stood out for them, what
tentative formulations they were making, what they
considered to be evidence for these formulations,
what responses they were inclined to make to the
patient, and so on. As the case is followed, optimal
strategies might emerge.

Many of the strategies to be discussed are understandable in light of the idea that information is
actually processed in complex multistages—an idea
now at the forefront of cognitive psychology. Although the data of introspection can lead us "intu-
itively" to such a conclusion, the conclusion is buttressed by recent developments in the information
sciences. We no longer think of the organism as a
passive recipient of information, with the flow of
information tending to be unidirectional. On the
contrary, it is now recognized that there is an active
search for information, active selections, and active
testing or evaluations of the information for relevance to any given need. As a result of such testing,
further information input can be allowed, selected,
or interrupted.

For example, the idea of perceptual defense—the
idea that information related to certain meanings
can be actively excluded—met with great objections
when first proposed. As Erdelyi (1974, p. 3) puts it,
in an article that reviews the literature, ". . . if perceptual defense is really perceptual, how can the
perceiver selectively defend himself against a particular stimulus unless he *first perceives* the stimulus against which he should defend himself?" How
can a homosexual man defend himself against perceiving an attractive woman unless he first perceives her? This apparent paradox is resolved when
it is recognized, as in an information-processing approach, that perception is viewed as taking place in
multistages and that the flow of information is not
unidirectional. At its simplest level, some information can be taken in and tested or evaluated; if ac-

ceptable, necessary, or relevant for whatever purpose, additional information is selected; if not, the information is excluded. As a result of the many stages of processing that actually take place, perception is now viewed very differently. Again, to quote Erdelyi (p. 13): "Broadly conceived, perceptual processes may be best thought of as spanning the full sequence of events associated with information intake and consolidation, beginning just after stimulus input and ending prior to permanent storage in long-term memory."

Clearly, to conceive of perception as a two-directional multistage process will have profound significance for our understanding of such things as the activity of both patient and analyst. The traditional description, derived from Freud (1912, 1913), is of the patient as a passive reporter who merely reports everything that comes to his mind while making no attempt to select, and of the analyst as listening passively, with evenly hovering or evenly suspended attention and with no expectations. Although such descriptions have been historically useful and necessary, I believe they are inaccurate; they oversimplify what are very complex processes.

It was necessary to be somewhat arbitrary in my selection of the strategies. I selected those that seemed to best reflect the actual work of the heuristic process. The strategies are grouped under five categories. The first four take up strategies of the analyst: general strategies; strategies as participant observer; strategies related to the patient as participant in the therapeutic process; strategies related to the establishment of meanings. The final category is strategies of the patient. Many subcategories could have been added, one related to the analysis of dreams, for example.

As with the strategies, the categories are somewhat arbitrary; they overlap, interrelate, and are to some extent repetitious. For example, the entire an-

alytic process and all of the strategies can be said to
be geared toward the goal of establishing unique,
personal meanings, although I have listed some of
the strategies more immediately related to this goal
in a separate category. Many of the strategies used
by the therapist have their counterparts in strategies of the patient. For example, I state as a strategy of the therapist that introspection should be fostered. The counterpart is the patient who is
developing the ability to introspect.

In general, I am writing for the practicing clinician who must work in the real world of extraordinary complexity and in the context of patient urgen-
cy. The strategies cannot therefore have anything
like the precision of those used, for example, in the
information sciences, where it is possible to select
the restricted problem to be worked on.

I list the following strategies and categories
mainly to facilitate discussion. I hope that other in-
vestigators will radically refine and revise the strategies suggested, alter the classifications, and present new and better ones.

13 Strategies of the Analyst: General Strategies

The first strategy in this category, (a) *focus on the analytic process,* refers to one of my basic themes, the comparison between stereotyped and heuristic approaches. The former focus on large-scale formulations made early in the analysis based on well-known or familiar stereotypes, part of the existing clinical theories. The latter focus on a process leading to discovery.

Here I repeat what Freud said about the analytic process. Freud, you recall, points out (1913, p. 130) that the analyst can but set in motion a process that, once begun, "goes its own way and does not allow either the direction it takes or the order in which it picks up its points to be prescribed for it." This statement might be said to form the keystone of the approach I am trying to articulate.

A phenomenon that can make its appearance at any time during the treatment (recall Mrs. A.) is the transference. The analyst should (b) *foster the development and verbalization of transference relationships.* In terms of my general operational approach, we can say, first, that the term refers to a mismatch between the actual relationship of the patient to the analyst—fantasies, feelings, behavior—and ones that models of normal adult relationships predict; and, second, that it refers to a relationship—fantasies, feelings, behavior—to the analyst or therapist that is related to the working models of the patient's infantile and childhood development, including his relation to important persons in his life.

Patients may begin treatment with the transference relationship at the immediate forefront, as with Mrs. A., where it was stormy, explosive, very open, and direct. In the case of Mrs. C., it emerged very early in an odd, indirect sort of way. Many patients can bring up transference thoughts and feelings on their own. Often, the analyst may point out possible transference phenomena that he has observed, or indicate to the patient, quite candidly, that experiences with regard to the analyst and the analytic process are crucial because they are active, current phenomena that can be observed by both parties. The latter activity is part of the education of a patient into the requirements of an optimal process. We often forget that patients initially do not understand what is expected of them in the therapeutic process—what they have to do to allow the process to work. In addition perhaps to finding it difficult to deal with the transference, many patients, even potentially able ones, may not realize the importance of working with it. Implicit in many of the strategies to be discussed is the education of the patient into the part that he must play in the process.

It is generally convincing when one can see transference manifestations that are closely related to the issues being discussed in the hour, issues that have a context other than the transference. In other words, the patient is "living out" in the hour exactly what he is saying about other areas of life. For example, a young anorexia-nervosa patient that I treated told of how self-conscious she is in a bus. She feels that people are wondering about "this disgusting creature." She looks at the advertisements while in a bus in a deliberately "nonchalant" way in order not to betray her self-consciousness. Immediately after telling me this, she spoke of the feeling that I also see her as a "disgusting creature" preoccupied with food and vomiting.

Another patient spoke of always being brought up with "shoulds," his mother telling him constantly that he "should" do this or "should" do that. He then immediately asked, "Now, tell me, what should I do about it?"

It is certainly useful to scan and test for transference manifestations as one listens to a patient. The therapist is implicitly asking: "Is what I am seeing a transference manifestation?" or "Is the transference at the forefront?" But note that I say "scan and test," implying that evidence must be forthcoming. Although some transference manifestations may be present, and undoubtedly always are present somewhere, it does not mean that the transference is the most important issue for the patient at the given moment. For example, when I picked up Mr. G.'s failure to deal with his full emotional reactions to his wife, transference issues were not at that moment paramount.

It may seem too obvious to say that one must (c) *recognize the suffering of the patient and the general family tragedy,* but the use of this strategy cannot be taken for granted. All too often, strategies are used based on the implicit attitude: in what way is the patient trying to manipulate the therapist or the therapeutic process?; watch out for the power struggle; don't let the patient control the situation, and so on. The first discussant of Case A., for example, apparently saw a patient interested only in trying to sexually seduce me. He never saw a person suffering profoundly and desperately trying to keep herself intact. He did not see the total family tragedy. It makes for a very different approach when we recognize a patient's suffering, wonder how it manifests itself, and how the patient is protecting him/herself.

I have frequently in hospital settings heard remarks about the "manipulating" patient and how it is necessary to prevent the patient from manipulating both staff and hospital. The patient's suffering tends not to be recognized, and all too often little attention is paid to what the supposed "manipulations" have to do with the patient's pain and anguish.

Recognizing the patient's suffering can allow us to tolerate some of the most difficult patients. One of my relatively successful patients, Mr. S., to be discussed at greater length later, was impossibly difficult at the beginning of treatment. He entered treatment because he could not concentrate and because of a "potency" problem. During the early months, I was subjected to a constant barrage of complaints. He rasped at me, screamed, told me he was getting nowhere because I was not making him potent and, at one point, even refused to talk until I made him potent. He felt that the whole treatment situation was simply absurd, humiliating, degrading. Coming to see me was a destruction of him, and he was afraid that I could take over his mind. I believe that I survived the early months and was able to turn the situation around mainly because I recognized this young man's profound suffering and deep anguish. I did not see our relationship as a "power struggle" or his behavior as any attempt to "manipulate" me.[1]

The analyst should (d) *build up his understanding, his working models, from within the data, basically from the "bottom up"—from simple generalizations about small units of sharply observed phenomena to more encompassing ones.* Because of the overwhelming complexity of the phenomena with which we deal, it is necessary to focus on only small, selected segments of experience. We try to maximize the informational context about them in order to reduce uncertainty and ambiguity. To enable a small segment to be understood, it is necessary for a patient to attend carefully to the phenomena being worked with, and to give full, free-associative details about the experiences—thus providing maximum informational context. The case of Mrs. D. is a good example: The patient detailed fully her objections to my use of the word *guarded*, a comparatively small segment of experiential phenomena, but it made for a very productive therapeutic situation. When we work with small units, sharply observed, with clearly delineated phenomena, the chances for true, convincing insight to emerge increase.

Finally, with regard to the strategy under discussion, case histories, even of the kind I have given, are generally crude and oversimplified. For example, the history I gave of Mrs. A.'s mother might have conveyed the idea that she was viewed by the patient as being all bad. Far from it! Actually, Mrs. A. also had an image of her mother as a most heroic and capable person who could virtually perform miracles, an image that had to be dealt with in great detail. We could not, therefore, merely speak of "mother" or analyze what "mother" in general meant. For Mrs. A., as with most patients, "mother" had very different disparate and even contradictory meanings. At different times, different attributes of "mother" were at the forefront. What "mother" meant at any given moment could be determined only by focusing on small segments of experience.

---

[1]I agree with those who consider the term *narcissistic personality disorder*, so commonly used and now part of DSM-III (1980), in many ways an unfortunate one. Though perhaps descriptively accurate in some ways, it has many pejorative connotations and tends to focus on external behavioral manifestations. For a psychodynamic approach it leaves much to be desired because it *does not focus on the suffering*, the conflicts, and the neediness of the patient.

(e) *Compare and match in different ways; use relatively random searches through segments of memory; test for goodness of fit using error-correcting feedback.* (f) *Interpret input through models of early infantile and childhood experience.*

The cases of Mrs. D. and Mr. E. are replete with examples of these strategies. Whereas many of what I am calling strategies are characteristic of human communication—we are always comparing and matching information in different ways, for example—the strategy of interpreting current input through working models of infantile experience is unique to psychoanalytic therapy and, indeed, may be said to be one way to define this kind of therapy.

One of my principal aims is to demonstrate operational approaches to Freudian clinical theoretical terms. The strategies of comparing and matching and of testing for goodness of fit offer operational approaches to such important clinical concepts as resistance and defense.

Thus, we can say that resistances can be detected by comparing or matching the observed existing analytic process with our model of an optimal one. We can recognize that a patient who refuses to talk about painful, embarrassing, or shameful experiences can be said to be resisting because our model of the optimal analytic process is one in which free association takes place and the patient is expected to try to tolerate such experiences. In brief, the mismatch between the existing analytic process and our working model of an optimal one, or the "error" in the existing process, represents the "resistance." Error-correcting feedback takes the form of interpretation by means of which the analyst attempts to correct the existing mismatch or "error," thus working toward the target of establishing an optimal process. The analyst may, for example, offer a patient the interpretation that he cannot allow full free association because of a fear of a loss of control, an interpretation that attempts to reduce the mismatch and correct the "error." If the interpretation is successful, there is a change in the target direction, a change toward the model of the optimum process where free association is not restricted by the patient's fears. In a sense, by error-correcting feedback, we attempt to enable the existing analytic process to become similar or identical to a working model of an optimal process.

The concept of "resistance" is a most useful one, but must be employed with great caution. For example, I cannot say that in his first hour, Mr. E. was resisting in any significant way. He came in paralyzed by tension. but he spoke about his emotional state. He reacted to and evalued my comments, and brought in memories—all of the things we expect a patient to do. Furthermore, as I have already said, if we speak of the resistances of the patient, there is no reason why we shouldn't also speak of the resistances of the therapist—the mismatch between actual performance and an optimum model of how a therapist should function. This "error," which represents the therapist's resistance, should be corrected, either by the patient or by the therapist himself. In the case of Mrs. B., for instance, resistance went on for some time; at the beginning of treatment I was not using anything resembling a heuristic approach.

It can be said that defenses may be present when an expected experience is not forthcoming. We can often detect such conditions by comparing the existing experience or reaction with those predictable from our models. The case of Mr. G. is a good example. I would have expected any husband and especially this patient, judging from his history, to have reacted more strongly to his wife's depression and suicidal ideation than he did. Actually, this concept of defense, though not formalized in psychoanalytic clinical theory, is one that is implicitly used by most therapists. A patient of mine who failed his doctoral examination had little to say about it in the following analytic session. I think most experienced analysts would wonder about this. They implicitly recognize that defenses were in all probability operating because, according to models of normal behavior and subjective experience, some expressible reaction, hurt, anger, disappointment, depression, should have been present.

Next in this category of strategies is to (g) *use generalizing and classifying processes*. One can think of generalizations as classifying processes. They are basic in all learning. Therapist and patient attempt to find general patterns. If, in a particular patient, it is noted that tension and depression are repeatedly associated with menstruation, we can say that tension and depression are members of the class of phenomena associated with menstruation. Typically, one seeks common patterns in a patient's associations. Mr. E.'s third illustrative hour exemplifies this process. The patient mentioned instances that could be classified as "rational, individual accomplishment being swept aside by appeal to authority or prestige."

In the case of Mrs. C., one can say that snakes and the patient's mother were found to be members of a class of vicious, destructive, cold, unrelated, and unresponsive creatures.

Mr. G. himself used generalizing processes. After pointing out that my comments were an accurate description of his father, he noted that he behaved similarly. Both he and his father were members of the class of people who "mute" their emotional responses.

My next strategy, (h) *use predictions from working models,* has already been described (see chap. 8). I would like only to add that this strategy, like so many others, is not unique to psychoanalysis or to psychoanalytic therapy; it is part of human communication, indeed, a part of life. We are always implicitly predicting from normal working models about every aspect of life. Someone who has different working models of the world—paranoid ones, for example—will obviously have different expectancies from the average person. Similarly when we communicate, we are looking ahead somewhat, predicting what is going to be said, preconsciously, to be sure. Such activity enables us to detect slips of the tongue, as previously discussed—for example, when current input does not match what normal linguistic models predict. Again, psychoanalytic therapy does not differ from ordinary communication in the use of such predictions; it differs in the nature of the models used from which the predictions are made.

When predicting from working models, two important regulatory processes are generally employed: error-correcting feedback and the process of looking ahead and predicting. Whereas in the first instance we make an error and correct it, in the second, we look ahead and prevent the error.

The strategy (i) *scan and test using clinical theoretical metamodels* brings up the important question of how the heuristic worker uses clinical theory. He certainly does use the theory, but in a very different way from the stereotyped worker.

Generalizations that are close to the empirical data, lower levels of theory, are essential parts of what I have called our fifth working model. We all have useful generalizations about paranoid personalities; we expect them to be hostile, angry, and to distort reality. We also have general ideas about alcoholics: that they tend to hide and deny their drinking. Such generalizations were immediately evoked in the cases of Mrs. A. and Mrs. C. when I heard of their respective mothers—not as established "truths," but as useful, reasonable, expectancies for which evidence would perhaps be forthcoming.

Other generalizations are more abstract in nature, but still relatively close to clinical data, and I have placed them in the seventh working model, which I have called a clinical theoretical metamodel. This working model includes concepts that refer to clinical theory as well as concepts referring to the theory of the therapeutic process—the concepts of resistance, defense, and so on. Obvious as it may be, it is most important to recognize that the concepts of resistance and defense are theoretical terms; they are abstractions about experience. I have tried to define these terms operationally, in terms of existing working models of experience, and strategies for their use. Certainly, therefore, such theoretical ideas as resistance and defense are constantly in use through their operational, experiential referents. Similarly, transference is an indispensable term referring to our theory of the process. It, too, is part of the seventh working model. Here again I have tried to deal with this concept in an operational, experiential way, in terms of working models and strategies.

It is a useful strategy in many cases, as already suggested, to ask ourselves about the current transference situation, to scan and test to see what may have not been picked up in relation to the transference, but such scanning and testing can only be done through the operational, experiential referents of the term "transference."

Similar comments can be made for clinical dream theory. Clinical generalizations of the following type are most useful: patients may represent themselves or some attribute of themselves through the representation of another person in a dream, A quick scan and test of a dream in light of this generalization is often very useful. Note that I say "scan and test." The therapist scans the dream reported and tests by simultaneously matching the dream to working models of the patient, including the current analytic material. A hypothesis may thereby be generated which may be good enough to suggest to the patient, "good enough" in the sense that the match was not only a relatively good one but involved a great deal of information. Evidence for the hypothesis must then be forthcoming.

A young woman patient reported a dream, "something about a dirty filthy child." I immediately scanned the recent analytic material to see if she was perhaps representing herself in some way in the dream. She had been having a sexual affair that week, an unusually free experience for this woman. She had even called in to work sick in order to spend more time with her lover—an unusual thing for this extremely dedicated, conscientious professional to do. I thought that, although she had been enjoying the affair immensely and that being able to have such an affair represented notable progress for her, she also probably felt exactly like what the dream portrayed, "a dirty filthy child." The patient agreed completely when I made some interpretations along these lines.

I hope it is clear that I am suggesting that for the heuristic worker there is a very close tie—an almost inseparable tie—between his experientially based working models and his clinical theoretical metamodel. Unless the clinical theoretical terms, whatever they may be, have operational or experiential referents, they can have no true meaning or use. I stress this issue because I have been suggesting throughout this volume that much of what is called Freudian therapy is done in an intellectualized way, divorced from experiential terms. Knowing about the "libido" theory, "drive" theory, and the associated psychic energies does not mean that one knows anything about sexuality in its human, experiential sense.

The analyst must (j) *recognize the power and the limitation of words*. The first part of this strategy needs little discussion. I think we all recognize how powerful words can be, and how much a given word can evoke, much more than one would expect from the lexical content alone. Recall the profound reaction evoked in Mrs. D. when I used the word *guarded*. We also generally recognize how important and powerful words are to a child; with the word *Momma*, a child can potentially mobilize his entire immediate world. Adaptation and even survival are involved in the child's ability to use this word.

But words are limited, very limited. A child's thoughts are well ahead of his ability to verbalize them. Observe how clumsy we all become when we try to use an unfamiliar language. And, most important for us, it is very difficult for the therapist to find the right words to express exactly what is going on in a patient. The traditional silence of the analyst has many rationales. One of these, usually not discussed, is that with many patients it is difficult to be accurate. Indeed, we are usually off target, more or less, when we try to verbalize a patient's experience. And I refer not only to those patients who are alienated from their inner lives, but to patients capable of expressing their inner lives, who can feel subtle shades and differences of experience, and who insist on accurate words to portray them. Some of the most analyzable patients I have ever had were those who told me to "shut up" and to let them tell me what was going on, because no matter what I might have said I could not possibly have been close enough to their experiences. Certainly it is true that early, archaic experiences are difficult to verbalize. And how does one even describe the feeling of normal adult love? As I have previously emphasized, a vast amount of what we all know and experience simply cannot be communicated by words.

The analyst must also (k) *not ignore common sense and the ordinary meanings of words.* This strategy is related to one to be mentioned later that "reality" must often be admitted and certainly not denied. All of these are seemingly obvious strategies, but, unfortunately, they are not. Psychoanalysis has the reputation of often violating common sense, and, I regret to say, the reputation is not undeserved.

Here is an example, A colleague reported a case of a painter who was depressed and complained that his recent painting was an "abortion." The analyst took the patient's description literally, and, because according to the analyst painting is a sublimation of smearing and anal impulses, the complaint about the painting being an "abortion" indicated an anal pregnancy wish. In other words, the patient was upset and disappointed because his wish for an anal baby was not being fulfilled. I believe such thinking is totally unsupportable; it can indeed be decidedly destructive to a patient. Any kind of project is commonly referred to as an "abortion" when it does not meet expectations. Even space flights have been known to "abort." About all the patient was telling the therapist is that he was depressed and upset, and one factor contributing to his mood was the feeling that his painting was not meeting some expectation. It would have been much wiser had the therapist inquired about the ways whereby the painting failed to meet expectations or what was meant by referring to the painting as an "abortion." At least this approach would not have abandoned ordinary meanings of words.

Here is another brief example. A colleague reported a case in which he claimed that the patient was "exhibitionistic" because of a memory, which might have been a fantasy, of saying to his dying grandmother, "Don't die, grandma, look at me in my new sailor suit." No evidence for the "exhibitionistic" nature of this statement was offered; it was as though the child's isolated statement spoke for itself and supported the interpretation of "exhibitionistic." I have asked several people what their reactions were to this statement. Almost uniformly, the response was "How sad!" How sad that an analyst cannot comprehend such simple, obvious human yearnings of a child for his grandmother, and his very understandable child-like way of trying to please her and to keep her alive and not lose her. To call such a statement exhibitionistic, with all of the implicit connotations of that term, violates our basic models of human experience.

To say that we must (1) *recognize the patient as a whole person with pathological and healthy attributes* may perhaps sound like a truism, but the strategy is not always easy to carry out. We are generally taught not to be "taken in" by a patient's "biased" point of view, the patient's view of a spouse, for example. This is certainly valuable advice. But simply because we are focusing on the pathological aspects of the patient, we can easily overlook the fact that there are areas in which the patient functions healthily, areas in which the patient is capable of realistically appraising his or her world. (Note the error with Mrs. C., as an example.) And just as we can fail to recognize the healthy aspects of patients, so we must guard against failure to recognize serious emotional illness in someone who is apparently functioning well in many ways.

Another strategy that may sound too simple and obvious to state is (m) *inquire of the patient if something is not understood.* I have nonetheless heard in case discussions all sorts of hypotheses formulated about what is going on in a patient when the simplest way to find out what is happening is to ask the patient. It is surprising how often the situation is clarified when this is done. The theoretical justification for this very simple strategy has been discussed earlier (see chap. 5).

Finally, in this category of general strategies, I would include (n) *recognize the uncertainties of the process.* I have already spoken of these uncertainties. They derive from many sources: the unbelievable complexity of mental phenomena; the multidetermined nature of any experience; the difficulties in capturing and verbalizing early experience; the difficulties of establishing an optimal analytic process; the inadequacy of working models available to the therapist, and so on. Interpretations, as I have constantly emphasized, are at best never more than tentative hypotheses. And I think it is a most reasonable strategy for any analyst or therapist to recognize the very tentative nature of what he thinks he has learned and understood from the therapeutic process, even in the best of circumstances.

In sum, the general strategies I am advocating are:

(a).–Focus on the analytic process.

(b).–Foster the development and verbalization of transference relationships.

(c).–Recognize the suffering of the patient and the general family tragedy.

(d).–Build up understanding from within the data, from simple generalizations about small units of sharply observed phenomena to more encompassing ones.

(e).–Compare and match in different ways; use relatively random searches through segments of memory; test for goodness of fit, using error-correcting feedback.

(f).–Interpret input through models of early infantile and childhood experience.

(g).–Use generalizing and classifying processes.

(h).–Use predictions from working models.

(i).–Scan and test, using clinical theoretical metamodels.

(j).–Recognize the power and the limitation of words.

(k).–Do not ignore common sense and ordinary meanings of words.

(l).–Recognize the patient as a whole person with both pathological and healthy attributes.

(m).–Inquire of the patient if something is not understood.

(n).–Recognize the uncertainties of the process.

14

Strategies of the Analyst: The Analyst as Participant Observer

The second category of strategies is of those related to the generally accepted nature of the analyst or therapist as participant observer.

Optimally, the analyst (a) *works closely to experience*. He attempts to *follow the patient's emotional line*. I think it necessary that any analyst, therapist, or even psychiatric interviewer must temporarily identify with his patient. For me, this activity is totally indispensable. Indeed, if I cannot to some degree project myself into a patient's world of experience—into the patient's emotional state—I generally find that I am at a loss, unable to comprehend what is going on.

Diesing, writing about case study methods several years ago (1971, p. 264), stressed the importance of the process I am describing:

> The kind of knowledge of a living system that case study methods provide is essentially suited to enabling a person to work within the system, to become an active participant in its self-development. The participant observer and the clinician work their way into the system they are studying and try to become an active part of it in order to understand it from the inside.

At this point, and at the risk of being repetitive, I wish to emphasize once again the limitations of words and what they can communicate, a crucial issue for understanding the therapeutic process and an issue that is generally not fully appreciated. The analogy that comes to mind is that of music. One must experience music actually being played to know and understand it; reading about music is not a substitute for this experience. Words alone simply cannot convey the full information available during the actual event. Furthermore, the evocative power of the actual musical event—the ability to evoke feelings, thoughts, fantasies, wishes, and memories in the listener—is much greater than the evocative power of words alone. As a result of the information available externally from the actual music and the information evoked internally during the experience, the total informational pool available is infinitely greater than what is available from mere words about music.

In the same way, words alone cannot give the therapist full knowledge of what is going on in a patient. They cannot convey the full informational content involved in the actual experience. To know, to understand, to capture the full experience, the therapist must live the patient's life himself—albeit, and of necessity, in a much attenuated form. The actual experience, in contrast to words about it, has much greater evocative power, and the total information available is therefore infinitely greater.

While identified with the patient, the therapist can allow himself to react freely and to experience various levels of thinking and feeling—all within the context of the patient's world. When such processes take place, there is an automatic filling in of the scene with a great many experiences, often much more than the patient may be able to do unaided. The therapist's experiences may be disordered as he allows the emergence of primitive, seemingly unrelated mental contents of a lower order of organization—thoughts, fantasies, and feelings that are related to the level or state of the patient's experience. Indeed, to analyze a dream it may well be necessary to enter into a state similar to the one we are in before falling asleep (see Freud, 1900, p. 102). The analyst can usually fill in the scene from multiple sources: models of the patient, other patients, his own life, general knowledge of the world. In brief, the analyst generates a great deal of information in addition to what is conveyed by the patient.

The fundamental reason for entering the patient's world is to obtain the relevant information to think about, organize, and generalize from—information based both on what the patient conveys and what the analyst fills in. The analyst uses himself as a basic model, which is necessary because no other model can conceivably encompass the complexity of the patient's experience. The resulting vast amount of information may make for a temporarily confused and disordered situation, but eventually, as the information is grouped and patterned and as hypotheses are formed and tested, uncertainty can be reduced. We then have a reasonable chance of being able to interpret something that is relatively on target, relatively accurate, and close to the patient's experience.

All the analyst's responses—all of the new informational input that he provides—must, of course, be evaluated, and these are complicated processes in themselves. If the analyst is annoyed or sexually aroused by a patient, it may or may not mean that the patient is being (consciously or without awareness) provocative or seductive. If an analyst finds a patient sexually arousing, the analyst should be able to activate a relatively complete self-model which can allow a recognition of personal needs, of what is causing the reaction, and what role the patient has in the arousal. Additional evaluations will be necessary to decide how the experiences can be used, if at all, to help the patient.

Thus, in addition to *working closely to the patient's experience and following the patient's emotional line,* we can speak of three other strategies: (b) *temporary identification with the patient (experiencing the patient's world);* (c) *free associative disordered experiences, which fill the scene;* and, finally, (d) *an evaluation of these experiences.*

Much of what I am describing here can be subsumed under the term "empathy." This term is a useful one, and a decade ago I had no hesitation about using it (Peterfreund, 1971, chap. 22), but it has since come to mean so many different things that I am restricting my use of it and discussing mainly some of its more detailed attributes.

One of the principal advantages of getting into a patient's world is that we can sense the full quality of the patient's state—its level of primitiveness, degree of chaos, degree of hopelessness, guilt, and so on. And such sensing of the depth and quality of a patient's state is most important—not only for psychoanalysis or analytic therapy, but also for general psychological understanding. It can guide our entire approach to a patient. It can mean, for example, the difference between advising hospitalization or not; it can help us evaluate the seriousness of suicidal ideation, and even lead us to be concerned about suicide when a patient denies any thought of it.

Here is a brief example. I was asked to see a research worker who was depressed. He expressed great hopelessness about his current situation and about his future. He felt very guilty that he had not supervised his students carefully enough and might therefore have hurt their careers. He completely denied any serious suicidal thoughts and refused to listen to any suggestion about possible hospitalization. He worried me deeply, and I found myself preoccupied with him throughout the week of the consultations. I knew there was very good reason to be concerned, but it took me a few days before I finally realized that within his world, within his frame of reference, suicide was the only "logical" way out. Therefore, despite all of his denials, I decided that I had better take action. I called in the family and expressed my concern. The patient was rescued because the family had been alerted and took appropriate action. For he was, in fact, making a very serious suicidal attempt during the very hour I was seeing the family.

Sensing the depth and totality of a patient's illness is not the same as gauging what or how much he can do about it. I have generally done fairly well with the first, but, at times, I expected too much of my patients, especially at the beginning of my career. I expected these patients to mobilize much more than they possibly could.

The ability to enter a patient's world, based on working models of the patient plus models of oneself that are similar to or related to those of the patient, can often lead to some of the most convincing experiences in analysis: accurate "predictions" in the form of images or thoughts of exactly what the patient has experienced and which they verbalize a moment later. When Mrs. C. spoke of dead abstract symbols I visualized scenes of her walking into her home and finding her mother drunk and stuporous on the floor—the exact scenes the patient verbalized a moment later. In the case of Mr. E., I caught the picture of the paralyzed man standing helplessly—just before the patient spoke of feeling how a catatonic might feel.

Here is another example of tuning into a patient's experience and getting strikingly similar images. A young adolescent patient was telling me of his fear of "that world," the orgastic world of extremely pleasurable fantasies, especially when he is high on marijuana. It is a "terrific experience," but it makes him anxious, afraid that he might not come back to "this world" where he has his "equilibrium." He then compared the anxiety he was talking about to the time when he was on LSD and had odd uncontrollable visual experiences and was afraid that he might not return to the everyday world that he knows. This patient had experiences during early adolescence when he did fear that he was going "crazy."

I remarked casually that his experiences were very frightening, yet extremely pleasurable, especially the heightened masturbatory, orgastic feelings. I then added, "You know, you speak of all of these things as though they had an enticing, satanic quality." My comment was in response not only to the content of what he was saying but to the way he was saying it: his gleeful laugh, the tone of his voice which evoked in me the image of a kind of wild, gleeful, satanic figure, totally lost in some frenetic, pleasurable activity. Of course, I also knew that when high on marijuana he would allow himself to indulge in some of his most exciting "perverse" masturbatory fantasies. The patient responded with a laugh and told me that I was absolutely right, and that before, while he was talking, he had the image of some "devil" figure.

A few additional examples should elucidate further aspects of the fruitfulness of employing the strategy of the analyst as participant observer. The first shows how a purely emotional response helped me understand what was going on.

One day, an obsessional patient casually mentioned that he had taken his young son to a doctor because of a lump that had been discovered on the child's arm a few weeks earlier, but all was well, the lump was benign. As he was speaking I experienced something that I can only describe as a startle reaction, something akin to a skipped heartbeat, a moment of alarm. I realized when I evaluated my response that I had partially identified with the patient as a parent and had become a bit anxious. But the patient had revealed no alarm. I then realized that he had never previously mentioned this incident. I checked with myself and decided that it was reasonable and "normal" enough for any father to experience anxiety in such circumstances. I asked the patient why he had never mentioned the incident and asked if he might be protecting himself against some painful experience. He replied by saying that he had tried to deny his knowledge of the boy's lump and had delayed somewhat in taking him to a doctor, reassuring himself that nothing was wrong. As he spoke, his anxiety became evident. He told of his inability to face the possibility of this child being ill once again. One of the most trying periods of his life had taken place a few years earlier: the child had nearly died from a very serious illness. By the end of the hour, the patient began to speak of his own fears of death and his concern about his advancing age.

Here is another example of how my personal reactions enabled me to make a helpful interpretation. On a snowy midwinter day some years ago, a young attractive patient came into the office wearing her big snow boots. After a few moments she removed the boots saying she had thought of taking them off earlier but hadn't because she didn't want to appear to be too informal and relaxed. Only when she realized that she was soiling my couch did she decide that she would have to remove them.

I interpreted to the patient that she was afraid of her seductive feelings toward me, and that taking off her boots in one sense meant undressing in the office. Of course, I was influenced by the entire context of the case. She had indicated in the past that she was afraid of her sexual feelings toward me; and she had had a seductive relationship with her father. Also, on more than one occasion she had spoken of having an affair with an older man—"it is something every young woman should experience." But the immediate stimulus for my particular interpretation (as an alternative I could have dealt with the fear of soiling) was that I recognized my own sexual feelings and fantasies stimulated by her taking off her boots. It seemed quite reasonable to me that she might be having similar feelings and fantasies.

I was evidently on the right track, for she said that she had noticed me coming down the hall after the previous patient left and I appeared to be younger than her inner image of me. This brought up the possibility of her having a sexual affair with me; if I were much older, the possibility would be diminished.

At times, accurate interpretations may be fostered by highly personal but relevant memories. One day a patient came in obviously tense and upset. She spoke of seeing her husband that week; they were in the midst of an unpleasant divorce after many years of marriage, and he asked her to return a gold watch he had given her as an engagement gift. As she spoke, my thoughts drifted to my own marital situation. The link here was that I too had given my wife a gold watch as an engagement present. I detected a note of sadness in myself and a sense of "what a waste of life" if I had been unfortunate enough to be in a situation comparable to that of the patient and her husband. I used my response. I said to the patient, "You probably felt horrible when returning the watch," and had a sense of "what a waste of years." She broke down and wept freely, while nodding to me, indicating that I had at least caught an important aspect of her feelings. The circumstances were especially painful to her because she was childless and wanted very much to become pregnant. But she was rapidly approaching an age when having a child is physiologically difficult and dangerous. For her, in an important sense, the years with her husband were a waste.

Identification with a patient can sometimes include direct imitation, unbeknown to the patient, of course. I have found that direct imitation can often help one understand what a patient cannot verbalize. For example, once, in a highly emotional context, the patient on the couch tensed and flexed his neck. It was a strange position as I observed it, and I couldn't imagine what he was doing. I could have asked him what was happening, but I did not think that he was capable of giving me a reasonable answer at that moment. When I imitated him, however, I realized that the patient was actually partly choking himself and restricting full expression of emotions. From the context of the hour it seemed that he was trying to prevent himself from crying. Later on, the patient confirmed that this indeed had been his intent.

Finally, although I have repeatedly stressed the importance of the analyst's spontaneous reactions as a useful strategy for understanding what is going on in a patient—provided these reactions are coupled with full evaluations—I want to stress again that no matter how careful and convinced the analyst may be that he is correct, the patient is always the final arbiter. Here is a good example.

A young married woman with several children developed breast cancer, and, although the pathology report after the mastectomy was favorable, she was preoccupied about the possibility of a recurrence of her disease.

Some time after the operation, she told one day of some vague worries about her health. And she then told of two "odd" preoccupations. While she was having her hair cut at a beauty parlor she left her purse on a couch. It contained an inexpensive piece of jewelry, but one she liked very much. As her hair was being cut, she could see another customer sitting on the couch. She was seized by the fear that the other woman would open the purse, take the piece of jewelry, and leave. The patient followed this with a report of how upset she had been at her country weekend house. When her family arrived they found that a mouse had been in the house, and eaten all the seeds her children had collected, and had left its droppings all over the living room floor. A trap was set for the mouse, but it managed to get the cheese and avoid being caught.

The central issue in this patient's life was cancer and anxieties about recurrences. As I listened, the hour seemed to deal with the sense of invasion, with things being taken from the patient. Indeed, as she spoke of the mouse I actually experienced a feeling of being eaten at, gnawed at, being invaded and eroded. I have no special personal anxieties of this nature, but I had on many occasions thought about how she experienced her cancer and about her fears as to what it might do to her. With no hesitation, I therefore suggested to the patient that perhaps her preoccupations had to do with her anxieties about a possible invading cancer. I felt very sure of myself even though I had not even asked for her associations.

The patient hesitated, thought for a while, decided that maybe I was correct, but that my remarks did not capture her experiences. She spoke further about her country house. She keeps a tight, safe, cozy home; it is a place where one can feel safe; one can even leave the door open and the keys to the ignition in the car. The experience with the mouse destroyed, in part, this safe, cozy image. She went on to talk of early memories about her home, a very large house in New York. She was an only child, and had often felt quite lonely and feared intruders.

In brief, my original interpretation may possibly have been accurate in some sense, but clearly, judging by her response, I was not close to her experience at the time; I was off target. It would have been much better had I not interpreted so rapidly. Although my personal "depth" responses and accompanying sense of conviction failed me in this case, I should add that I did not lose much by my interpretation because I did not insist on it and error-correcting feedback was allowed. And had I been wrong with the patient mentioned earlier when I interpreted her fear of her seductive feelings to me, again not much would have been lost.

I wish to stress one important point. I have been very critical of stereotyped approaches that mechanically translate experiences reported by patients into existing clinical theories. True empathy is minimal in such approaches. But even approaches that stress the significance of empathy may be no better than mechanized stereotyped approaches unless the experiences that emerge from the therapist's empathic activities are fully evaluated by the therapist before an interpretation is made and unless the patient can accept and support the interpretation offered. *Empathy alone does not automatically guarantee validity.*

In summary, the strategies that I advocate for the analyst as participant observer are:

(a).–Work closely to experience; follow the patient's emotional line.

(b).–Identify temporarily with the patient; experience the patient's world.

(c).–Allow free-associative disordered experiences which fill in the scene.

(d).–Evaluate these experiences.

15

Strategies of the Analyst: The Patient as Participant in the Therapeutic Process

One of the great differences between psychoanalysis or analytically oriented therapy and the therapies that are devoted to immediate goals, such as behavior modification therapies that focus on a symptom, is that the former (a) *foster the primacy of inquiry and understanding*. In analysis and analytic therapy the attempt to understand the patient and his symptoms takes precedence over eliminating the symptom. The therapist tries to arouse the patient's curiosity and interest in himself as a person, in his past, and in his psychological development. He attempts to get the patient to see himself as more than merely a carrier of a symptom complex to be gotten rid of. Indeed, many detours may have to be taken before the symptoms or the original presenting complaints are dealt with. Frequently, a symptom may be modified even though never directly worked on—a result that is understandable if we recognize how multidetermined and complex symptoms actually are and how much can change if only some of the determining factors are dealt with. One's self image—how one feels about one's body, for instance—is crucial in adequate sexual functioning. Changes in sexual experiences can be observed if body-image disturbances are dealt with, although sexual activity per se may not have been worked on.

A strategy generally accepted in psychoanalysis and requiring little elaboration at the present time is that of (b) *fostering introspection and free-associative disordered experiences in the patient, accompanied by emotional expression*. Patients must learn to tolerate the emergence of disordered experiences: odd, bizarre, and apparently random and "crazy" thoughts and impulses; strange and inexplicable sensations; deeply painful feelings of anguish, terror, and loss; feelings of being dead, unreal, depersonalized; phenomena that can be called "altered states of awareness." It should be added, though, that many experiences that patients often find intolerable are not necessarily of this category. They may often find intolerable simpler, tender feelings of love and trust for the therapist, for example.

Because we want patients to attend very carefully to their inner processes and to remember in detail, we try to avoid questions that will encourage patients merely to infer. Hence, the nature of the inquiries made by the analyst are of great importance. Such questions as "Why are you depressed?" or "Why are you anxious?" usually cannot be answered and may only encourage speculative inferences. Open-ended inquiries of the following kind are to be preferred: "Tell me about your depression," or "Tell me about your anxious state." I often suggest to patients that they go back and try to recapture exactly what they felt, thought, fantasied, or feared during a disturbing incident which they are reporting. Implicitly, or even explicitly, one tries to get across to the patient the need to attend carefully to specific events in great detail, to remember and verbalize whatever emerges in a free-associative way. We can thereby approach getting the full detailed content and context of the psychological state with which we are working. In brief, the aim of our inquiries is to activate relevant memory organizations and to avoid circumventing them.[1]

The strategy of (c) *fostering active, independent, analytic work on the part of the patient* has long been understood to be essential to establishing the therapeutic alliance. It may seem to be an obvious strategy; unfortunately, according to my observation, it is all too often disregarded.

Patients should be encouraged to assume some initiative in anal-

---

[1]To further the understanding of psychological processes and fostered by the information-processing paradigm, cognitive psychologists have been studying introspection and the nature of inquiries that lead subjects to infer rather than remember their mental processes (see, for example, Ericsson & Simon, 1980). Future developments in this area should be of great interest to psychoanalysis.

ysis, encouraged to bring in whatever is bothering them, what interests them, what has come to their attention that may seem odd, unique, irrational, out of keeping with their ordinary experience or the experience of others. Patients must be encouraged to recognize their inner states and be active in delineating them. Optimally, they take an active role in remembering and in connecting and organizing their experiences. They should be able to both experience and reflect on their experiences. In brief, optimally they take an active role in the process of achieving insight. Meaningful working through, for example, can take place only when interpretations are understandable and when patients take an active role in the process. It is always a good sign for any treatment when a patient comes into an hour having independently made some discovery about her/himself.

Encouraging the patient to take the initiative has many important implications, in addition to fostering the search for "truth." Just as a child, and indeed everyone, learns through his own efforts, so must a patient learn. It is crucial in "differentiation," in the development of one's sense of self, in developing a sense of "I am confident that I can do it because I have done it before or because I have learned that I can learn how to do new things." Making a patient into a passive receiver of analytic "wisdom" tends to duplicate what many parents unfortunately do: take over a child's right to discover, learn on his own, make his own errors, and recognize his own uniqueness.

To (d) *develop an awareness of different levels of experience, different states of cognitive and emotional organization* is a most important strategy. Patients are often embarrassed by their archaic feelings, irrational thoughts, and "perverse" fantasies. It is most helpful to convey to them the idea that we all have different levels, layers, or states of experience, which generally have different origins and meanings. As a result, patients can see themselves as adults who may also have archaic feelings and fantasies, and not as "nothing but" degraded, perverse creatures. Some therapists play into the debased images that patients have of themselves. The "real truth" the "deep unconscious stuff" about patients, these therapists think, is merely the discovery of their nastiness, perversions, anal and oral sadistic feelings, and bizarre fantasies. It is not recognized that these may be only partial truths, and that it is also a "real truth" and also "deep unconscious stuff" for a patient to recognize that he or she has a tender feeling for the therapist.

With regard to the strategy under discussion, the therapist should not overemphasize the reasonable, realistic point of view of an adult. We are not trying to push our patients into sweet reasonableness. We want them to know themselves, to find out what has happened to them. Many of our patients are afraid to evaluate their experiences; they are afraid of being unfair to important figures in their lives; they feel guilty about saying "bad" things about them. For example, a patient of mine found it very difficult to talk about her experiences with a previous therapist who had died during her treatment. He had done very well with her, but had not dealt adequately with her during his illness. She was left confused, bewildered, and unnecessarily traumatized by his illness. She had difficulty talking about him because of her deep devotion to him and also because she felt that she had to be forgiving. His illness made his behavior "understandable," she felt. True, ultimately, what he did was understandable and certainly forgivable, but these considerations are irrelevant for our understanding of what effect his actions had on her and what specific meaning they had for her. For such understanding, all realistic, adult, humane evaluations of his behavior must temporarily be set aside.

In this connection, I have on several occasions treated patients whose parents were physically ill, depressed, alcoholic, or schizophrenic and who were reluctant to talk about what happened in their home. Typically, they might say, "I am an adult now and must understand that my parents were troubled and could not help being what they were." Here one can point out that an infant or a child does not know why parents act the way they do, has no adult knowledge to help understanding, and reacts only as a very young person can to the world around him. To understand the effect of the parent, one must capture that early infantile or childhood experience, setting aside today's adult point of view. All too often, I have heard of therapists who quickly point out to a patient that "you must understand that your mother and father really loved you and couldn't help doing what they did," an approach that stifles the therapeutic process and closes off whole segments of emotional life.

If reality is acknowledged and not denied, archaic and unreasonable reactions can then be better dealt with. Note that in the illustrative hour of Mr. E. I acknowledged to the patient that he was indeed having enormous and unusual reality difficulties, but that these had evoked early, frightening, archaic reactions. I was, in effect, attempting to help the patient recognize different levels or states of cognitive and emotional experience. He could not cope with the reality problems on a reasonable, adaptive level: primitive meanings had been evoked, related to an archaic experiential state.

A fundamental strategy and a basic aspect of the therapeutic alliance is to (e) *foster error-correcting feedback.* The final arbiter of much of what happens in an analysis is the patient. Ultimately, it is only the patient who knows the truth about what he is thinking and feeling. An analysis cannot proceed unless a patient feels free to accept, reject, refine, or revise the analyst's interpretations. Such corrections are absolutely essential for any analytic process. As I have already suggested, it is most important therapeutically for a patient to be able to detect and delineate his own inner states, to verbalize awarenesses, and not be merely a passive receiver of what the analyst says he is experiencing. To state the issue in another way: when a patient is unable to accept an analytic interpretation, the rejection of it may be due not to resistance or to the patient's unwillingness to understand the analyst, but simply to the fact that the analyst is wrong.

In brief, an interpretation is never more than a hypothesis, as I have repeatedly emphasized, and the analytic process must allow for the full range of confirmation or refutation. Error-correcting feedback is an intrinsic part of the process; it is a basic constraint in the scientific system, it represents a fundamental "checkpoint," a term used by Diesing (1971).

In the seven case illustrations previously presented, except for those of Mrs. A. and Mr. F., the strategies in this category were eventually relatively successful. I was able to get the patients actively engaged in a working process; they had "learned" through interpretation how to be good patients. Mrs. C. was able to correct a very serious error that had been made throughout the early part of the analysis—an error for which three analysts were responsible. Error-correcting feedback was nicely revealed in the hour of Mrs. D. when she corrected me on my use of term "guarded," and in the second hour of Mr. E. when he gave a more exact description of his experiences, correcting my earlier comments, which were only roughly accurate. Mr. G., too, used his own term, *mute,* to describe what he does with emotional experiences—a better term than the one I had used because it represented something emotionally meaningful to him; it was his language. All of these patients had the ability to do independent work, to both experience and reflect about their inner life.

Mrs. A. and Mr. F. were different. Mrs. A. was a frantic woman trying to survive. For many months I heard an outpouring of anxieties, fears, fantasies, hypochondriacal preoccupations, and so on. But there was no true therapeutic process. Never once in those many months did she refer to a previous hour, reflect, and make meaningful connections. This was owing to her feeling that she could not think and that her mind had been destroyed. She was waiting for a God-like figure to organize her from the outside, a "beginnor" [sic] who would enable her to begin living. Until some inroads were made into these basic problems, the semblance of a meaningful, optimal analytic therapeutic process of the type that I have tried to describe was not possible.

Mr. F., as mentioned earlier, was all action. He truly never developed an attitude of inquiry or of reflection. He could pour out his anxieties about finances, his troubles with the business world, his frustrations about things not moving quickly enough, but he seemed unable to go further. Except fleetingly, he rarely wondered why he was so ambitious, why it was so important for him to amass a fortune so early in life. And, even when offered some reasonably convincing leads about these issues, little was changed. Understanding one's inner life, connecting past to present, wondering about one's motivations—all were fairly alien attitudes for him, and I could find no way to develop them.

In considering the patient as participant in the analytic process, heuristic psychoanalysts will, then:

(a).—Foster the primacy of inquiry and understanding.
(b).—Foster introspection and free-associative disordered experiences in the patient, accompanied by emotional expression.
(c).—Foster in the patient active, independent, analytic work.
(d).—Develop in the patient the awareness of different levels of experience, different states of cognitive and emotional organization.
(e).—Foster error-correcting feedback.

16 Strategies of the Analyst: The Establishment of Meanings

The issue of meanings is basic in psychoanalytic therapy. The analyst tries to (a) *discover unique and personal meanings* and to (b) *establish full emotional and cognitive contexts.*

Of special interest to analysts are "emotional" or the so-called "unconscious" meanings—unique, private, personal, connotative meanings. Analysts are usually not especially interested in general denotative meanings or in generally accepted connotative meanings, although these are certainly never ruled out.

Insofar as the same lexical term can mean different things in different contexts, meanings can be said to be context dependent. A ball can, in one context, refer to a round body used in various games and, in another, to a large and formal assembly for social dancing. To obtain the highly personal meanings of terms or expressions, the kind that are of interest to us in analysis, we need informational context too, but of a very special kind. We need free-associative detailing of the full personal, cognitive, and emotional experiences related to the given term or expression.

For example, four different patients have asked me if I was a Jew. Superficially the questions were very similar, but analytic work revealed that in each case the term *Jew* had a different meaning—a unique, personal, individual "unconscious" meaning. One patient, a young woman, asked me if I was a Jew because to her the term *Jew* at that time meant someone who can engage in "perverse" sexual acitivity, unlike her image of the well-spoken, Ivy League WASP. If I was a Jew, in her sense of the word, I would not condemn her interest in "perverse" sexual activity. Another patient asked me if I was a Jew at a time when she felt guilty about her sexual activities. If I was a Jew, a "member of the tribe," I would tend not to condemn her as a gentile might have. A third patient asked me if I was a Jew because he did not wish to associate with Jews. For this patient, a Jew was someone who rots, unlike gentile Englishmen. When he was young he thought he saw his dead grandmother "thrown" into a grave without a coffin, according to what he thought, inaccurately, was the custom of Orthodox Jews, to be "eaten by the worms and to rot." In his mind, Jews rot, elegant Englishmen live in airtight mausoleums after death. A fourth patient asked me if I was Jewish because he felt rootless, uncontrollable, and without a conscience. He wanted a Jewish analyst because he felt that someone brought up with the Jewish ethic might bring something to the analytic situation that would enable him to control himself.

My discovery of the meaning of the snake fear for Mrs. C. is another example. There are no generally accepted denotative or connotative meanings for the word snake that have much to do with the highly personal meaning this term had for her.

I cannot overemphasize how necessary it is not to take for granted even fairly common or ordinary words, how necessary it is not to assume that we understand what these words mean to the patient. One day, a patient told me that she went into a temper tantrum because her husband said to her, "I know you are pissed." "I can't stand such words," she told me. I asked her what the word "pissed" meant to her. She replied, "I function at a higher level than that word indicates; he makes me seem like his mother, that I go around angry at the world, as though that is my personality, that I am comfortable being that way, and as though he had no role in provoking me or giving me any cause."

A few additional brief examples will support my contention that we should not assume too quickly that we know what the patient means.

One day a young woman patient told of being like a cactus in her marriage. I did not know what she meant. Did she mean prickly? Untouchable? Unable to be fondled? Something that keeps others away? She elaborated on her own the full context of her use of the term. She felt that she needed little to exist on in her marriage; she did not have to be tended to; she could live in relatively adverse situations. She felt that she survived although she was getting little from her husband. In brief, both she in her marriage and a cactus were members of a class of entities that need little, receive little, and yet survive.

Another young woman patient came in one day and said simply, "Here I am; I feel like oatmeal; that is all that I have to say." I had no idea what the oatmeal simile meant, and so I asked her. She replied, "Oatmeal is oatmeal; it is always the same, forever; it never changes; there is nothing ever different about it. What can possibly be interesting about oatmeal?"

A patient told me that on coming into the office she felt as though she were going into the water in the summer. Her analogy could have had any one of innumerable meanings, and so I asked her about it. She told me that when she comes into the office it is like putting her toe into the water to test the temperature. She gauges my mood, my reactions, my "temperature." She is concerned that perhaps I see her as a nuisance or a bore. She talks very slowly and owes me money, and she always wonders how that is affecting me.

A young married patient spoke one day of his male friends who seem to be homosexual. He told of his great curiosity about female homosexuality. He wondered about his own homosexuality and that of a member of his family. Then, with very considerable embarrassment, he told of having "homosexual" fantasies when having intercourse with his wife. When I inquired about these fantasies he said that while having "straight" sex he often fantasies having anal intercourse. When I asked him why he referred to anal intercourse as homosexual, he replied that it was only because he imagined that "that was how homosexuals do it." Clearly, the patient was using the term "homosexual" in a unique way.

Not only do we look for the personal meanings of words in psychoanalytic therapy, we also attempt to find out what different events mean to a patient. Thus, with Mr. E. special meanings were discovered. It seemed that his current reality difficulties had the meaning of an enema experience.

As we listen with our habitual free-floating attention we should (c) *scan for the unusual, the odd, and the unique, for those phenomena that do not fit the normal flow of experience.* This strategy leads to the interruption of free-floating attention, to alertness, to the focusing of attention, and, finally, to specific expectations.

Analysts follow this strategy constantly. Included here is the detection of slips of the tongue. For instance, a patient told of his boss "salvaging" him. This is an unusual expression; it does not match what we would anticipate from normal models. We generally speak of a boss hiring, not "salvaging." A response to such a verbalization is called for, even if the analyst only calls it to the patient's attention by repeating the word with a questioning inflection. We can reasonably assume that the term "salvaging" was loaded with personal meaning for this patient.

Another patient spoke of his sperm count after vasectomy and wondered if he were "still sterile." Then he corrected himself and said, "again sterile." What he was trying to say, of course, was "now sterile." The third expression would have fit the context of everyday familiar speech; the former two did not. Another patient spoke of her genitals as looking "used," an odd expression, probably loaded with personal meaning. Such instances should alert the analyst. A response is called for, even if only to ask for associations.

An otherwise energetic, slightly hypomanic patient who was in a period of severe anxiety and depression told of having to urge herself to get some food for dinner. She spoke of being unable to face the "trip," surely an inappropriate term for simple, everyday marketing. The term "trip" indicated that for her the experience was probably overwhelming. When I simply echoed back the word "trip" to highlight it, she replied, "Yes, I know, it felt like one."

Scanning for the unusual can include odd ways whereby patients verbalize their presenting complaints. I recall vividly one of my very earliest cases, a young man who came for treatment because of a potency disturbance. Thinking that I had a good workable, analytic case, I eagerly presented him to an experienced supervisor. I recall her grimace when she heard me say that the patient was concerned about his penis being small or "rotting." The word "rotting"—the patient's own term—disturbed her, and rightfully so. It was a most unusual way to describe how one feels about one's genitals, unusual even for the average patient with a potency disturbance. Indeed, this patient's problem was not a "simple" analyzable potency disturbance. His concern about his penis reflected a very profound body image disturbance.

Another strategy, similar to the preceeding one, also leads to the interruption of free-floating attention. To (d) *scan for signs of signif-*

icant phenomena also leads to the emergence of alertness, a focusing of attention, and specific expectations. This strategy is so automatic that we are usually hardly aware of the process. An internist may scan a patient for skin color, weight changes, and so on. He will be alerted if he notes deep pallor and great weight loss. He may then have many expectations, and on the basis of these expectations he may take appropriate action. Experience and a generally accepted body of knowledge in internal medicine have taught the internist what signs are significant and what the expectations may be. So, too, the psychiatrist learns to scan a patient for his mental status. Suspiciousness and arrogance, for example, alert him to expect serious psychopathology. It is generally accepted that such signs may indicate the presence of paranoia.

Psychoanalytic therapists work similarly. Most analysts, for example, upon hearing of an unusual childhood masturbatory history, will be alerted to wonder about its significance, how it may live on in adult sexual life, or how it may be defended against. Let me give a few examples, taken from clinical cases, of the kinds of phenomena that I see as significant and the nature of some of the expectations.

If I hear that a patient is constantly working endlessly long hours, I am alerted to expect that he may possibly be defending against a depression. Excessive activity of any kind, beyond the bounds of reasonable norms, alerts me to suspect the presence of defenses. When I hear that a patient had alcoholic or psychotic parents or that he suffered early illnesses and surgery, I am alerted to the possibility of finding serious problems related to attachment, separation, body imagery, and the sense of psychological and physical organization. If I hear that a patient feels deeply hopeless, empty, unreal, or that his life is meaningless, I am once again alerted. I expect to find some serious problems rooted in the first years of life. When I hear of someone relentlessly pursuing a career, sacrificing everything to be a writer, an artist, or anything else, I am alerted to understand the motivations, and I expect to find very important fantasies, perhaps even restitutional ones.

The illustrative cases presented in the earlier chapters contained numerous alerting significant signs: the history of Mrs. A.'s mother's severe depression; the history of Mrs. C.'s mother being paranoid and alcoholic; Mrs. D.'s early strabismus; Mr. F.'s asthmatic history; the suicide of Mr. G.'s sister, as well as the severe physical illness of the father when the patient was an infant. Some of these apparently significant signs proved to be of no profound consequence though hardly unimportant. For example, Mrs. D.'s strabismus was important in many ways but was never a basic issue in the patient's difficulties. Significant signs can also include recent events, such as the depression of the wife in the case of Mr. G.

These significant signs are of enormous importance in the treatment process. The phenomena they alert us to become parts of our working models of a patient, but especially significant parts. As already suggested, we can say that they are "flagged" in memory and therefore stand out for special attention. They become nodal points for organizing what we hear, foci for our attempts to understand how a patient may interpret an event. And it is through such interpretations that events take on special meanings.

Paying attention to these significant signs allows us to reduce uncertainty, to cut down on the vast complexity before us. In general, as noted earlier, working models highlight and select input; the significant signs are especially highlighting and selective. They may direct paths for further inquiry; they may reduce search in a meaningful way; they may help make selections for emerging hypotheses and, consequently, aid in possible discoveries.

What I have said about the strategy of scanning for signs of significant phenomena in no way contradicts what I wrote earlier (see chap. 13) about a "bottom up" approach where I suggested as an important strategy that the analyst should build up his understanding from within the data, from simple generalizations about small units of sharply observed phenomena to more encompassing ones. The former strategy can be thought of as a "top down" approach. We are alerted to expect certain important events even before we have direct evidence for them, but the direct evidence for any expectation will generally come from small units—sharply observed. Thus, the two strategies work together. We can generalize from small units of phenomena without previous expectations, as when we observe repeated lateness, repeated ways by which a patient greets or responds to the therapist. We can also generalize from small units of phenomena, using some previous expectations that have become part of the general context with which we approach a patient—expectations that may come from significant signs. The two types of strategies that I am suggesting might be thought of as "bottom up" and "top down" can also be thought of as "data driven" and "conceptually driven" strategies, to use terms employed by cognitive psychologists. Processing that starts with certain conceptualizations and expectations is thought of as conceptually driven. As Lindsay and Norman (1977, p. 13) write: "Whenever knowledge of the possible interpretations or *conceptualization* of something helps in perceiving that thing, we say the processing is conceptually driven."

In summary, the strategies I suggest that are related to the establishment of meaning are:

(a).–Discover unique and personal meanings.
(b).–Establish full emotional and cognitive contexts.
(c).–Scan for the unusual, the odd, and the unique, for those phenomena that do not fit the normal flow of experience.
(d).–Scan for signs of significant phenomena.

The last two strategies lead, first, to the interruption of free-floating attention, then to alertness and the focusing of attention, and, finally, to specific expectations.

17

Strategies Used by the Patient

As I have said earlier, whether we realize it or not, we use strategies in all walks of life. Patients are therefore using strategies of different kinds from the moment therapy begins. In this chapter I focus on a small group of strategies the patient should be encouraged to employ. Many patients adopt these strategies naturally in response to being told about the basic rule of free association (which itself is essentially a strategy) and in response to the entire therapeutic climate. Others need to have them spelled out. Exactly when to talk to the patient about strategies depends on the circumstances. A patient suffering from overwhelming anxiety will not be able to pay much heed to the idea of how to establish a process of investigation leading to discovery. In such instances, considerable preliminary work may be required and in some cases medication may have to be used. But I cannot imagine the existence of even a reasonably good therapeutic process unless the strategies to be mentioned eventually become operative.

I think it most important for patients to (a) *focus on working in a process of learning, investigating and understanding—a process leading to discovery*. I earlier called attention to what Freud (1913, p. 130) wrote about the therapeutic process—that it is set in motion and "goes its own way and does not allow either the direction it takes or the order in which it picks up its points to be prescribed for it." Patients must also *develop alertness to odd, unusual, extreme, unexplained experiences*.

Though they may reasonably expect eventual relief, patients must abandon any expectation of immediate relief. As already indicated, patients in acute distress have trouble with this approach. A deeply depressed, profoundly anxious anorexia-nervosa patient evaluated every word and every moment with "Am I getting better? or "Am I doing the right thing to get better?" A frantic attitude such as hers is not compatible with the experiencing and reflecting attitude required for establishing a good treatment process.

If the patients' curiosity is not present from the very beginning, it may develop as the therapeutic process moves on, provided they have a degree of trust and can see something begin to happen that has some meaning to them. Actually, patients who come to and remain in treatment generally do have such attitudes to begin with. Often, years of trouble have forced them to look inward to some degree. Optimally, most patients do become alerted to odd, unusual, extreme, puzzling, and unexplained experiences. Such activity implies a matching against norms—either general norms, or the particular norms of the patient.

With regard to the strategy of focusing on the process, patients must take the initiative in introducing meaningful, relevant issues for therapeutic work. Only the patient knows what is on his mind and what concerns him most. As noted earlier, it is hard to imagine any sequence of inquiries by the therapist that can be as meaningful to a patient and that can reduce existing uncertainty and complexity as much as spontaneous input by the patient himself. Here, as previously indicated (see chap. 5), the "classical," silent, passive therapist who listens and lets the patient take the lead has ample justification from theoretical informational considerations.

Closely related to the analyst's strategy of putting himself into the patient's world is a group of strategies that apply to the patient. The patient should learn to (b) *introspect, scan, and allow free-associative detailing of current experiences; allow disordered experiences.* The patient should try to *relive and revive segments of recent and remote past experiences, to evoke and get into a segment of his own past world.*

Psychoanalysis or analytic therapy is an invitation to a patient to take a chance; of necessity, it is often stressful. Patients must allow themselves detailed fantasies and feelings of all kinds, even those that may be judged bizarre, "crazy," and "perverse." They have to attempt to capture what I heard Eugene Gendlin call "the vague edge of experience; the felt but not yet understood, not-yet-defined texture of experience." Indeed, as I said earlier, to analyze a dream it is probably necessary to enter into something close to a sleeplike state, as Freud (1900, p. 102) emphasized. Malcove (1975 p. 9), writing on Isakower's ideas about analyzing dreams, states: "He has found that a successful analytic investigation of a dream is possible only when the patient, at the time of presenting the dream in the session, happens to become re-immersed, however mildly, into a dreamy state; thus evoking, in varying degrees of vividness, the dreaming experience."

It is a constant struggle to avoid the automatic censoring that is so necessary and characteristic of everyday communication. And it seems generally true that when patients do take a chance and do allow themselves to capture fully what is going on, our data base is markedly enhanced and there is a notable meaningfulness and richness to the hours, with consequent greater clarity about what is going on. For example, a patient told the following dream: "I was sexually aroused, and while my husband was in the bathroom, I began to masturbate. When he came out he saw me, and then he began to look like my father." Subsequently, the patient told me that while lying on the couch, she found herself editing her remarks, but caught herself. With great embarrassment she told me what she had begun to edit. She had noticed that her knees were upright and apart, and she had the thought, "too seductive and not ladylike. I should be more ladylike, delicate, and close my legs and turn to the side, to a less crotch-oriented position." Certainly, had she allowed herself to edit her thoughts, the chance to understand the dream would have been markedly decreased.

Here is another brief example where close attention to inner experience lends greater meaning, conviction, "confirmation," and "reality" to what is being said. A patient was telling of her tendency to pick on herself, a general impatience and dissatisfaction with herself. She found that she was constantly urging herself to do things faster and constantly dissatisfied with her accomplishments, although she was a well-functioning professional. And anything brought up in treatment was greeted by an inner reproachful voice that said, "Big deal! So you finally brought this up; it's about time." Or else, "What are you talking about this for? You already discussed it." The pervasiveness of the self-belittlement emerged with even greater clarity and conviction because, as a result of the patient's close attention to her inner experience, she could discern that an inner voice was belittling the very accomplishment of becoming increasingly aware of how she belittles accomplishments—the phenomenon of an ad infinitum inner voice commenting on an inner voice, like looking into a mirror that simultaneously reflects one's reflection in another mirror, resulting in an endless series of images within images.

The strategies I am describing are intended to encourage the patient to deal with specific details, rather than generalizations. It is one thing to say that you have an evil mother and an ugly body, generalizations that are important and meaningful. But it is another thing—and a necessary step—to go into details. In exactly what ways the mother is experienced as "evil," and in what ways the body is experienced as "ugly." It is one thing to say that you felt depressed at work prior to the session; it is another thing to give full details of exactly what happened and when—the full context of events, feelings, thoughts.

Finally, it is important to recognize that it is one thing to *talk* about remote experiences in a rather general way, and another to *revive* and *relive* details of the experience. It is one thing to say, "I had an operation when I was small, and I remember that it was a horrible experience." It is another thing to revive the full details of the experience, and to "relive" and "reexperience" it as though it were happening now—a kind of replay of the event. The differences may well be related to how the memories in question were stored—whether episodically or semantically (see chap. 6; see also Bowlby, 1980).

It should be emphasized that to capture an experience accurately, the limitation of words must be recognized and many metaphors and images may have to be used. Some patients find it necessary to close their eyes to shut out current, immediate, visual input in order to attend to or focus on an experience. Also, in order to carry out a full reliving or reactivation of a segment of past experience, patients must allow themselves to be one-sided, not subject to adult, "reasonable" evaluations. If a wife, for example, wishes to tell of painful experiences evoked by her husband's behavior, she must allow her painful state to become fully active, as "childish," "unfair," or "unreasonable" as it may be, and not inhibit herself by adult, fair, reasonable views of the situation. This strategy is the counterpart of one of the analyst's strategies discussed earlier, that of developing the awareness of different levels of experience, different states of cognitive and emotional organization.

Patients vary in their ability to carry out the strategies discussed so far. The severely obsessional patients, though perhaps successful in some areas of life—in business or in a profession, for example— are typically difficult in this respect. Some are so remote, distanced, out of contact with their inner lives, and so completely under control that often they do not know what they feel; shades, subtleties, and differences of feeling tone seem to be virtually absent; and few feelings exist with sufficient intensity to allow them to know which are "hotter," more urgent, or more meaningful. Often these patients may feel only a diffuse tension, a sense of anxiety, a low level of chronic depression, a vague sense of general dissatisfaction. It is very difficult for them to give details of current experiences or to revive and relive recent or remote past experiences with any of the richness or vividness often available to others. As a result, the relevant information they convey is minimal, and ambiguity and uncertainty are not reduced. If we try to work with these patients, we get little sense of understanding or of truly knowing what may be going on. Because they are so unable to get in touch with their inner life, to know what they feel, these patients generally tend to intellectualize and speculate about what "might be" or about what "could be." But they have too little access to raw data—alive, vivid, recognizable, discernible, detectable feelings and fantasies—to be able to tell which of the speculated possibilities is indeed the case. Few of us do well with such patients; I certainly do not.

Here are two brief examples from an obsessive young businessman, Mr. Q. In his typical dry, flat style, he told of his interest in Betty, an attractive secretary in his office. He found himself hesitant about offering her an open invitation. When he did ask her out for a drink, she was cool to him. He was upset to see flowers on her desk, an obvious gift. He was bothered to see her go out for lunch with one of the handsome salesmen in the office. He found himself often passing by her desk to gauge her mood.

Mr. Q. differs from other patients in that, in pursuing the events reported, the therapist can learn almost nothing more about them—

no further detail, no further feeling or fantasy. Meanings or true connections to the past are therefore not established. It was indeed difficult for me to enter Mr. Q.'s world. Actually, I found it disorienting when I tried to do so because everything was so flat, gray, murky—truly passionless. After some floundering on my part, I suggested to Mr. Q. that perhaps envy was an important feeling here. He agreed, envy was important; he envied others because they, not he, caught Betty's attention. He went on to tell of reading about children who were left when young. His father died when Mr. Q. was 3 years old. "I guess I envied others who had fathers, and so the pattern persists; I envy what others have."

The patient's apparent insight was actually intellectualized, vague, devoid of details. He did not give any direct memories of being envious of other children who had fathers. Furthermore, even if he was envious in this regard—as is highly likely—this fact does not necessarily explain his envy concerning Betty. After all, he doesn't report being envious about everything that others have; obviously, there must have been particular aspects to the situation with Betty. But I learned little about his personal reactions concerning Betty, the inner meaning of his observing her going out to lunch with the handsome salesman in the office. In brief, he was merely speculating, "guessing" in a kind of empty way. Even if envy was an important or significant issue, he was incapable of dealing with the subtlety and complexity of the emotion.

On another occasion Mr. Q. spoke of several things that bothered him in his office. A co-worker went to lunch and did not ask the patient to accompany him. He was unhappy with his secretary and asked the personnel officer to transfer her, but his request was being disregarded. He mentioned one or two other similar incidents and then went on to say that maybe everything could be explained by the fact that mother had given him everything after his father died and maybe "I want everyone to love me as mother did." Note again the absence of details. I couldn't find out what went on in him when not asked to lunch, and just what he experienced when his request to transfer the secretary was disregarded. Had he perhaps felt helpless, powerless, too insignificant, not enough of a man to be listened to (I knew that he felt short in height, and also important was his feeling that his penis was not large)? Again, what is significant in this case is that I could not get sufficient relevant input to reduce the uncertainty and to give me some feeling that I understood what was happening.

Other patients can capture, revive, and relive experiences in varying degrees and express their inner lives quite accurately. Mrs. C. and Mrs. D. were both able to bring in a great deal of relevant information about any given experience, making a considerable reduction of uncertainty and ambiguity possible. As therapist, I could fairly easily enter their worlds and not get a feeling of disorientation, murkiness, and grayness, as with the obsessional Mr. Q.

Here is an example from a patient who could capture in depth the fullness of an emotional life. This is the kind of simple "living," believable, sensitive good hour that is in sharp contrast to some that I have just mentioned. There is no high drama in this hour, and little in the case in general, but experienced clinicians would say that this is the kind of hour which indicates that the patient probably has a good prognosis for treatment.

A young woman came in after a weekend and talked about her dog. She had been very attached to Ruff, who had died suddenly a few months previously. She and her husband had him cremated but never got the ashes. It was finally decided that they would get his ashes and drop them from their boat on the weekend. Ruff had spent a great deal of time on this boat with the patient and her husband—all very pleasurable experiences. She then spoke of how important it seems to be to know where a dead person "is" even though one knows that there is no longer a real person. "But still," she said, "there is something concrete about it and if one knows where they are buried, then there is still some connection; they are not completely gone." She then told of how she and her mother were on a trip several years before and they stopped, though late in the day and despite a terrible storm, to be able to get to the cemetery before it closed in order to see grandfather's grave. Finally, the patient told me that though they took the dog's ashes out on the boat to scatter them into the water, they could not go through with it. I said very quietly, "It was too difficult for you to give up Ruff." She agreed; her voice became husky, and she sobbed quietly.

Some patients, in contrast to the obsessional Mr. Q. mentioned earlier, can allow various kinds of primitive archaic experiences—states of depersonalization on the couch, for example. One of my patients could allow himself to enter into a hypnagogic-like state, permitting the emergence of a typical Isakower phenomenon (Isakower, 1938), with the characteristic feeling of being all head and mouth. In his case the phenomenon seemed to be defensive against massive, disorganizing, primitive, rage, pain, and anxiety. When he allowed the latter to emerge, the Isakower phenomenon dissipated.

Some patients can go well beyond words, capture primitive sensations, and even dramatize in a physical, sensorimotor way what is going on—all under control, of course. For example, after much work, Mr. R., a patient already mentioned a few times in passing, was able to sense a deep urge to wail, a very vague, almost undiscernible edge of experience, which proved to be of great importance. Another patient, who had a history of an early walking disturbance, was able to get off the couch and, with eyes closed—a necessary condition—capture in a purely sensorimotor way the faltering movements of an infant attempting to stand and walk. These were not efforts to imitate anything that he had seen or knew about intellectually. He could predict what was going to happen only in a general way, devoid of details. He had to allow his body to express itself, allow his body to "talk" and to present the full details of the experience.

Most patients are unable to capture levels of experience such as those just mentioned, and many need not do so because their early life may not have been very traumatic.

Only once did I have to stop a patient from dramatizing a very primitive experience. This patient, Mr. T., started to slap himself in the face to demonstrate how he felt about himself. The slapping became increasingly wild, and I became very uncomfortable, fearing that he might be getting out of control. When I found the situation intolerable, I intervened and insisted that he stop. As he did so, Mr. T. told me that I had stopped him just in time; he was about to run and smash himself, head first, into the wall of my office. Mr. T. had great limitations as a patient. He never could truly introspect, revive and relive recent and remote past experiences in a detailed, controlled sort of way. Slapping himself violently was a frightening eruption of uncontrolled experience. His early life was apparently very traumatic, as best as I could judge from his history, but it was not possible to work it out in any detail.

I believe we can say that we work with a *spectrum* of situations with respect to the kind and amount of data, as well as our understanding of it. At one extreme, we have great uncertainty and ambiguity, which persists and cannot be reduced very much; at the other, much of the uncertainty and ambiguity can be reduced. Thus, we cannot speak of the validity of psychoanalytic findings or of the efficacy of analytic therapy in any generalized or simplistic way. When I treat obsessional patients of the kind discussed, my "index of confidence" in the situation is low. In contrast, the analytic treatment of patients such as Mrs. C. and Mrs. D. left me with much greater confidence that I understood a fair amount, that I had some firm knowledge and grasp of the situation. In the latter cases, even when I did not understand, I at least had an idea of what I was not understanding, what had to be worked on, and the confidence that, given time, things might work out. With the obsessional of Mr. Q's type it is hard to say that one has a firm grasp even on what one doesn't know, and there is little confidence that the situation will change significantly. The ability of patients to carry out the strategies under discussion is crucial in giving the therapist the sense of confidence I mentioned.

Free association is hardly a totally wild, random, or chaotic process. Of the infinite number of things that can be talked about, optimally, only certain relevant things are selected. What determines such selections? First, patients are aware, or should quickly become aware, that in therapy or analysis we are interested in their emotional life—personal thoughts, fantasies, feelings. A selection is hence implicit. Patients should not talk about business or professional matters unless these have relevance to some personal emotional issues. Second, the patient brings up material that the patient feels is important to be understood—an unusual, odd, unexplained, bizarre experience, situations of turmoil and anxiety. Further selections are implicit in such activities. Third, when the analyst scans for the unusual, the odd, and the unique experiences that do not fit the normal flow of experience and when he inquires about these, again a selective procedure is implicit.

But still further selections must be made. If a patient wishes to recount a recent experience and capture all of the associated feelings and thoughts, or if the patient is responding with spontaneous associations to something the therapist has asked about, the arena for selection is still enormous—especially in patients with rich inner lives. As Mrs. D. once said when I asked her to respond with her associations to some experiential element, "It is as though a stone were thrown into water and there are ripples or waves in all directions." (Contrast this statement with that of the patient who told me that her thoughts were like "cement blocks," meaning unrelated and unconnected.)

Which to select, which line of associations to be followed is a basic problem. It is also very true that a patient with a rich inner life may find it hard to begin an hour because so many things might have happened since the previous session or there are so many things to report that the patient does not know where to begin. It is often the case that it makes no difference where one begins, especially when a highly emotional event is being reported because the different paths eventually point in the same direction. But this does not always happen, and when it does not, strategies must be employed.

One strategy to help determine selections for "free association" is for the patient to (c) *test by looking ahead and evaluating. He follows the associative line that is most evocative,* most emotionally arousing—of tears, depression, anxiety—or of new associative lines.

What I am suggesting is very close to one of Freud's recommendations (1913, p. 135). Speaking of the importance of free association, he suggests what we might say to a patient: "You will be tempted to say to yourself that this or that is irrelevant here, or is quite unimportant, or nonsensical, so that there is no need to say it. You must never give in to these criticisms, but must say it in spite of them—indeed, you must say it precisely *because* you feel an aversion to doing so." Essentially Freud is suggesting that it is useful to look ahead, test, and select the very line of association that is most aversive.

Here, once again, a strategy of importance in analytic therapy is a general strategy, found in all walks of life. We are constantly testing by looking ahead and evaluating using different standards. Do we wish to have fish or meat for dinner? We look ahead to both possibilities, evaluate how we feel about each experience, and then decide. Of course, the evoked experiences that we evaluate will depend on past history in similar or related contexts. And again, we look ahead constantly when communicating; when we carry on a rational, ordinary conversation, we may have innumerable associations. We test them by looking ahead and evaluating them for relevance, pertinence, and logical relationship to previous comments and to the general theme. And, of course, we are constantly looking ahead and evaluating for the possible effects on the listener of anything that we say; we judge how he may react, based on our working models of people in general and of the listener in particular.

The difference between looking-ahead strategies used in ordinary communication and those a patient may profitably use lies in the standards for evaluating. In ordinary communication we evaluate for relevance, logic, and the like. A "good" patient will evaluate and select what is odd, unusual, "crazy", or, as Freud suggests, most aversive.

Testing procedures of the kind just discussed can take place with astonishing speed. Very rapidly, several steps of each of multiple lines of associations can be allowed and the responses to each line evaluated. The rapidity of these responses and their preconscious nature blinds us to the astonishing complexity of the events that are actually taking place. (One advantage of attempting to simulate such experiences artificially is that we are forced to attend to so much that we generally take for granted.) But again, I emphasize that such activities are possible only in patients who have rich emotional reactions available and are capable of detecting degrees of response. Mr. R., who could capture early archaic, primitive experiences, could rapidly evaluate multiple lines and detect the most arousing, the most evocative. He could select lines of associations not only because they were "hot" in terms of intensity of emotional arousal, but "hot," too, in terms of the flooding of new, relevant associations—-memories and fantasies—that, on even quick inspection, seemed possibly relevant. He could therefore very often zero in on aspects of recent events that were most directly and immediately connected to significant events of the past. When such activities are being carried out, the therapeutic situation is exciting; one feels involved as one sits behind the couch; and one has a sense of participating in discovery in statu nascendi—in a most convincing way. Such reactions on the part of the therapist are a far cry from his reactions as he hears the flat, dry, monotonous report of the obsessional.

At times, with "good" involved patients, we can see the interesting phenomenon of a "prepared hour." Prior to the hour, the patient recognizes the general direction that the hour may take. He has a general sense of the topic, the thoughts, fantasies, feelings, and bodily movements that need to be expressed. All of this is based on a process of anticipation and an evaluation for significance and degree of emotional arousal. But the patient holds back full expression of the entire experience until the analytic session begins. Mr. R. was one such patient. He could anticipate broadly what was going to happen—could feel it in his whole body; presumably, there was low-level arousal in advance. But the full expression in the hour—full arousal—brought unexpected details that he could not sense before the hour actually began—details of the emerging experience took unpredictable paths.

Patients must (d) *sort out, group, compare, and match experiences; they must generalize and classify.* Patients detect subtle differences in attributes of many apparently similar experiences. These processes take place when, for example, a patient says, "I love both of my children, but in very different ways."

Patients are generalizing when they detect common attributes and often will then test to see if the generalizations hold true with other experiences. Such activities have taken place when a patient makes the simple statement, "I was always a self-conscious, unhappy child, bored in school, but things are very different now."

Patients must carefully match words against experiences they are trying to express and test to see if the words express their intent. As already mentioned, "good" patients grope to find the exact words to portray well-delineated feelings. Commonly we hear from them, "That is not what I was trying to say," a statement indicating that some matching has taken place and the words are judged not to have expressed the patient's intent.

Careful attention to one's inner life, sorting and comparing of inner experiences allow the ranking of experiences—which ones are more intense, urgent, and meaningful. One establishes "an intensity dimension," as a patient put it. Often, after a highly emotional experience, patients use the therapy session to sort out what happened. This commonly occurs with patients who may be flooded by feelings, fantasies, and memories. But note, here the confusion results from too much happening too soon; it is a confusion that can be resolved over time as the recent experiences are revived, the multiple reactions examined, and many hypotheses tested. A good example where both patient and therapist felt confused when too much had happened too soon was when Mrs. C. flooded the hour with fantasies and anxieties about a snake. This confusion was resolved by sorting out the multiple attributes of her experiences and testing several hypotheses.

Sorting out of experiences, comparing, matching, generalizing, and classifying—all are basic activities, and not just because they are essential steps in therapy. They are actually growth experiences in themselves; they are strengthening and adaptive; they are differentiating; they contribute immensely to the patient's sense of self. They represent the paths whereby human beings in general learn about themselves and their world, learn about their own uniqueness. Although often difficult, frustrating, and stressful, the final result can be most gratifying, comparable to the delight of the child who, on his own, has explored some part of his world, erred, faltered, felt frustrated, but who has finally discovered something meaningful to him.

One of the very serious problems with Mrs. A. was that she was not generalizing, classifying, or finding patterns or relationships. During those early months, she was merely expressing fantasies, fears, chaotic emotions, and hypochondriacal preoccupations. She was not reflecting on her experiences, and therefore no true learning took place.

Finally, it should be noted that working through, generally recognized to be an essential part of the psychoanalytic process, is based on generalizing and classifying. A given generalization, a good hypothesis, should have broad applicability. Classifying other events under the generalization, and thus widening its scope, is basic to working through and to updating and revising working models.

The patient should become aware that (e) *patient and analyst are partners in a process of investigation that can lead to discovery.*

It is necessary that a patient evaluate the analyst's interpretations. As I have repeatedly emphasized, these are only tentative hypotheses, and must allow for the full range of confirmation and refutation, refinement, and revision. Such error-correcting feedback is essential. The therapist must make sense to the patient at the moment, and the patient is the final arbiter of the truth or falsity of whatever the analyst claims is taking place in him. And I will say once again that if the patient does not understand the analyst it does not necessarily mean that he is resisting; it may mean only that the analyst is not making good sense.

Error-correcting feedback by the patient is so crucial that I wish to give a few additional examples of it. Here is one where I was just about totally wrong in what I said, and the patient rightfully told me so.

He was an adolescent boy who was to start school in about a week, after having been out of school for some time. When he came in I casually remarked, "So, one more week of freedom." He replied, "Well you can put it that way, I guess. But I don't see it that way. I don't even think that way. The weeks just melt into each other. I am in limbo and have been there for a long time. I see school as time for a new beginning, something is going to happen, and there are now possibilities for the future." I was making the mistake of not thinking from within the patient's experience. Actually, as the session went on we used the term "delimbotizing" to describe what school might be for him. But I should add that the hour was turned to advantage; we did learn something because error-correction was allowed.

Here is another example of error-correction wherein the patient refined my remarks, which were only partly accurate, and then elaborated on the material—typical of a decent therapeutic situation.

The patient, a young woman, spoke of her boyfriend, who is romantic, "who can make one feel wonderful." In contrast, her exhusband was a cold person who didn't talk much; and sex for him was little more than a release of tension. He did not give her the "personal" feeling of "the two of us" that her boyfriend now gives her. She said too that her exhusband was the one who, when they were young, told his sister that there was really no Santa Claus. I commented casually, "He takes the romance out of things." The patient replied, "True, but more than that. He uses words to hurt, and always did. Words are weapons for him. I could never argue with him; I never had the ability." She then told of how her exhusband was called "swordmouth" when young.

When patients are using their full faculties to evaluate an interpretation, we can often get not only agreement, elaboration of the interpretation, and so on, we can also get a marked change in the mood of the session—an important "marker" for a good hour. Here is an example.

At the beginning of the hour a young college student spoke some-what quietly of arranging for the purchase of cocaine. He then went on to tell of how well he did in school, how well he had done on a test and in class recitation. He commented that he "would have loved it" had I heard the praise heaped on him for his class work. He spoke of his need to be admired, liked, and praised by his professors.

I was struck by the slightly giddy, "high" state he seemed to be in, accompanied by much laughter as the hour went on. I knew this patient well, and the issue of drug use had often come up. He had occasionally come into sessions high on marijuana. I said, "All of the experiences that you mention—how well thought of you were in school, how you would have liked me to hear how much you were praised—I wonder if your telling me these things helps you deal with your concern about buying cocaine and your great concern about what I might think of you for doing so." The patient's mood changed sharply. He became quite "sober" and quietly said he thought I was quite right. He then went on to elaborate extensively about his use of drugs and his concern about my opinion.

Patients are frequently much better than we are at finding the right words to describe what is going on in them, as I have noted earlier. Competent therapists recognize how remote their own words appear to patients, an unavoidable situation even under the best of circumstances, especially with early and primitive states.

When patients are well tuned in to the analytic process, they can find connections, relationships, and generalizations that have gone unrecognized by the analyst, and can compare and match against working models and achieve insights that the analyst may never have thought of himself—all an excellent sign of the health of the therapeutic process. Indeed, it is an important growth and learning experience if patients are able to do this, and are allowed to do it, just as it is an important growth and learning experience for the child to discover himself.

Here is a simple example. A patient was planning a trip, but felt great guilt about it. She felt that it was too expensive and that she should be helping a man, Samuel, in whom she was interested and who was having some serious career and financial problems. She saw him as somewhat helpless, disorganized, and confused, but a decent and brilliant man. Her guilt was profound and preoccupied her a great deal. She could not understand what this man meant to her. Marriage was not a likely possibility with him, though they had

had a brief and enjoyable affair. I was puzzled about her guilt, and as I reviewed my model of her early life I began to think about her father who, in some ways, resembled Samuel. There was presumably some marital difficulty when the patient was young, and, as far as we could tell, there was a separation. But I was on the wrong track, and the patient came up with a much better idea on her own. She realized that, in many ways, she saw Samuel as her "baby," the child she always longed for, and "one doesn't abandon one's baby." After she said this, she broke into tears and wept for some time.

In short, most activities performed by a therapist can be performed by a patient, and often much better.

In summary, strategies used by the patient include:

(a).–Focus on working in a process leading to discovery; develop alertness to odd, unusual, extreme, unexplained experiences.
(b).–Introspect, scan, and allow free-associative detailing of current experiences; allow disordered experiences. Relive and revive segments of recent and remote past experiences.
(c).–Follow the associative path that is most evocative; test by looking ahead and evaluating.
(d).–Sort out, group, compare, and match experiences; generalize and classify.
(e).–Recognize that patient and analyst are partners in a process of investigation that can lead to discovery. [1,2]

---

[1] I have oversimplified my discussion concerning the nature of memory in the therapeutic process, and I believe it important to recognize the complexities because so much of Freudian therapy involves memory organization. A case discussed elsewhere in greater detail (Peterfreund and Franceschini, 1973) raises important issues. The patient, referred to earlier, came into treatment with anxieties about his penis "rotting" and equated Jews with people who rot because he had a memory of his grandmother supposedly being thrown into a grave without a coffin (see chap. 16, p. 175).

At times, while on the couch, he experienced an urge to vomit uncontrollably and to curl up in the manner of a very ill child attempting to deal with a loss of bowel control. This repeated experience combined with a working model of the patient built up over many months led me to suggest to him that he might have once experienced some traumatic event or events involving a loss of consciousness with associated symptoms, such as vomiting and loss of bowel control. Direct inquiry of the parents by the patient produced reasonably good confirmation for the surmise. He had indeed early in life had a serious, acute febrile illness with the symptoms mentioned.

If we recognize the reasonable possibility that every event is interpreted or takes on meaning in the context of existing working models or existing memory, then we can say that the death of the grandmother took on meaning in terms of what had been learned from previous traumatic episodes.

What can we reasonably say about the memory structure here? The term *Jew* had a place in semantic memory, a unique place with all of the idiosyncratic meanings for this man. About the episodic or detailed memory, there are some very interesting questions. Certainly, he may have misperceived the burial of the grandmother; there is no custom among orthodox Jews to bury bodies without coffins, as the patient claimed, or else the idea of her being buried without a coffin may represent a "re-working" of an earlier accurately perceived event. About other aspects of the grand-mother's death and burial, when the patient recounted the details of these events and his reactions to them—his episodic memory—are we truly getting details of the events as experienced by the child at the time or are we getting some subsequent reinterpretation of those events, perhaps "reworked" many times over? I tend to believe the latter is generally the case (Peterfreund, 1971, p. 214). Memories of old events are probably "reworked" many times over and thereby acquire new meanings and new nuances. I agree with Freud (1899, p. 322) that: "It may indeed be ques-tioned whether we have any memories at all *from* our childhood: memories *relating* to our childhood may be all that we possess."

It seems reasonable to suggest that what this patient tells us about his grand-mother's death and burial represents aspects of the *detailed* record of the experience only as this *detailed record now exists*. The early detailed memory has probably been "revised" and reinterpreted in many ways. In contrast, the personal connotative meanings of the term *Jew* represent what he learned, what he abstracted from his experiences; they represent selected information from the early pathogenic events. The term *Jew* gives no detailed picture of any sort, "reworked" or not "reworked," "revised" or not "revised." However, the experiences that emerged in bodily form— seen in this patient and at times in other patients with early traumatic histories, as I have indicated throughout this book—may possibly be relatively undistorted, unre-worked, direct "replays" of some part of the past febrile illness, the result, perhaps, of some special storage of sensorimotor experience which remains relatively unmodified.

---

[2]On reading the final page proofs of this work I was astonished to find that I had failed to be specific about strategies concerning conflict. Certainly, it is a basic strategy for patient and analyst to *focus on obvious conflict-laden situa-tions,* as, e.g., a patient conflicted about leaving a spouse, having a sexual affair, changing jobs, disciplining children, caring for elderly parents. As mentioned (pp. 87-88), conflict may be related to memory organization. Conflict is rarely a simple A versus B phenomenon. Conflict usually involves multiple, hierarchically organized, contingently related experiential phenomena (Peterfreund, 1971, pp. 172-174; 1980). A patient may be conflicted about leaving a spouse because of multiple possible consequences, each of which may be fruitful issues for analysis.

18

Some General Characteristics of Heuristic Analytic Sessions

Given the models and strategies discussed and assuming that they are fundamentally operative, what are some of the characteristics of the resulting therapeutic sessions?

First, the heuristic process is nonconfrontational. The therapist's role is not to do battle with a "resistant" patient. The adversary is not the patient but the patient's illness. The equation for the process is therapist plus patient versus the illness and not therapist versus patient.

Lest I be misunderstood, let me quickly say that I believe a therapist must demonstrate to a patient the reality of his illness, and there are many distressing and difficult times for patients in any good treatment process. But if patients suffer and are hurt during treatment, it should not be because of what the therapist does, but only because of the nature of the illness and how it manifests itself in the therapeutic situation—recollections of painful memories, reawakened traumata, awareness of lost opportunities. Our patients are unhappy, suffering, and needy people; they would not be in treatment if this were not so. It is not the task of the therapist to add to the burden of already overwhelmed patients.

In this connection, a basic point deserves to be emphasized about the use of the term *resistance* when a patient is unable to accept the analytic interpretation offered. Often, the patient is told, "You cannot accept my interpretation because you are resistant." What can a patient do under such circumstances if the interpretation offered does not fit the patient's experiences? How can the patient not hear the term *resistance* as an accusation, part of an adversarial approach with analyst as adversary? In response, patients naturally tend to feel defeated, hopeless, and stupid—a totally unnecessary, iatrogenic cause for suffering.

Certainly, the *idea* of resistance is always used in heuristic work but *only* in a full *experiential context* and preferably when a full statement can be made which includes *what* is being resisted, *how,* and *why,* thereby giving a patient a meaningful statement with which to work, one that is not accusatory, and that doesn't take an adversarial position against him. We can, for example, say to a patient, "I think that you give generalities about your sex life because you find it too embarrassing to give details." The patient is here implicitly being told that he is resisting giving details of his sex life (the *what* of the resistance) by speaking in generalities (the *how* of the resistance) because of embarrassment (the *why* of the resistance). This form of interpretation is not accusatory; it is actually an attempt to understand what is going on, and a patient can work with such a statement in many ways. Furthermore, it is nonauthoritarian.

This last point leads to another fundamental characteristic of a heuristic technique. I cannot emphasize too strongly that the analyst does not possess "truths" and does not possess "answers" to a patient's problems; at best the analyst has only a *method to discover* some answers and possible truths; success depends to a large extent on the ability of the patient to work with the analyst. At bottom, it is the nonconfrontational and nonauthoritarian atmosphere of the therapeutic situation that sets the stage for a therapeutic dialogue and permits error-correction and hypothesis-testing—fundamental aspects of the multiple automatic regulations of the therapeutic "system."

At the termination of a good therapeutic process, both patient and therapist should have a sense of mutual respect, an awareness of the limitations and frailties on both sides; and the patient should retain no great ambivalence to the therapist and certainly no sense of awe for the therapist or the process.

And what about Freud's advice (1912, p. 118) that "The doctor should be opaque to his patients and, like a mirror, should show them nothing but what is shown to him"? As an attempt to counteract treatment by suggestion, one can well understand why Freud wrote such remarks in 1912, but at the present time I can only judge this advice to be unsatisfactory. The therapist is performing a unique professional task, working with the models that have developed from both personal and professional experiences. Of necessity, in every word and gesture the therapist conveys some information from these complex models. We cannot say that the therapist should be "opaque" and show patients "nothing"; attitudes, beliefs, a personal philosophy, and the like, are always being conveyed, and the question to be answered is *what* attitudes, beliefs, and personal philosophy are indeed being conveyed.

Certainly, an image of reasonableness should be presented to a patient, one of awareness of the wide range of human experience, and a nonjudgmental attitude. Much of this is conveyed implicitly. Returning to the interpretation mentioned earlier, "I think that you give generalities about your sex life because you find it too embarrassing to give details," the therapist is actually conveying a message well beyond the ordinary meanings of the words employed. The implicit message is, "You are free to talk about your sex life here; I am familiar with such things and will not be shocked by anything that you say; I will not be condemning or guilt-provoking." And there is even a larger implicit message, "I believe that sexuality in all its forms is a fact of life and should be talked about." In brief, the therapist is conveying a set of attitudes, a system of beliefs, and something of a philosophy of life. Of course this does not mean that the details of his own sex life should be talked about, although patients are free to speculate about these.

The therapist is a professional with a task to perform, not a friend, which does not mean he is not friendly in manner. Fundamentally, as is generally recognized, it is necessary to frustrate. Gratifying many of the patient's wishes is totally impossible, and attempting to do so is counterproductive for it obviates analytic understanding. Instead of gratifying the patient's wishes we attempt to understand their many meanings. But we do provide many important gratifications. Patients are entitled to our full attention and our maximal effort to understand them; they are entitled to have their suffering recognized and taken seriously; and they are entitled to have their needs be our primary concern in the therapeutic hour. The therapeutic value of these gratifications should not be underestimated.

The use of psychoanalytic jargon is not at all characteristic of heuristic therapy. The use of such terms as *phallic mother, castration anxiety, incest wishes, masochism* have no place in the treatment situation, as I understand it. Indeed, the use of such terms generally serves only to divert patients from experiencing feelings and memories we are trying to elicit to further our understanding. If a patient has an image of mother as "beating," "screaming," "controlling, "demanding," or "overpowering," these are the things to be talked about, not "phallic mother." If he has a fear that his penis will be injured in some way, or of its being too small, vulnerable, ineffectual—these are the things to be talked about, not "castration anxiety." If he has wishes to touch and fondle his mother; smell her genitals, body, and clothing; penetrate her in some way—these are the things to be talked about, not "incest wishes." Finally, if a patient has arousing and exciting masturbatory fantasies of being tied up, made helpless, and of being penetrated "up the ass"—these are the things to be talked about, not "masochism."

In favorable cases, heuristic therapeutic hours are characterized by the emergence of almost an infinite variety of specific and individual experiences from multiple levels and innumerable areas of the patient's life. Similarly, we find an almost infinite variety of specific and individual formulations or interpretations. The therapist who employs the heuristic approach does not operate from a procrustean bed of stereotypes into which the data is forced. The heuristic therapist operates from the infinite variety of experiences reported by the patient as these impinge on the therapist's broad-based working models of the world.

PART FIVE

EVIDENCE, EXPLANATION, AND EFFECTIVENESS

19 Evidence and Explanation in Psychoanalytic Therapy

This book has been devoted to the formation of explanatory hypotheses in psychoanalytic therapy and the nature of evidence that supports or confirms the hypotheses.[1]

Typically we can discern the following pattern for hypothesis-formation and evidence. A hypothesis is generated from different sources of information. One of the principal sources is information from the patient—observations of the patient by the analyst and reports by the patient. The hypothesis generated is suggested to the patient in the form of an interpretation. If the patient—who is aware of the right to refute the interpretation and indeed does not hestitate to do it—does indeed accept the interpretation and gives confirming evidence, we say that the initial explanatory hypothesis is supported. The process is even more convincing if the patient actively refines and revises the interpretation to make it more exact and personally meaningful. When the patient goes on to generalize the interpretation (the explanatory hypothesis) even further, to view different aspects of his or her life from the standpoint of the interpretation—the process of working through—we feel that we now have even greater substantiation of the original hypothesis

---

[1]I speak of "confirmation" of a hypothesis, a common acceptable usage of the term provided we recognize that the term is used in a weak sense, closer to the meaning of "substantiate." It can be said that we never truly confirm our hypotheses in the sense of establishing their ultimate truth.

suggested. I have given several examples in which this basic pattern is discernible: the hour concerning the feeding experience in the case of Mrs. D., the sessions concerning the enema experiences in the case of Mr. E., and others.

When substantiation or confirmation of an interpretation/explanatory hypothesis is received, the information from the patient originally used to generate the hypothesis now becomes evidence to support the hypothesis, together with the additional evidence items that the interpretation itself evoked. And substantiated hypotheses can, in turn, become evidence for other, perhaps more encompassing hypotheses.

It is most important to recognize that the information based on the patient is only part of the information that enters into hypothesis-formation. As I have emphasized (see chap. 14), the analyst enters the patient's world and fills in the scene with many associations while identified with the patient's life as well as with personal associations. I gave examples where my own reactions of alarm, sexual arousal, and personal memories all helped me reach hypotheses that were subsequently accepted by the patients. It can be said that "anything goes" for hypothesis-formation, any thought, fantasy, feeling, the wildest of speculations—any source of information can be used. But not a shred of such information constitutes *evidence* for any hypothesis about the patient. Evidence for a hypothesis comes *only from the patient,* someone who is a working partner in a process and who can evaluate the *truth for him* of the explanatory hypotheses offered. I stress these points, as I have before, because there seems to be a tendency to think that the therapist's empathic experiences are synonymous with evidence. Not at all! And unless the fallacy of this thinking is recognized, the resultant work may be no better than the stereotyped approaches I have criticized.

It would be gratifying to be able to say that all of our cases follow the neat schematic outline just mentioned for hypotheses-formation, interpretation, and confirmation. If only this were so! Life, however, generally does not usually conform to our neat schematic representations of it. I have repeatedly emphasized that many patients can not give us good reliable data to substantiate significant hypotheses, the obsessive Mr. Q., for example. But even with those patients who give us what I have called a "high index of confidence," sessions do not generally work out simply and we do not get neat step-by-step confirmation of hypotheses, although with such patients we can get the "good" hours which I have described. We almost always work in a context of great uncertainty, even under the best of circumstances. We have to keep in mind innumerable hypotheses with some rank order of how significant each may be, how much evidence there is for each one. Often we are bewildered and confused—even for years— and have much evidence for something, but have no idea what that something is (as in the bottle-feeding reconstruction with Mrs. D.). Often, we can get a great deal of material about our patients life, even be able to get into their world and feel that we have a genuine "handle" on their experiences, but have no reasonable explanatory hypothesis to put any of it together in any meaningful way. For example, for several years I treated a highly intelligent, verbal anorexia-nervosa patient in psychoanalytic therapy. I used various psychotropic drugs with her. I could get an extremely vivid picture of her current state, both from her description of herself and my observation of her. I could capture her dramatic helplessness and depressiveness, her extreme anguish, which she described as feeling as though "a meat hook was buried in her chest." She felt like an amoeba, given shape by the external environment, and potentially able to disintegrate completely in the absence of constant external supports. Separations were extremely traumatic for her. Uncontrolled urges to eat emerged during several types of stressful experiences. The urge to eat seemed to have a life of its own. Anorexic episodes apparently served to control the violent urges to eat "everything in the world." Although I could capture many aspects of her world, although the raw data about her current experiences was vivid enough, I had enormous difficulty developing reasonable hypotheses to explain why she was so ill. The early history and whatever problems existed in the family simply did not even come close to offering reasonable hypotheses.

One very important point deserves to be stressed. We need *sufficient relevant information for any given hypothesis*. If data are limited, we can test and perhaps support only very weak, limited hypotheses. The better the data, the broader the hypotheses they can support. An example from my own experience will serve to illustrate the point. A dream I had during World War II supports some Freudian hypotheses about dreams in a most convincing way, but gives insufficient information to substantiate or refute other Freudian hypotheses about dreams.

> In the dream, I was in a field on a hillside. I picked up some pieces of wood that were lying around in the field and, with the aid of my axe, I also took some pieces from a big barn on the top of the hill. I put the pieces into two small wagons, using some of the pieces to connect the wagons so that they moved simultaneously when I pulled on one of them. The moustached captain was there laughing at me. I waved my arm in greeting, but paid no further attention to him.

The dream occurred at the time of the Battle of the Bulge. I was in a radio intelligence company which had two basic tasks: to intercept and decipher German radio messages, and to identify and locate enemy radio stations. Before the dream, I had been very active for several hours trying to identify the source of some radio signals that had been heard for several days. Using various clues from radio messages intercepted by my own company and by headquarters, I began to suspect that the unknown radio network was coming from a Panzer unit connected to one already known and identified. When I telephoned headquarters early in the evening to discuss my hunches, the captain (the moustached captain of the dream) scoffed at me because the identification seemed improbable. I paid no attention to him and continued my work until I found some fairly good evidence for what I suspected. Meanwhile, headquarters began to investigate the whole problem more carefully. In the middle of the night, the captain called, this time to congratulate me instead of to scoff. I went to sleep in a state of elation. My work held the promise of being important. Codes had been captured on the previously identified Panzer unit, and if the new network was indeed part of the same radio complex, then the messages being received from this new network could possibly be easily deciphered. While I was sleeping, the decoding unit at headquarters was checking out the messages, using the captured codes. The results would be known by morning.

Unquestionably, I was excited when I went to sleep and preoccupied with the day's events: I even wondered if I would be able to fall asleep. I could hardly wait for the morning to arrive when I would find out if the captured codes were applicable to the newly identified radio network. I must add that in my spare moments I was then reading Freud's *Interpretation of Dreams* for the first time. Very impressed with what I read, I said to myself before going to sleep, "If this guy Freud is correct, I simply must have a dream about what happened today."

Upon awakening, I was momentarily disappointed; but then I recognized the relationship of the dream to the events of the day. The dream took place "in the field," just as the day's events went on "in the field"—a military expression for an actual military operation. Two wagons were connected and made to move by pulling on one of them, just as I had connected two Panzer units during the previous evening, and just as it was hoped that the captured codes of one of them would work for both. The captain's behavior in the dream was very much what it had been during the previous evening. And in actuality, I used clues that were "lying around," in the radio messages picked up by my own company as well as in information from headquarters (the pieces from the big barn on the top of the hill). Finally, the hypothesis that the dream was related to the day's events is made almost certain by the fact that the code name used to identify my company was Tomahawk (the axe in the dream), and the code name for headquarters was Barn (the big barn on the top of the hill)—code names in constant use whenever phone calls were made. The previous evening had been typically full of calls that began with "Hello Tomahawk, this is Barn" or vice versa.

I have never since discussed this dream with anyone without getting a positive response—a laugh of recognition, or a comment such as "Oh yes," or "That's a good one," or "Isn't that funny." What was so believable here, to me and to everyone? What became so clear, obvious, and convincing to me almost immediately upon awakening from the dream? First, the dream was too closely related to the events of the day to be the product of a random or fortuitous process. Second, the dream portrays the abstract events of the day in easily recognizable, concrete, visual form. The dream was actually a naive, childlike or cartoonlike replay of the theme of the day. Thus, mere reporting of the dream and the facts of the day are sufficient to give very strong support to some basic Freudian hypotheses about dreams: that dreams are not random, meaningless phenomena; that they are often related to events of the preceding day; and that they often apparently employ pictorial representations for the more abstract ideas of the waking state. In brief, if judged by a jury of reasonable men, the information provided was sufficient and relevant to support these relatively basic Freudian hypotheses about dreams. The dream certainly supported the test that I mentioned before I went to sleep. It did turn out that "this guy Freud" was correct. But, I hasten to add, the information provided is not at all sufficient or even relevant to support many other Freudian hypotheses about dreams. (For my reservations concerning Freudian hypotheses about dreams see Peterfreund, 1971, chap. 21).

Recognizing that we need sufficient relevant information to support a given hypothesis, I turn now to the next issue: what kinds of hypotheses are of interest to the clinician and what information is sufficient and relevant to support them? I distinguish four kinds of hypotheses.

There are, to begin with, the group of hypotheses generated in the initial clinical interview. It usually requires comparatively little information for one to say that we have evidence for these types of hypotheses, and an extended investigatory process—a therapeutic process—is not needed to provide adequate evidence. If the patient is hyperactive, for example, if his speech is pressured, he has flights of ideas and grandiose ideation, and he reports racing thoughts, little need for sleep, and reckless buying sprees, we have sufficient evidence to suggest that the patient is suffering from a manic episode. No therapeutic process is required for such a hypothesis. Indeed, such hypotheses are typical of the kind formed in any initial clinical interview situation, whether in psychiatry or internal medicine.

Second are the innumerable limited hypotheses, the kind that may be generated from small segments of data, the kind that may depend only on direct observables in the immediate hour. For example, the therapist may say, "I think you are tense today," or "I think you may have come late today to avoid dealing with the very painful issues that we discussed yesterday," or "I think you reacted sharply to my comments because you felt criticized by me," or "I think you are annoyed by my lateness and are having trouble dealing with your feelings." Much, if not most, of our analytic work takes place at this level of limited hypotheses. And our confidence in the work that we do with any given patient emerges from the interactions with the patient about these types of hypotheses. For such hypotheses to be substantiated, we do need a therapeutic process and a patient capable of reliably detecting what is going on inside of him.

Third, are clinical hypotheses based on clinical theory that the therapist can test and get evidence to support or refute. For example, the hypothesis that in a dream, one may represent oneself or an attribute of oneself in the form of another person or thing. Earlier I gave an example (chap. 13,) of a patient who represented herself in a dream as a dirty, filthy child after having had a sexual affair and missing work the next day. Certainly a therapeutic process is required to substantiate these hypotheses.

Fourth are the hypotheses that have greater explanatory value; they are more general, more encompassing than the hypotheses already discussed. But to formulate these hypotheses, relevant information of a highly reliable and specific kind is needed, and a heuristic process is required with the characteristics I have discussed. These hypotheses go well beyond any of the hypotheses that can be supported by data from the initial interview; and they go beyond the limited hypotheses, discussed previously, that can be supported by material from an immediate session. The hypotheses I am now discussing generally require a process that has extended over time. The time factor in a good process is vitally important because, even under the best of circumstances, there is no way to hasten the emergence of good reliable data, the sorting out and testing that a patient must do to see if he is reporting experiences accurately, the generation of many hypotheses. And there is no way to hasten the testing of hypotheses, including refuting, refining, and revising them, as well as providing further evidence to support them. The cases of Mrs. C. and D. and that of Mr. E. illustrate these processes.

The issue of explanation in psychoanalysis is inextricably related to the problem of evidence. Indeed, when we obtain good evidence for any hypothesis, no matter how limited, we have in effect built up part of an explanatory system, and the new substantiated hypothesis can now become evidence for more extensive explanatory hypotheses.

We explain clinical phenomena by constructing a working model of the patient, showing the relationship of any given phenomenon to a larger world of events. During the therapeutic process, substantiated hypotheses and associated evidence are woven into larger and larger themes and relationships, into complex patterns. The large complex pattern constitutes the explanatory working model. Pattern explanations encompass the well-known psychoanalytic idea of multideterminism.[2]

The relationship of the phenomena to each other in a working model—a pattern model—serves to explain, interpret, or give meaning to the phenomena to be explained. It is important to note that we always explain by bringing the phenomena to be explained into a larger context. A patient's report of a memory of his mother's face being "blotchy" with purple, yellow, and green discoloration, made little sense until the patient pointed out that father beat mother on the face unmercifully and that the blotches were probably bruise marks. The phenomenon to be explained, the blotchy face, was related to a larger world of specific events in the patient's life and was to that degree thereby explained. It had already been fairly well established from assorted lines of evidence that father was psychotic, and so the explanation was a very plausible one. Other explanations may also have been possible, nor were they completely ruled out. It was known that mother was seriously ill and died when the patient was very young. The remembered blotchy face may have been related to mother's terminal illness. But in either case, the event to be explained was placed in the context of a larger world of events.

In pattern explanations the elements of the network serve both descriptive and explanatory functions, depending on how they are viewed. Thus, the recollection of mother's blotchy face as well as the recollection of father's psychotic behavior represented the patient's reports: they were descriptions of aspects of her life, descriptions of remembered experience. But the second phenomenon is also in an explanatory relationship to the first: father's psychotic behavior explains the existence of mother's blotchy face.

---

[2]I find Diesing's (1971) discussion of pattern and concatenated models of explanation (following Kaplan [1964]) to be most persuasive. I have borrowed freely from his discussion, adapting much, revising some, and adding what I feel is especially relevant for psychoanalysis.

The validity of pattern explanations is not based on any one component. There is much contextual validation (Diesing, 1971). Weak evidence items can be supported by their relationship to other items. And interpretations of any given phenomenon which may be questionable if viewed in isolation, because innumerable alternative interpretations may be possible, can nevertheless be buttressed and supported by convergence with other hypotheses and by the establishment of many interrelationships, as well as relationships to the whole. We have here the well-known jig-saw puzzle effect that Freud (1923) mentions or the crossword-puzzle effect, to use Matthew Erdelyi's (personal communication) analogy. We may be doubtful about a given word in a crossword puzzle, but we gain increasing conviction about that particular word as we complete the puzzle and observe how the questionable word gets cross-linked to neighboring words as well as into the entire puzzle. Indeed, as a result of such context, the original doubts about the word may dissipate.

Briefly put, evidence for any hypothesis can be buttressed by convergence and interrelationships with other evidence; and, likewise, hypotheses can be buttressed by convergence and interrelationships with other hypotheses.

Thus, it is the patient's large network or pattern that forms the ultimate believable picture. The complete pattern represents our best ultimate validation for the process and serves to buttress questionable observations and questionable interpretations of innumerable events. But it must be emphasized that such ultimate believable patterns or explanations emerge only from an optimal therapeutic process, which provides multiple checkpoints, and with a dependable patient who supplies reliable data. As a result, over time, one can eliminate many alternative plausible interpretations of individual phenomena. A good overall pattern explanation emerges only from multiple, relatively well substantiated hypotheses.

When the process meets these criteria, we may say that an explanation is believable because it is difficult to imagine alternative explanations that include all of the individual observations, events, and relationships that have already been more or less reasonably well established. The reconstruction concerning Mrs. D.'s early feeding experience represents such a believable explanatory situation.

The process was a good one, and the explanation that emerged was believable on the basis of what we know about human beings in general, and the nature of early pathological mother-infant interactions in particular.

Mr. R., the musician mentioned several times earlier, offers another example of how multiple confusing phenomena finally coalesce into a believable explanatory pattern.

Mr. R. originally came for treatment because of anxiety that interfered in many areas of his life. During the course of treatment he was able to capture for the first time some very primitive, archaic states. Each of these states was originally experienced only vaguely and was poorly delineated. It required prolonged effort to experience them clearly, but once Mr. R. could experience them clearly, he could recapture them with great reliability. Mr. R. first experienced one of these states outside the analytic situation and without obvious context, and he therefore found the experience totally puzzling. He described the state as a feeling of deadness on both cheeks in an area near the rear of his gums. Subsequently, when feeling upset and frustrated while on the couch, in the somewhat hypnagogic state he was able to capture in that posture, a violent, agitated feeling involving his whole head emerged. It was as though his head was being pushed into the couch. Simultaneously, he would have the feeling of his cheeks being pinched together (at the very same spots where, outside of the analytic session, he had had the sensation of deadness), thus forcing his mouth open. On other occasions he would feel as though something was being forced into his mouth while simultaneously he choked, was unable to swallow, and had difficulty breathing—feeling states he could dramatize very vividly. He could also capture a violent, tense feeling in his whole body and demonstrated how he felt by bringing a doll to the sessions, holding it in a tense and agitated manner, and then slamming it against his chest. He, of course, felt like the doll.

It took some time to piece together into a meaningful pattern these sensations, which, separately, seemed so bizarre, confusing, and unfathomable. Each of these states, as it unfolded, was at first so unclear that it was "at the edge of experience." The picture slowly began to make sense when we finally recognized that the phenomena may have been the sensorimotor residues or memories of repeated violent feeding as well as of other highly traumatic early experiences.

His mother's pregnancy had been a very difficult one; she apparently had to remain in bed for several months because of continual vaginal bleeding, while also caring for an older child. She had already had one miscarriage prior to the patient's birth, and she was determined to sacrifice everything to have this baby, the patient. His mother directly confirmed that there were many phenomena indicative of a severe postpartum, agitated depression after his birth, and, in addition, she suffered from very frequent, severe, incapacitating migraine headaches. She informed him later in life that she did not know what to do with him during infancy because of her emotional and physical state. Despite all of her difficulties she insisted on breast-feeding the patient, and we both thought that he was probably force-fed whenever she felt that feeding should take place. Presumably, she jammed the infant to her breast and jammed her breast into his mouth despite his unwillingness and consequent frantic protests. It was also our surmise that she got the patient's mouth open by pressing on both of his cheeks, much as she often claimed she had done with barnyard animals when she was young.

Even early in the treatment Mr. R. could easily capture an inner, screeching, tense, agitated maternal voice—an actual, almost identifiable voicelike sound, and not just a vague feeling—which was simply "EAT! EAT!" It was a reasonable surmise, too, that, when solids were introduced, they were also jammed into the patient's mouth regardless of his protests. Certainly, feeding experiences and the entire early relationship were extremely stressful, hardly pleasurable, to say the least. It was our surmise too that these difficulties were in part responsible for many problems in learning. He had difficulty in quietly appreciating, taking in, and "savoring" the world about him without overwhelming anxiety. One of his early models for learning was to "cram" it all in and then "spit" it out on exams. Fortunately, he also had other models for learning that served him much better.

One phenomenon puzzled us for years. After an immense amount of work, Mr. R. was able to delineate a sensation of falling backward and of slamming the rear of his head and back against something solid, resulting in his slumping to the floor feeling dazed and bewildered. He could capture the full feeling, but could not actually dramatize it because he would have seriously injured himself had he done so. It took some time to figure out what this might have meant, and the patient arrived at the following explanation completely on his own. He thought it likely that when he was an infant, his mother, when in a highly agitated migrainous state, may have pushed or slammed him against some object, the side of the crib, perhaps, when he balked about conforming to her wishes.

The mother's behavior in later life fit very well what she told the patient about her behavior when he was an infant and also fit with what we surmised about her. Throughout life, she was compulsive, tense, and high-strung. Typically, later in life, when she had a migraine episode, she would force herself to function.

It should be emphasized that the explanations offered regarding Mr. R. are not clear-cut "truths." As usual, when we deal with human phenomena we struggle with possibilities. Although the observed phenomena were real, dramatic, and clear, the explanations offered can only be said to be reasonable, plausible, believable; they make a coherent picture and unite many disparate and confusing phenomena. But conclusive evidence was never obtained. The patient failed in his efforts to get from his mother exact *details* about the feeding experience in his first year of life.[3]

As an analysis proceeds, patterns emerge and enlarge over time as details of a life are filled in. Interpretations are refined, revised, and further generalized. Indeed, good interpretations open new paths and foster the input of new information, allowing ever more encompassing explanatory interpretations to be generated and the

---

[3]Although I have spoken of defenses and resistances in this book and have attempted to define these terms operationally, I have said nothing about the concept of repression, a concept generally deemed to be basic in psychoanalysis. Although the case of Mr. R. can be said to exemplify the removal or lifting of repressions, I have nevertheless even here avoided the concept because I believe that it has become something of a catchall for many diverse phenomena, the unhappy fate of many psychoanalytic ideas. The phenomena deemed to demonstrate the removal of repression are not always easily distinguished from new learning. And many unacceptable theoretical ideas—psychic energy, for example—are associated with the concept. Elsewhere (Peterfreund, 1971, 1980; Peterfreund and Franceschini, 1973) I have atttempted to show how some of the phenomena subsumed under the concept of repression can be conceptualized in an information-processing frame of reference.

overall pattern explanation to be broadened and filled in. And when a process is working well, both patient and therapist get the increasing sense that more is understood over time. There is learning, genuine communication, and enlargement of the scope of awareness. I strongly suspect that these basic activities are fundamentally true of any process that leads to discovery, in any scientific enterprise.

But pattern explanations are always incomplete. There is no end to the ways whereby they can be extended and elaborated. New information may require dramatic changes, revisions of old meanings, reinterpretations of earlier events. In analysis, we always see new links and new relationships. In a sense, psychoanalysis, like learning, is a never-ending process. Unfolding life events, changing biology, and changing life circumstances continually force us to revise and review our understanding. Pattern explanations represent the outcome of such learning.[4]

---

[4]Two points can be made here. As Diesing (1971) suggests, classical deductive hierarchical models of explanation, common in the more exact sciences, such as physics, may be subclasses of pattern explanations. Second, owing to the interrelationship of phenomena and the complexity and uncertainties at any given time, pattern explanations generally do not lend themselves to predictions of future phenomena in novel circumstances.

20 Evaluating the Effectiveness of Psychoanalytic Therapy

Do our patients improve, do they get better, and if they do, is it causally related to the therapeutic process that we carry out? To put it simply, the issue is "does psychoanalytic therapy work"? My answer is "Yes, psychoanalytic therapy can be effective." In this chapter, after considering the question of ongoing evaluations of effectiveness during the course of therapy, I present reports of several long-term follow-ups, which more or less speak for themselves.

The problem of efficacy is one that every clinical discipline faces, and the experienced clinician becomes cautious about his claims. I once treated a highly intelligent, well-educated, black man who was born in the Caribbean Islands and who spent his earliest years there. He suffered from anxiety, depression, and dizzy spells. A neurological workup was essentially negative. I treated him with antidepressant medications and saw him once or twice a week for psychotherapy. After a reasonable period he seemed to be doing well, and I began to congratulate myself a bit, until one day with great embarrassment he informed me that in addition to seeing me, he had also, at the insistence of his very superstitious mother, regularly been seeing a spiritualist healer. This healer employed a host of magical incantations and rituals to exorcise the bad spirits that were supposedly making him ill. Deep down, the patient felt that there was indeed some validity to this kind of therapy. A sobering experience for the psychoanalytic clinician!

Several important points about the issue of effectiveness deserve to be emphasized.

First, when we evaluate the effectiveness of psychoanalytic therapy we must consider whether the patient had the capacity for analytic work. The patient lacking this capacity will not be likely to benefit from psychoanalytic therapy. Writing on the efficacy of psychotherapy, Greenspan and Sharfstein (1981, p. 1218) make the following relevant point: ". . . the issue of efficacy does not depend on demonstrating that a technique is applicable to a large number of persons. As long as one can specify which persons are likely to benefit and/or not benefit from a given technique and in what way, one has a scientific clinical approach." After preliminary interviews, it is often possible to predict, at least in a general way, if the patient will benefit from analytic therapy and in what ways he might benefit.

Second, we cannot speak about the effectiveness of psychoanalytic therapy solely in terms of specific symptoms or presenting complaints; we can talk meaningfully only about the total clinical context of which symptoms or presenting complaints are aspects. Recall the patient who entered treatment for a "potency" disturbance, and who subsequently described his penis as "rotting. (see chap. 16)" This patient had a severe body-image disturbance and his complaint of "impotence" had a totally different meaning and a very different prognosis from a presenting complaint of "impotence" from a patient who was not as ill as my patient.

Third, when we speak of effectiveness we must recognize *the spectrum of possible outcomes in a large number of patients,* a general truth in all clinical work. Greenspan and Sharfstein (1981, p. 1214) state this issue nicely when they write: "In clinical practice, when one speaks of efficacy, one speaks of being able to alter in a favorable direction the *otherwise natural course of an illness,* which includes slowing down the rate of deterioration, stabilizing the patient, or simply reducing pain and suffering, as well as 'curing' or improving functioning."

Fourth, when we speak of effectiveness we must also recognize a *spectrum of possible outcomes for any given patient.* Even in favorable therapeutic situations, we often see only partial improvements in a given patient, a favorable outcome in some areas, but only minimal improvement or no change at all in others.

Ongoing Evaluations Of Effectiveness

Keeping in mind the factors just discussed, it is nonetheless necessary, as in other clinical disciplines, for the therapist to have some means of evaluating the effectiveness of the treatment during the course of the therapeutic work, some "measure" of ongoing therapeutic progress. These evaluations tell us whether the patient is capable of benefiting from our treatment process and they provide us with a way of checking our work.

Frequently the therapist can observe gradual changes over time; often, patients look back, take stock, and themselves offer an evaluation of their progress. I believe, however, that the most convincing means of evaluating the effectiveness of our treatment is by the presence of what I have called "good hours." These hours give us the opportunity to observe effective experiences in an immediate and vivid way. And, most important, they occur in a context that allows us to observe the causal relationship between effective experiences and different aspects of the therapeutic process.

For the most part, *the criteria or characteristics of the good hour are actually criteria or characteristics for an effective therapeutic experience.* Thus, we need only a reasonable model of human experience to recognize that it is effective therapeutically for a patient to be understood; to express his emotions; to experience some relief of tension and anxiety; to achieve new awarenesses about current life situations; to be an active participant in a process of learning and understanding his own life history; to have corrective emotional experiences. Indeed, instead of the term *good* hour, I could have substituted the term *effective* hour.

Patients often report feeling better as a result of good/effective hours. But even if they do not give us such information directly, we often can tell that change for the better has taken place by noting the reduction in anxiety, the diminution of depression, the return of a note of optimism, and the like.

In brief, the good/effective hour is a marker of the progress of a psychoanalytic treatment process. It provides both a "measure" of the state of the process and a "measure" of ongoing effectiveness.

Follow-ups Of Analytic Cases

I now report on follow-ups of six cases that were in long-term treatment, focusing especially on clinical material that relates to the problem of efficacy. The follow-ups were handled very informally. I asked each patient what he or she got out of treatment, if anything; in what way treatment was meaningful; in what way it failed; what was recalled of the treatment sessions—did anything especially stand out, for example. With the three patients interviewed face to face it was possible to continue with appropriate questions. I was especially challenging whenever they reported some positive change as being the outcome of treatment. I asked why they thought the positive change could not have occurred in the absence of any treatment—as a result, perhaps, of normal psychological growth and maturity.

I think it important to say that I conducted these follow-ups when the manuscript for this book was close to completion. Nothing was changed in what I initially wrote about these patients, in view of the follow-up findings, except for Mrs. C., who corrected a few details. These corrections are incorporated in the description of her treatment.

Mrs. A.

Mrs. A. was interviewed in two long tape-recorded sessions. The interviews took place about 15 years after her treatment of about 9 years was terminated. In the intervening time I had seen her only once, approximately 5 years after treatment ended, when she came in because of some depressive symptoms. Additional treatment was under consideration at that time. The follow-up interview revealed that she had seen a therapist near her home and had taken Elavil for a very brief period. I think the follow-up report will be more meaningful to the reader if it is recognized that when she first came into treatment Mrs. A. was profoundly ill and her condition was deteriorating. Indeed, she was then in a state of total desperation.

Mrs. A. looked relaxed, much less tense and anxious than I recalled her to have been. She looked younger than her age, now about 60. She reported that in general she was reasonably satisfied with her life. Her children had done well; her marriage was satisfactory. The symptom picture with which she entered treatment was markedly improved. She had a very positive feeling about her treatment, though difficulties remained. Depression was still a problem, and upon awakening in the morning she generally had trouble getting started with the day's activities, but usually felt better toward the latter part of the day. She was even now still considering returning for some kind of therapy because of anxieties about aging and about time passing too quickly. "Time is rushing over me like Niagara."

The very first thing she told me was that the analysis had been a "nonintellectual" experience for her. One of the most striking things was the marked reduction of the florid symptom picture that characterized the early treatment situation. She herself now spoke of the "extraordinary panic" which lasted for quite a while during treatment, though the intensity diminished almost immediately. She saw the New York Psychoanalytic Institute as the "guardian angel." She saw herself as adrift, afloat, a "survivor" and the Institute the "anchor," and the analysis as a "huge life raft." The agoraphobia had disappeared almost immediately, and she was now generally comfortable enough when traveling and getting around by herself. Even the hypochondriacal preoccupations, including the extreme anxiety about dying, diminished over time; they still existed to some extent but were not crippling. She felt that perhaps some of these changes were explainable by normal maturational processes. She noted that as one gets older one "accepts the inevitability of life processes" and also that one's fears about death may naturally diminish—one's children are older and the thought of dying in one's 60's is not as horrible as the thought of dying in one's 30's. But she felt that treatment was, in general, most important in the general improvement that had taken place.

Mrs. A. was quite aware of how ill she had been when she first entered treatment. She commented that she was then essentially "moving through a nightmare." She reminded me that when she went on her first vacation, a few months after analysis started, she was so upset that she wanted morphine to calm her down and to reduce her pain, anguish, and terror. When I read to her the entire report I wrote on her for this work, she felt that my portrayal of her was accurate, but she was now so distant from the person portrayed that she felt as though I was speaking of someone else.

She felt that her "self-image" was helped considerably as a result of treatment, that it was most important to her to have been able to "articulate" in the sessions. With considerable emphasis she added, "I loved being able to be articulate and get subtle nuances." She told of losing the sense of being an "inarticulate person in the real world." Treatment allowed her to think about herself and alleviated her sense of worthlessness. "I could talk of seemingly trivial things as though everything counted. I was able to see myself as more important. I always felt that something was wrong with my mind, and you seemed to point out that I was as intelligent as I had to be and that I am able to compete with others." When I challenged the patient that perhaps such changes could have taken place without treatment, she replied that I had sat with her for 5 days a week and heard her talk about herself. "Something seemed to grow as a result of my being worth your time." She pointed out that she became more comfortable in social situations, less self-conscious about expressing herself, less concerned about her intellect and how it would be judged.

Mrs. A. reported that her whole image of her mother was now "reversed." "I saw her as someone with immense and mysterious power. I was attached to her in a destructive way. There was immense attachment and immense rage. I saw her as a positive person despite her endless depression." The patient saw mother as "murderous" and felt linked to her in a "Siamese connection," that whatever mother was, she, the patient, would also eventually be. The patient had an urge to "hack" herself away from mother, but this urge was not clear-cut because "so much ambivalence was there." Mrs. A. emphasized her earlier feeling that she had not tried hard enough to help her mother. At the beginning of treatment she was operating on the premise that she could make mother happy, and if she only did the right thing mother's whole life would be changed. "Her happiness was my responsibility and I was in control of making her happy. I raced around like crazy to find the panacea to make her normal. I did not acknowledge her terrible personality problems which were so destructive to me. She always belittled my friends. If I said that I was going to do something for someone, she would say, 'You have time for everyone, but not for me.'"

Her attitude to her mother changed significantly during treatment, and the "tentacles" that held them together loosened. She no longer feels rage now. She doesn't like her mother; she feels sorry for her, sorry for her suffering. "I see her now as sick and terrible, but I had nothing to do with it. It isn't possible to please her. She is a miserable woman. She has been generous to me and to my family in some ways, but she is a hateful, paranoid, unlovable depressive. I am dutiful still, and I take her as my responsibility."

The patient credits treatment for making the difference in her changed view of her mother. It was important to her that she was able to talk about her mother without startling me and without getting the sense that I saw her—Mrs. A.—as a terrible person. As a result, she was encouraged to keep talking about her. "I felt that you were leading me to see that I could never turn her around and that I was not responsible for her illness." She recalled my saying to her, "It may be that you don't love your mother because she just is not lovable. Not all people can be loved, and your mother is just a person." Mrs. A. found this a startling notion. "It was a totally new way of looking at one's parent. Maybe I was beating my head against the wall; she is impossible in part of her personality. The awful thing was that she had stretches of niceness, real caring, and sweetness, but nothing to hang onto, and it was like a light switch— the next moment it was off and she was utterly hateful." She added, "I felt like Hercules holding up the world; I was trying to lift that mother into the world, to make her smile, to make her happy. That was what I was supposed to be doing. This changed greatly in the analysis."

The patient confirmed that her mother had had several courses of electroconvulsive therapy before Mrs. A. started her analysis. And in the late 1960's the patient saw to it that mother was treated with lithium. The mother had no recurrences of depression after this treatment was begun.

About her husband, she felt that here, too, things improved and she has been able to stand up for herself. She always felt intellectually inferior to him and often felt "ground down" and "bullied" by him. But she had to hold him up as a God-like intellectual, a pillar of strength who would maintain her—the woman with "wild terrors." For this she was willing to pay the price of enormous rage at him and a demeaned self-image. There were many battles with him which ended up with her feeling even more intellectually inferior than before. She feels analysis helped her greatly to recognize her own sense of reality, her own worth, and her own abilities to think. She could give no specific examples dealt with during the treatment situation, but offered the following more recent one as being typical. She spoke to her husband about having something taken care of on the right side of the car. He informed her that the term "right" side was ambiguous, that it depended on how one looks at a car. From the driver's seat, what may be the right side would be the left side for someone looking at the car from the front. An argument ensued; she vehemently insisting that "right" and "left" in relation to a car were fixed, that one doesn't tell a mechanic to fix the right front wheel and then tell him which wheel one means. She tends to avoid such battles with her husband and has learned to accept him for what he is, even though she has had to forfeit having someone to talk to. She has learned to go her own way, separate from her husband when necessary, and to pursue those interests he does not share with her. Although he has "skewed" ways of viewing things and is rigid, authoritarian, and inflexible, she recognizes that he is brilliant, creative, sincere, decent, well-meaning, steady, predictable, basically rational. And, above all perhaps, he is a man of integrity and loyalty—all traits that were generally unknown in her own family, traits that she values most highly.

She feels that she acquired new, more realistic, humane, and reasonable ways of looking at her mother and her husband, the two principal sources of conflict when she started treatment.

She had strong doubts about me when she began treatment. She wondered if I was "up to" dealing with her. But her doubts were generally allayed during treatment whenever I came through with "startling moments of insight." She was unaware of any of the difficulties going on between me and my supervisor in the early months of the analysis and did not recall the dream that I reported about her. However, in the early months she felt that I was "going by the book" and she suffered from my silences, which she referred to as "cruel and inhumane tortures." She hopes that analysts have now modified these methods. These difficulties lasted only during the first few months.

Incidentally, the patient was quite "shocked" when I read her my reports of the supervisor's comments and those of the first two discussants. She found it hard to understand how they could have so completely neglected her history of having a grossly psychotic parent. She found the supervisor's comments incomprehensible.

In one very important area—the sexual one—she felt that analysis failed her completely. She never developed a good sense of herself as a woman. She knew, first of all, that she did not "use the transference" as much as she could have; she had to avoid the "male-female" aspect. But, and about this issue she was quite vehement, she also felt that the analytic technique employed was wrong for her, and if she were young and in treatment today she would undoubtedly consult someone who dealt actively with couples, educating them about sexual techniques, etc. She felt that I merely interpreted her anxieties, her fears of disorganization on orgasm or sexual excitement, for example—all of which was true. But what I did not do was to *actively* suggest, for example, that she try to masturbate or take a look at her genitals with a mirror. It would have helped her greatly had I been active in this way because it had not occurred to her to do these things.

Mrs. B.

Mrs. B. was seen in one long tape-recorded interview. Her analysis, which began over 25 years ago, lasted more than 8 years. Subsequently, she was seen several times by me for once-per-week therapy for periods of up to 1 or 2 years. On one occasion her anxiety and depression were so great that Elavil was prescribed. She was last seen by me about 1 year before the interview being reported.

Mrs. B. was fairly satisfied with her life and spoke positively about her treatment. At first she found it difficult to recall why she had initially come for help. "It is hard to remember who I was." She finally did recall her anxiety, her feelings of inferiority, fears of traveling and of being away from home, and preoccupation with fears of killing both her husband and her mother. She said that she had had a "lifetime of experiences on the couch" and wondered how one sums this up. She added, "You and the process gave me a chance to have another beginning. I have more that is me now."

She felt that treatment had helped her grow up, helped her to feel better about herself. She emphasized that it had allowed her to acquire a new "guide" for life, a "perspective," a "yardstick"; she began to see things in newer ways. If, for example, she felt panicky and upset, she came to realize during treatment that her distress would not last forever and need not necessarily have to be acted upon immediately. She lost many of the worshipful attitudes she formerly had toward others. Life experiences helped her grow, she said, but treatment helped her enter into and make use of these experiences. She emphasized that she became more aware of her separateness, stopped living vicariously through others, and built up respect for herself. Being able to take a trip to Europe in the past year was, she pointed out, a "monumental" event for her, considering her earlier anxieties.

Important for her, she noted, was her perception of me as steady, consistent, patient, and nonjudgmental. "You were there, but didn't take over for me." And she didn't feel pushed during treatment. She learned to respect time, that one cannot undo a lifetime of trouble in five or 10 sessions, or even in a year. She felt that it was most important that she have the time to experience the "different levels" of her life.

She remembered one particular event in the analysis. She recalled that very early in analysis, when she was age 26, she got her driver's license. She remembered feeling as though she had climbed Mt. Everest, and she came into the session proud and wanting me to praise her. Instead, she got a matter-of-fact response from me which, in effect, said, "O.K., you got your drivers license; that is what one expects of someone your age." She recalled that she thought, "God, what a crumb." Only later did she understand and appreciate that I was implicitly giving her reasonable "guidelines" or "yardsticks" for someone of her age and intelligence. "Before coming into treatment," she noted, "I felt like such a nothing that every accomplishment was monumental to me."

Of great importance was her understanding of her relationship to her mother. Father was frequently away for long periods when she was young, and mother was the dominant figure in her life. She told of coming into treatment with a very strong bond to her mother. Consciously, she saw mother as good, close, caring, someone who did everything for her, and who therefore must have loved her a great deal. On the other hand, the patient had thoughts of killing mother.

She commented, "I could never put the two together, and I could never have known the underpinnings of all of that without treatment." She was able to see that her mother, for her own needs, had to keep her dependent. It took a long time to unraval how her relationship to her mother had affected her as a person, woman, mother, and wife. The past year had been very important; mother died of cancer. Although the patient felt that her dying was "horrible," she added, "I could live with myself. I was there for her." Her mother was fully aware of what was happening, handled it bravely, and the patient felt that she and her mother grew closer during the period of illness.

Mrs. B. went to graduate school after completing the initial lengthy period of treatment and received a degree in social work. Her work has been enjoyable, gratifying, and most important in changing her self-image. She feels that she does a good job and has received tangible rewards in the form of promotions to buttress her own self-esteem.

Her relationship to her husband improved primarily because she learned to allow him to be a separate person who didn't have to meet impossible, unreal standards. And she also felt that she no longer held onto him in a "childlike way."

As for the negative side of her treatment, she felt that it was very demanding, time-consuming, and often painful and frustrating. She was frequently annoyed when I was somewhat distant and not quick to reassure her or to grant what she felt she needed. It was difficult to experience long periods of treatment when little seemed to be happening. She felt that treatment fosters a degree of self-involvement and self-preoccupation that can be difficult for other members of the family. She felt that important issues had not been fully worked out, for example, some important early traumatic events.

Mrs. C.

Mrs. C., who originally came for treatment because of anxiety and depression, was seen for about 8 years in psychoanalysis, four sessions a week. After an interruption of some 4 years she was seen again for about 3½ years. About 5½ years after having last seen her, I received a phone call from her. She and her husband had left New York and she was apparently doing well, busy with her work, and involved in bringing up her young child. She had had some troublesome physical symptoms and was afraid she might be seriously ill; she asked me for advice on whom she might consult. She said that she had thought of me in her anxiety because she trusted me. In the course of our telephone conversation she spoke about her work and her child. She was especially delighted and gratified by how well her daughter was doing. Having a child and being a mother were extremely important to her. Because she and her husband had moved, my follow-up contact with Mrs. C. was by phone and mail. She was on the staff of a university and had teaching and research responsibilities. She was obviously depressed when I contacted her, though friendly, and she seemed pleased to hear from me. She sent me pictures of her daughter. She wrote the following:

These are some of the positive things I believe happened in analysis.

I ended up feeling more connected to the world. My parents' alcoholism had made it impossible for me to form a relationship where I could be heard and understood and responded to, and this caused me no end of pain and confusion. My feeling that I was real was always under siege—I think because I knew that my parents had no clear image of me in their minds. I used to feel that *I* had to hold the "idea" of me, that if I didn't, no one else would. There was a feeling that I would vanish if no one had me in mind. When I came to feel that you had a clear, sober perception of me, I was able to relax in some profound way.

I believe too that many memories I had were "defused" so to speak. By that I mean that there were many unhappy events in my past which could only lead me to despair if I allowed myself to think freely about them. (For example—my mother's like this, my father doesn't care, I have no one, nothing to hold onto, therefore I can't bear to live anymore.) I believe I had to struggle very hard to keep these thoughts at bay—to stop from making the natural connections. I think in analysis I was able to pursue these memories and the thoughts they gave rise to—but with you there to keep them from overwhelming and destroying me.

So I feel that I came out of analysis more stable, "grounded," more resilient, less threatened. I think I came to see more clearly many of my mother's destructive acts and attitudes toward me, and to acquiesce less in them. She had such an unrealistic attitude about how to achieve anything. It virtually boiled down to "ignore the facts and just do it." I can see now that this had to do with "drunken courage," and of course it was little good to me. She had a contempt for "mere facts" and honest effort. The idea was to be above it all and sail through everything. I had to take a lot of ridicule from her for my plodding efforts, which, thank goodness, I never abandoned—but her mockery was part of my inner weather—especially when I applied myself—and I think this was ameliorated a great deal in analysis. I have your attitudes about "reality" and work and effort more in mind than hers now.

As different as I always was from my mother in this way, I wish I had been still more different. I realize now that I was severely limited intellectually by a deadening of my interest in "mere facts." In college I always preferred to study rather small closed systems, literary and philosophical works, psychoanalytic theory, for that matter, chemistry at an elementary level—and had a real aversion to studies where there was a vast amount of data—history or biology, for example. I felt uncomfortable when there was so much to take in, so little chance of organizing it "perfectly." I think this changed in analysis too— because of your example (being open to facts and being comfortable, or at least fairly comfortable with them even when they didn't lead to any certain conclusions). I think too the problem I mentioned before— of having to isolate or compartmentalize a lot of memories in my mind may have made it difficult for me to deal with a lot of new facts. I feel that I'm different now, after analysis, in that I do take an interest in these things. It makes the enormous variety of the world a positive force in one's life rather than something threatening disruption.

Another thing that comes to mind is just a kind of osmosis of feeling and mood. I certainly picked up a lot of unhappiness from my parents in this way, and I think there was the same kind of gradual influence in analysis with you, but of a positive kind.

I remember feeling terrible guilt about my mother's drinking. I believe this was very changed by analysis—by analyzing many of the things she said to me that were intended to make me feel responsible, and by analyzing my own irrational thought (wish) that I could influence her—and also because my own feelings and needs became more real (or valuable) to me. Hers had always taken precedence before, in my mind as well as hers.

By the way, to bring you up to date, both my parents died since I saw you last. My mother's death didn't upset me a great deal. In fact, to be frank, I felt a certain relief. I feel that I had already mourned her over many years, a lot of it in analysis. I remember thinking that she had died silently when I was about 10, without anyone marking it—

and I only realized later that I never saw my "good mother" again. I think this must have been about the time the alcohol had really destroyed something vital in her. I cried when my father died. His life seemed more tragic to me than hers. He struggled with the practical problems of keeping a family supported, the sort of efforts she found so beneath contempt. Compared to him, I feel that my mother had a "full life," however unhappy. Her impulses and feelings had full play, and there wasn't a person close to her that she didn't hurt badly, except her own parents, I suppose.

A couple of miscellaneous things. I have no real fear of snakes anymore. There are some around where we live, and I don't avoid those areas. I have a feeling if I really wanted to I could get rid of any remaining aversion by gradual deconditioning—seeing them, handling them, and so on. I can also drive without any anxiety now (at least in reasonably familiar territory). I don't know if you remember—I had a terrible fear of driving that persisted even after I got my driver's license when I was 20 or 21. I had to learn all over again when we left the city. I got an instructor from a driving school. The fear was virtually paralyzing to me when the car started to move—a feeling of disorientation and lack of control. After a session like this I took some Valium before my lessons. That calmed me down enough for me to get the feeling of what it was to drive without these incapacitating feelings. I also tried to analyze the thoughts and fantasies I had—I recall thinking of my mother in the back seat doing something to upset me at a crucial moment and make me have an accident. When I passed the driver's test, I had a strange reaction. I cried and cried, not with relief—I don't really know why. Maybe it seemed very anticlimactic after overcoming all that terror that the only outcome was that I could drive. Anyway, I drive normally now, and I had no trouble dispensing with the tranquilizers after the four or five sessions of instruction. I know that I often related my fear to being in the car with my mother when she was drunk, but I'm inclined to think now that this wasn't very important. No one else in my family had this fear, and they'd all had hair-raising experiences with her in the car. . . . I've often wondered if this was something innate. Have you followed some of the research on identical twins? I've seen a couple of programs on television that mentioned similar phobias, among other things, in twins reared apart.

I do feel that something went very wrong in my analysis. To pinpoint a time, I think maybe it was in the later years of my first analysis. The second analysis I can't really regret because I was in such bad shape I had no other options. I'm glad that you were able to keep seeing me then. In your place, I would have felt so guilty that I think I would have had to cut off the relationship. . . . At some point I believe much of my effort became misdirected, and the drift of the analysis became harmful to me. I feel very painful regrets about this. The time, of course, is irrecoverable.

I've tried to formulate in my own mind what went wrong. I believe my fundamental mistake was to believe that my husband was the kind of man I could have a close relationship with if I could only overcome my inner problems. Why I believed it and continued to believe it over so many years is, I think, related to a predisposition I have that was unfortunately reinforced in analysis.

I have always had much more faith in my own abilities—what I can call on in myself—than in what is "out there." I've always been willing to work, and didn't at all mind the idea of working on myself in analysis. I much preferred to think the remedy lay in me—and in that spirit I think I became a "good patient"—very willing to remember and discuss painful things and to connect past experiences with present ones. You know, whatever may be said about the terrors of confronting the past, it's undeniably a happy thought that the real sources of misery lie there and not in the present. I think my greatest fear has always been that other people would fail me and that there would be nothing whatever I could do about it. These feelings I can quickly relate—as I write this—to experiences with my parents. And yet I think you'd agree that the escapist solution, thinking of unhappiness in terms of inner problems, is powerfully reinforced by notions of "illness" and "cure." I can recall your use of these words, and of the word "treatment"—I remember your saying once, in a sympathetic voice, "You are very, very ill, but you can be helped"—and you used words similar to "partial cure" or something like that. These words, I believe now, fostered both an ill-founded despair and ill-founded hopes in me, both at the same time, and they implied a precision that doesn't exist.

I think it must be quite tempting, since an analyst has very limited power to solve real problems in the present, to focus on a person as a kind of portable "mind" that's right there in the office, and to try to change that mind, so to speak. What was really "wrong" with me when I started analysis? I think you saw it largely as a problem of distorted perceptions on my part—that I saw other people and situations in terms of my past family relationships, and therefore that I falsely perceived the world as a very frightening place. I wouldn't deny that this could happen and did happen, but I don't think it was the central problem. I think what was "wrong" with me—it's very hard to find words—was a kind of weakness and, even more than fear, a loss of heart. I'll try to explain what I mean. I think that my parents, far from giving me a feeling of protection and support, forced me to knuckle under to them, and to give up any show of will. There was tremendous anger behind this, and always the threat of violence because of their drunkeness. I think I developed a terrifying sense of aloneness, the feeling that there was no one behind me, that if I were attacked, no one would help me—that I could be quickly isolated and overwhelmed by an enemy—and that I lacked the nerve, the strength, the will (whatever) needed to protect myself. There was already a Trojan horse inside me, so that the enemy at the gates was a terrible threat. I think maybe my father's indifference was even more frightening than my mother's aggression. He really didn't care about me. I didn't figure in his imagination the way my brothers did. Quite frankly, I don't know if the kind of weakness I'm talking about can be "fixed." I'm completely serious about this, and don't say it in a despairing mood. I don't see how I could ever be as strong as someone who had real support from their family. At any rate, I think that my fearfulness—what you saw when I came to your office—came from this "weakness," and that, far from attributing all kinds of evil intent to other people, I've very often underestimated people's capacity for aggression and deception and cruelty—simply because it frightened me so much.

To give an example—say, in my first job I felt that someone in my office was hostile, and it frightened me and made me unhappy. I think typically your interpretation was that I was "reliving" something from the past. If in the course of talking I then recalled a similar incident with my mother, this would be taken to validate this interpretation. And if I felt better afterward, this would be taken as further confirmation that this was the right interpretation. I think now that this was usually wrong. I believe that, when I found people to be cruel and unfriendly, they *were*. What was abnormal was my excessive fear of it. . . . I think it's obvious that if there is hostility out there, and if one's efforts are directed at seeing it as "not real"— obviously the situation isn't going to improve, and a person's self-confidence can only be further undermined in the end.

. . . I still think it's meaningful to talk about a reality that resists one's mental predispositions. I think that my own reality was too bleak for me or for you to see clearly. If I had, I don't know if I could have borne it. I don't know if I could have done anything to become "stronger"—but I do know that efforts to think of my frightening perceptions as illusory, or manifestations of an illness, were doomed to failure.

I think that my sexual problem was somehow misconceived. I tended to think of it, and I think you, too, as a problem of conditioned responses resulting from my mother's mistreatment. I don't know how much this contributed to my unhappiness—but I do think now that my husband hurt me psychologically, and that the fear and misgivings I had about being close to him were well-founded. I believed then that they were neurotic. . . . I'm not even certain that my mother's mistreatment inevitably led to sexual problems that could only have been solved through reliving and discussing them. The fact that I came from an unhappy encounter with my husband, then recalled a somewhat similar experience with my mother—and then felt better— I don't take as evidence. Do you?

I used to believe that sexual feelings were "primary." I conceived of orgasm as a kind of natural physiological function that was somehow blocked in me because of my experiences as a child. I felt that, if I could somehow undo this harmful conditioning, I would perceive the world differently and live more happily. It seems to me now that this was a mistaken way to look at it, almost a reversal of the way things are. I think that sexual feelings, at least for me, are more like a summation of many particular feelings about life and another person. This isn't a perfect analogy, but the other approach is a little like saying if a person can learn how to smile they'll be happy. I know it must be difficult for a person in your position to assess what's going on in these situations. The only things I can think of to which you might have given more weight were the common-sense realities of my husband's and my relationship that you knew about. You knew that I supported him for many years and encouraged him in his research work. In other words, I think a common-sense approach, rather than the presumably more sophisticated psychoanalytic approach might have taken that as evidence that I had warm feelings toward him, and loved him. Other questions that might have been relevant were—who was getting the greater advantage out of the relationship? Who was in more trouble in terms of functioning in the world? I was in the strange position of giving him a great deal, getting very little from him, and yet I was the one being criticized as emotionally inadequate.

I don't think anyone should ever be encouraged to have intercourse if they don't want to. I often did in the belief that I had to confront irrational negative feelings in this way and that they would be dissipated somehow. I think now that these experiences were not only painful but harmful. Maybe they hurt me as much as anything my mother ever did. I think it's unfortunate that sex tends to become a 'should' in analysis—conceived of as something healthful, normal, understood by doctors, etc. This may be a good antidote to beliefs that it's evil or dirty, but in my opinion it tends to take something vital out of it to hash it over in analysis for many years. The point is the sense of "ought to" that becomes attached to it. . . . As you know, I was in analysis a total of 11 years, and my husband 8, with two different analysts.

. . . When I look at my life today in terms of what I had hoped for while I was in analysis, I feel I've certainly failed. I have no close relationship with my husband—he doesn't want one—but we're business partners, so to speak, in our research work, and he's an extremely good father. When I compare my life to those of other people I know (instead of to an ideal I had) I feel I have much to be grateful for. One realization that hit me very hard in my early 30's (my second analysis) was that I've controlled events much less than I had thought I could. My marriage I really worked at, and haven't been able to make it what I wanted. My daughter was born when I was past the best age and might have expected trouble, and she turned out better than I had dared hope. I don't mean that I find things totally unrelated to my efforts—but I feel grateful rather than proud when things go right. Actually I think this feeling is happier and more realistic. . . .

We were lucky when we moved here to find a terrific school for Emily [the patient's daughter]. Two of the teachers there are some of the most decent people I've ever met. They really love Emily and she them. It means so much to me to find this kindness. I think one thing that's good about me as a mother is that, as much as I love her, I'm not possessive or jealous. My mother used to resent my having friends for some reason. . . .

Mrs. D.

Mrs. D. came for analysis because she felt that there was much confusion and uncertainty in her life. She felt that she was excessively tense and hyperemotional. There were serious difficulties with her marriage; and she was divorced during the analysis. Treatment, which lasted over seven years, was terminated over 14 years ago when she left New York to remarry. My follow-up of Mrs. D. was conducted by phone and by mail. She seemed to have done quite

well; her second marriage appeared to be quite successful. She had
two children by her present husband and she had also earned a
graduate degree. She wrote the following:

> I was delighted to talk with you and hear of your project. [She spoke of
> unavoidable delays in responding to me and continued:] During that
> time span I jotted down ideas. At first I imagined I would have a
> myriad of memories connected with your basic questions. When I
> looked at my notes, I discovered that my free-floating thoughts had
> repeated themselves and that I could boil them down to three areas.
> Here they are, all influenced by time and experience of 14 years.
>
> Next to the many personal reasons for my analysis, the actual
> process of the analysis stands out as the most important factor. The
> combination of your professional listening and my patient revelations
> built solid flooring on which to gauge insights. It was crucial to me to
> repeatedly sense such flooring in order to work in the analysis. A
> stable, purposeful working relationship with you was extremely
> meaningful to me. The process of together studying seemingly bizarre
> images or interacting about their value was itself a healthy, integrat-
> ing experience. I realized over and over that an instinct, insight,
> simple thought was to be highly respected. The opportunity to concen-
> trate on ongoing life themes was at times magnificent. The cyclical
> process of not passing over an innermost thought but (torturously)
> verbalizing it and knowing that you would help me include it with
> other thoughts was fundamentally life-giving. The gradual knowl-
> edge that I could transfer a similar relating style to other people was
> the grandest reward. It was the best educational experience I ever
> had, and in many forms the process has been everlasting.
>
> Within the analysis I would have liked more challenge. I wished
> that I could have asked you to take more risks with me as a patient. I
> wish that I could have taken more risks too. I felt a note of restraint,
> which I could attribute to myself partially, but from which I would
> have liked to have been rescued or pushed. I might have been better in
> this direction had I been married and with children because as a
> single woman (in that decade) I felt quite fragile. (I know that I was
> legally married when I began with you. Were it today, I would have
> been trying out living with him.) Nevertheless, I think I would have
> preferred more "threat" in the atmosphere or less allowance for self-
> protection, which in turn might have given me a feeling of you re-
> specting that I could make it through rough periods. This is a delicate
> line to traverse but one that I sense is important in the analyst-

patient relationship; important enough to consciously test in more ways than I remember experiencing during my analysis.

I continue to be interested in finding ways that people can be a part of a process and also know about the process as a structure, making it less mysterious. That is, I would have liked to make a contract with you not only because we estimated that we could work together and about time and fees, but about the process itself. The conversation might have been something like "this is how we work as analysts; this is what we would be aiming for; these are some of the areas we'll be exploring together; how would you feel about working that way;" etc. My tentative feeling is that such an introduction might have made me more valuable as a patient/partner initially. Woven through the analysis were moments of changing from a patient-like feeling to one of mutuality, and perhaps if I had comprehended more about the foundation on which we were working together I might have grown more quickly.

These are my responses to your questions. I have not concentrated on the endless number of personal shifts and changes that were made during and after the analysis. I am unable and have no inclination to summarize such meaningful angles. My analysis with you was an extraordinary experience which has permanently influenced my personal and professional life.

Mr. R.

Mr. R. had been in a lengthy analysis, lasting over 14 years. He too had left New York and could be contacted only by phone and mail. He was married and doing well personally and professionally. I sent him a copy of what I wrote about him. Here is his brief letter in reply.

What can I say about one of the most meaningful experiences in my life? I was a mass (I almost typed "mess") of anxiety and confusion when I first came to see you, with a hell of a lot of rage and irritability, and I really knew little about myself. Much changed.

I never understood anything about my mother, about my whole relationship to her—all of the things you mentioned. My father was less of a puzzle. I had so many cockeyed ideas about things, I was so uncertain about everything, that every time we made some connection, whether it was about her directly, or what resulted from my experiences with her, or, for that matter, any other connection—every bit of understanding—well, it was like adding a small piece in the composition of me. Every bit made me feel stronger, gave me a sense of who I am and what the world was all about; every bit, no matter how tiny, reduced the confusion.

And all of that crazy physical business that you wrote up, I certainly had not the slightest idea that any of it existed in me, that I even had the potential to bring any of it out. It is true what you wrote that we never got conclusive evidence for what it all meant, but the pieces fit together quite convincingly, to me anyway. And the ability to bring all of that stuff out helped enormously. I always felt a craziness inside of me, as you know, a wildness, a great fear of losing control. It was extremely helpful that we found out what that craziness was all about. Bringing it out always made me feel better, immediately. You may remember that I often came into a session feeling upset and depressed, but I felt better after bringing up the physical stuff that you described. It was extremely helpful to see that all of that diffuse crazy feeling in me, that sense of potential physical wildness, actually had a basic structure that made sense in relation to my life. When I first began to get hold of it, it came in bits and pieces, as you indicated in your writeup. For a very long time, it was like listening to a barely audible melody from far away; one can make out only parts, fragments, as the melody fades in and out. One doesn't know what one is hearing until one gets enough fragments. Then they begin to get together, and the underlying themes stand out.

I think it was crucial that I was not rushed, or pushed by you. That there was time, time, time—time to sort things out, to work carefully, to get a convincing sense of what I felt and what the connections to other things might be. I can't imagine anything important happening without all of that time; and I don't know where, except in analysis, I could bring out all of the things that you wrote about—things which surprised me, and, if I am right, also surprised you. Who would ever listen to or even be interested in all of that stuff?

There was always a sense of peace and safety as soon as I entered your office, together with that sense of endless time. For me these were terribly important, as you know. It may all look so "easy" and "obvious" to others when you write it up as you did. But, as you know, it was not that way at all. For a long time I didn't have the foggiest notion as to where I was going or what was to come up next. I learned to trust my gut feelings, let my body talk, and follow these wherever they went. And I am very grateful that you allowed this to happen and weren't afraid of them. And, in turn, that allowed me to trust you.

Mr. S.

Mr. S., mentioned briefly in chapter 13, began analysis over 25 years ago when he was about age 22. He was seen for over 15 years, often six times a week.

Mr. S. came into treatment at the suggestion of a friend. After graduating from college, he spent a year traveling in Europe and Israel. He told of being upset because he had great difficulties concentrating and therefore could not work—he was a writer; he had a severe potency problem; and he was petrified about being drafted for military service and wanted to find a way to avoid it. He was seen by several experienced senior psychiatrists before being referred to me: psychological testing fully confirmed the clinical impression that the patient was quite ill. Indeed, his situation was deteriorating when treatment began.

Mr. S. was an angry, bitter, cynical, suspicious, rebellious, agitated, anxious, intellectualized, young man who felt that life was passing him by. He emitted an all-pervasive sense of doom. When he found himself unable to concentrate he would pick at his body, masturbate, and fall asleep. He usually slept about 12 hours each day and felt that he was unable to do anything unless pushed and prodded. Suicidal thoughts were prominent, and he spoke of having some hope of getting his head shot off in Israel. His trip to Europe was taken primarily to give himself time to think things through and to solve his problems by philosophical analysis. While still in college he had begun to feel that there was no order in the world, and he wanted to establish order through his own mind. He succeeded in developing a philosophical system that reduced everything to absurdity. But then he realized that even this system was unsatisfactory because, by its own logic, it had to lead to its own annihilation. When philosophy did not seem to be the answer, he felt that he had to try something else. He therefore took the advice of his friend and sought psychiatric help. He told me almost from the moment he came into the office that "potency" was his problem and absolutely nothing else was to be touched.

The early months of treatment were, as I said earlier, almost unbelievably difficult, and it is not easy to reproduce the full flavor of what went on. I was subjected to a constant barrage of complaints. He rasped at me, screamed, told me he was getting nowhere in treatment because I was not making him potent and at one point even refused to talk until I made him potent. At times he screamed that all he wanted to do was to "get the son-of-a-bitch" who had made him impotent. He felt that the whole treatment situation was absurd, humiliating, degrading. Psychiatry was nothing but a cult. He mocked dream analysis. "How do I know if a dream is from me or from the fact that I am in the business and will dream in the appropriate system?" He felt that he had been "mousetrapped" into treatment, forced, and commanded to talk about masturbation. He wanted to keep away from treatment as much as possible. "Everything is shit; all is shit"; there was no point in talking; he knew enough about himself. "Why adapt and adjust to the world and become money-minded like everyone else?" He insisted that he would never allow himself to talk freely here. To do so would plunge him into an endless void. He certainly would never cry; if he did, I would listen only because I was being paid.

He felt completely at my mercy; everything was being ripped away from him, and I was pulling everything out of him. He felt that his thoughts, once told, were no longer his own; they were lost. Coming to see me was destroying him. I could take over his mind, tell him to "eat shit," make him "kiss a cross," and in 6 months he would be told that he is hopeless and would be left, abandoned and doomed as an impotent. At times when he came into the office he insisted on walking behind me down the corridor from the waiting room, afraid that I might do him some harm and afraid of what he might do to me in retaliation.

He wanted only to avoid people. The world was unfair; it had never given him anything. He trusted no one; and he could allow no one to have any power over him. He hated doctors. No doctor had ever been able to help him with his enuresis, which lasted about 18 years, so how could another doctor now be of help. He hated himself for coming to see me; it was the ultimate humiliation, the final proof that he couldn't solve his problems through philosophy. His intelligence was all that he felt he had; his body had always been weak, inept, and impotent; and, now that his mind had failed to help him, he felt totally worthless. A "real man" doesn't need to be helped. He was petrified of being drafted into the army and was afraid he wasn't strong enough; he feared being helpless, being "banged around" and hurt. He got out of the draft by showing up at the draft board deliberately looking hunched over, "like a mess," wearing an old jacket. He told of frequently standing in front of buses "defiantly," half wishing that he would be run over.

Session after session went on with the basic theme unchanged. He parried my every attempt to make some genuine contact with him. Often I confronted him in the bluntest terms about what he was doing to me and to himself. Often I was ready to give up, and I told him so. Session after session ended with his saying, "What good is all this?" On rechecking my notes for this write-up I found them filled with such comments as: "another wrestling match today," "another impossible session," "I cannot reach this man." Generally, I stumbled along, trying to deal with his enormous fears, trying to make some connections between his moods in an hour and the day's events; trying to educate him into being a workable patient; attempting to show him some of the contradictions in his own thinking, while respecting his logic and intellect; attempting to show him the unreasonableness of his self-reproaches.

Despite all of the problems, I felt that slowly something was happening for the better. Bits and pieces of history were emerging about his previous traumas and humiliations; and easily detectable was the panic-ridden, terrorized, lonely infant behind all of the angry outbursts at the world. Indeed, the barrage from him was often akin to a petulant, infantile temper tantrum, and at times it was so patent that it could even be seen as funny. For example, he once told me that he wanted nothing to do with me, and that he would certainly never see me as his father because to do so would be an "insult" to his father. And here and there sessions took place which gave me some hope that perhaps there was light ahead, albeit far away. He seemed to be getting attached to me. For example, one day after going on ad nauseum with mockery, belittlement, and berating of me, I told him simply that he really wanted very much for me to like him and that all of the aggressive façade indicated that he feared that I might not and that I might even belittle and demean him. His reply was, "Of course, I want to be liked, but it is still dangerous. I can't trust. How do I know that you won't call a halt in a few months. I can be fair. I will declare peace when I trust you."

After some months I even insisted that he try the couch, and I lowered his fee to enable him to increase the number of sessions per week. This gesture made some difference to Mr. S. Although he complained about the couch, the ultimate humiliation for this man, he did indicate that he was impressed by my lowering the fee; perhaps I was an honorable person after all. Although his relationship to his father was not a warm one, he admired the father to some extent. He was a physician who spent a good deal of time writing scholarly works and was not totally absorbed in earning a huge income, contrary to the wishes of the patient's mother. Incidentally, my own motivation for putting the patient on the couch was simple: I couldn't tolerate the face-to-face barrage that I was getting from him, and he was so ill that any regression that might take place because of being on the couch could not, I felt, make things much worse than they already were.

Slowly, very slowly, over the course of many months, and in fits and starts, the frightened, panic-ridden infant emerged in an appropriate therapeutic alliance. Mr. S. became a good patient. It is totally impossible for me to report in any detail what happened in the many years of treatment. I will focus only briefly on what turned out to be the central theme—the very disturbed mother-child relationship. His mother was apparently a carping, complaining, accusing, controlling woman, dissatisfied with everything in life. She could lash out at the patient, pummel him, and even throw things at him. Apparently, marriage and having a child was for her merely an interference with her career ambitions. It seemed that there was little that the patient could do to please her, and whatever difficulties he had were greeted with a barrage of reproaches. For example, his bedwetting—a central problem in his life—was a source of endless arguments in the family. She could never see the shame and total humiliation that he suffered when, for instance, he went to camp. Instead she belittled and screamed at him and told him constantly that his room was a "stinking mess" and that he was "smelly," that he was bedwetting deliberately to hurt her, and that he could control it if he only wanted to. She did not hesitate to tell him that he would obviously never get married if he was a bedwetter. Her reproaches often took the form of "look how much we have done for you, the good schools we sent you, and look what you are doing to us." Many of the patient's self-reproaches seemed to be based directly on mother's endless reproaches.

Mr. S. seemed to be the focus of all of his mother's dissatisfactions in life. She apparently had only the most demeaned image of him, no pride and joy in him whatever. For example, he recalled bringing home a simple construction built when about age 12. She put it in the living room for 2 hours and then moved it into the attic. Mr. S. felt that she could not stand it because it did not fit in with her elegant antiques. The experience left him feeling hopeless. She finally later disowned him completely when he married a woman she felt was not socially and religiously appropriate. I recall the letter he showed me from her in which it was obvious that she took his marriage as a deliberate attempt to humiliate her.

In general, he saw women as the powerful ones; they petrified him. He felt that, sexually, one could lose oneself with a woman, one could "fall into an abyss." If a woman were to put her legs around him, he feared that he "could fall into the hole." He feared that on sexual intercourse one's penis could be injured and be caught in a woman's vagina. A woman's breasts were like two hostile eyes. He told of a Japanese torture where the victim's penis is tied up with a wire and he is then placed in front of young, naked dancing girls; as he gets an erection, his penis is cut off. Anxieties about homosexuality were very prominent and recurred throughout treatment. His "sexual" urges often turned out to be urges to urinate.

His fears about body intactness were extremely primitive. He recalled seeing a cross section of a human body in a museum when he was five years old. It was not until he went to college that he realized that the man was probably dead before being cut up and that "they did not put the screaming slob into an egg cutter." Anxieties about death were extremely prominent throughout treatment. And to complicate the early traumatic history, there was a severe illness at about age 5 from which he was reported to have almost died.

In the therapeutic situation that was finally established, he could bring out his panic and despair, his screaming for his mother, and his deep sense of loneliness when she would daily go off, leaving him in the hands of others. He would express his rage by shrieks and by screaming at the top of his lungs, banging on the walls of my office. His general feeling about life was, "I trust no one; no one ever believed in me; no one ever listened to me; no one ever had any faith in me." He had to develop a belligerent attitude toward the world to protect himself.

It appeared that the patient probably reflected in his self-image what his mother may have felt about herself and about raising a child. She was a very efficient, tense woman, an "expediter," who could only go through the motions when it came to any true maternal relationship to the patient. She was devoid of any real warmth toward him, any pride or joy in him, as I have already indicated. He experienced her as essentially dead in regard to him. His entire self-image was that of a mechanical man; he felt that he had to press buttons to make his limbs move; he felt dead and empty inside; and had no spontaneous feeling of joy and life. Only occasionally, certainly at the beginning of treatment, could he truly hear my voice. On one such occasion he said, "When your voice is soft, I can hear the world through it."

In general, his wish to be "potent," the wish expressed when treatment was begun, meant more than sexual potency in the usual sense. It was actually a cry for life, a cry to be seen as a person, to be in the world, to have a sense of himself and of connection to others. Asking to be made "potent" had all of the meanings of a rebirth, a restitution of both himself and the object world.

I saw Mr. S. in one long tape-recorded, follow-up interview. The sentences he left unfinished, his groping for the words to express exactly what he wanted to say conveyed the feeling that Mr. S. was emotionally upset, although he spoke quietly and was in obvious control of himself. I hope my report conveys at least some of the emotional quality of this very moving interview.

Ten years had passed since I had last seen Mr. S. It was hard to believe that this fit-looking man was the very disturbed young man I had known. I was seeing him, he said, at a "bad time." He was somewhat depressed; there had been problems in recent years.

He reported,

> On some levels I am doing well; on some levels I am in a great deal of pain. I am a successful member of the community and I have a lovely family with two children with whom I am very pleased. I love my wife, but there is trouble.
>
> I was at the end of the line when I came to you. I have always been very clear about that. I am now able to live a respectable life. I am not on the run. I have a place, some security, a certain amount of pride, and I can support myself. And these are not small things.

Slowly, tearfully, and with difficulty, he went on: "I think of you often. There really has never been much in my head except my little dog, and I feel you present as somebody besides my dog. I still have my dog too.

"I have no feeling for my mother; she is still alive; my father died. I have no internal feeling for her as a person. I don't see much of her, and for about 10 to 15 years I didn't see her at all. When my father died we set up a perfunctory relationship at the funeral." He then told of his mother's trying to cut him off from a small inheritance from his father. He had to threaten to take her to court before she allowed him to have it. He felt something when his father died, but, he commented,

If mother were to die I would feel nothing. I don't hate her now, but there is no sympathy. I don't have any sense of being raised by my parents. The fulfillment of my relationship with my mother is an absolute brick wall. It isn't pleasant to feel that way. Friends tell me that some day I will grow to appreciate her, but I don't think so, and it is irrelevant now. I paid my dues.

It is tragic to grow up without any people in you. I think about you and feel you as a person. I am more judgmental of myself as a person than you would be. I know that you are present in me; I am very clear about that. You're honest. I feel you as structure and dimension and honesty. I feel reassured when I need to consult with you or myself as to what I am doing.

Treatment, he said, was painful.

I remember my mind being joggled apart and forming in new ways, with your help. People who know me now, even my wife, don't understand how disturbed I was. I was incredibly disturbed. Where could I have gone? There was no place to go. What could I have ended up doing? Selling newspapers on a streetcorner, living in a room eating canned soup? I was totally dysfunctional. I couldn't have done anything at all. Would I have stabilized in some way without treatment? I don't know. I don't know if I would have committed suicide or died. And if I stabilized, it would have been at a very low level. I just had nothing going for me. I had no way to work.

I wish I had solved more of my sexual problems; I would be more satisfied. On the other hand, I have a life. I wouldn't knock that for a minute, and I am very proud of that. I was fortunate. I liked the cut of your jib. A lot of this is personalities. I never felt that I could snow you, and I never had the desire to do that. I don't think you deal with bullshit, and I appreciate that. I feel in you a certain strength which I have never lost sight of.

He said that the enormous "psychic pain" so prominent when he started treatment was no longer present. He added that his banging on my wall and screaming was out of anguish and not anger. And he is free of that now.

When I inquired what he had learned in treatment about himself or his family, he said,

I didn't know anything about myself; I didn't know who I was. Even now I have difficulty. I hear myself better in here than I do at home. I was a wreck, a wreck of a human being at age 21. I didn't have any idea why I was here or what was wrong with me. I knew that I was sick—that was the only piece of insight I had. You were offering to do something, and I had no other way to go, and it was my job to stay.

He objected to my use of the word "learning" to describe treatment. "Learning" for him implied something discrete "like learning the three R's or like helping a child 'learn' not to be too aggressive in class." For him, treatment was a "deeper learning"; it was a "megalearning." He was dealing with "a level of shattering" that was enormous. He referred to it as "destructive chaos." Finally, he added,

What we did here was a process. It took 10 years of cutting before we were through to a level in me that could just listen to your chair or listen to you being quiet. And that is when things could turn around; it couldn't turn around before that.

I don't know what kind of a person I was before you started diddling with me, but I was a hell of a mess, and I continued to be until I was able to listen, to hear myself, and to hear other things. For me to have the intellectual knowledge that my mother was this or that wouldn't have helped me a bit. That is why I don't like the word *learning*. How could that have helped me?

The area of dealing with my mother was so primitive that it was never possible to link up the feelings with the person. If someone said that I wasn't raised by Vivian S. but by Jane Doe, it would have made no difference because it was all so totally global that it never related to a human being.

All that pain, pathos, and screaming was at such a level that it never reached the identification of a human being in terms of a name, a face, or who they are. Then you are left with the fact that you keep going on through it, but what forms as you do it is a structure that was internal between you and me, a structure that came out of me and reflected your patience. If you had been in a hell of a hurry, I would have been in a hell of a mess. I am glad that you weren't. You could have rushed me a little, but I would have gotten skittish and panicked. I wasn't letting anybody near. How could I? Look how crazy I was. I had no way of accepting anybody. I wouldn't lie to you or blow your horn, but I don't like the word *education* or *learning* to describe treatment.

Everyone is in a big hurry these days. I was never in an experience where I was allowed time. You were patient and willing to sit and listen. But it wasn't just the sitting and listening. You were there with your structure with whoever you are and whatever you know.

As I sit here I have a feeling as we talk that I have dimension in space, structure in space, and you gave me the opportunity to allow that to develop. Even today it is hard for me to realize that I am not the alien, the loner.

I feel good about you and comfortable. Not intimate though. There was no dogmatism here. You could have killed me off, with 'Believe this, David' or 'Believe that, David.' I don't think you ever asked me to believe anything, except that I had to mind my manners here.

He spoke of his work. He had done well; he was successful. He felt that he was "a leader" in his community. He loved his wife and was proud of his family; his children were doing well. But there were troubles. First, there were economic difficulties, temporary ones he hoped, but these bothered him. More important, his wife had developed a chronic illness and seemed to have aged prematurely. As a result, he had to take over more of the parental functions. And especially distressing to him was the fact that their sex life had fallen off because of her illness.

He felt that he had not truly matured sexually. This was a serious problem for him, and his wife's illness compounded his difficulties. "I was never a boy, never a young man. I am still sexually only 9 years old. I would like to have the experience of being young, and in love, and exploring. I never had the opportunity and it makes me desperately upset. It is a grievous loss." He told of fantasies of having affairs with young women, but he could never allow himself to be unfaithful to his wife.

With some pride, at the end of our session, Mr. S. volunteered the fact that he had become athletic and runs five or six miles several times each week. His pride was understandable in view of the massive anxiety, primitive fears, and very debased body- and self-image that characterized his early years.

21

What Makes Psychoanalytic Therapy Effective?

The goal of psychoanalytic therapy is to initiate an optimal process of which the good/effective hour is a marker. Many hours may be seen (generally only retrospectively) as setting the stage for good/ effective hours (the session with Mrs. D., for example, when she objected to my use of the word *guarded*). Many hours that follow a good/effective hour are devoted primarily to refinements, elaborations, generalizations of the insights of the good hour—the process of working through, the importance of which psychoanalysis has rightfully emphasized. Certainly, those hours dominated by working-through activities are important and are therapeutically effective, although I have not focused on them.

A process takes time, and a good/effective hour is only a cross section of time—*an hour in the life of a process*. Though we can only work from moment to moment, from hour to hour, guided by our existing models and strategies, a long-range view over time is essential for a more complete understanding of what makes therapy effective. The long-term follow-ups are of special interest in this regard.

That *time itself is a crucial issue in effectiveness* was spontaneously emphasized by several patients in the follow-up. Mrs. B. spoke of how one cannot undo a lifetime of trouble even in years and how important it is to have the time to experience different levels of one's life. Mr. R. spoke of how important time was for him, time to work carefully and to get a convincing sense of what he felt and of what the connections to other things might be. Mr. S. said that if I had been "in a hell of a hurry" he would "have been in a hell of a mess." It took him a great deal of time to build up a sense of trust in me.

Time is necessary to get relevant, reliable data. It takes time to detect many kinds of experiences, time to sort these out and to be able to articulate them. We cannot barge into the confused lives of our patients with global interpretations based on very little data. It took years before Mr. R. was able to detect the sensorimotor phenomena described. Once detected, he could slowly and with great effort attend to them and finally capture them completely. I do not know how to hasten such work.

As the therapeutic process moves on, there is a *vast input of new information* from the patient, who may be "reliving" an experience, or from the analyst as he fills in the scene when he enters the patient's world. As a result, *new awarenesses* can occur, *new learning* can take place, and *working models can be updated, revised, and enriched*. There is constant working and reworking as new connections and generalizations are formed, and as the patient's models become more detailed and more encompassing—processes that constitute working through.

Several of the patients who were followed up emphasized how important the new awarenesses were. Mrs. A. spoke of how her "image" of her mother was reversed; as a result of treatment she no longer felt responsible for her mother's illness. Mrs. B. became aware of how her mother, for her own needs, had to keep her dependent. Mrs. C.'s guilt about her mother's drinking diminished as she became increasingly aware during therapy of the things that mother had said to her that were intended to make her feel responsible. Before treatment, Mr. R. understood virtually nothing about his grossly pathological relationship to his mother. For Mr. R. it was of immense importance to become aware that all of the inner sense of wildness and craziness actually had a basic structure that made sense in relation to his life experiences. Mr. R. also emphasized how every connection and every bit of understanding made him feel stronger, gave him a sense of who he was, and reduced his feeling of confusion. The supportive role of the therapist in enabling patients to attain painful awarenesses should not be underestimated. Mrs. C. spoke of how she was able to pursue memories and thoughts about her early life because I was there to keep these painful experiences from overwhelming and destroying her.

Learning and becoming aware are important as activities in and of themselves, regardless of the content. Many of our patients are so doubtful about themselves, so mistrustful of their own abilities, that the very activity of being allowed to learn during therapy that they have the ability to think and learn is of immense help. One of the serious problems in the early analysis of Mrs. A. was the fact that she felt she couldn't think, that her mind had been destroyed, and therefore she could do nothing to help herself.

The *expression of emotions* of all kinds is of immense therapeutic effectiveness. Mr. S. had to scream and bang the walls to express his deep sense of anguish, pain, despair. Something important happened to him as a result. He referred to it as a "structure" that came from him and reflected my "patience." Mr. R. could get considerable relief from anxiety and depression evoked by some current life situation when he allowed expression to the sensorimotor experiences described. It is always a good sign of progress in a treatment situation when formerly inhibited patients become free to express their emotions, whatever they may be, tears, anger, anguish.

Corrective emotional experiences that occur over time are crucial in therapy and may well be the single most important aspect of psychoanalytic effectiveness. It seems to me that the expression *corrective emotional experience* expresses what actually takes place in a good treatment situation. The phrase has been anathema to most analysts ever since Alexander (1948, p. 287) used it to mean "a consciously planned regulation of the therapist's own emotional responses to the patient's material (countertransference) in such a way as to counteract the harmful effects of the parental attitudes." As I have already mentioned, when I speak of a corrective emotional experience I am *not* referring to a consciously planned emotional reaction.

It is *in the context of the relationship to the therapist that we see the most important corrective emotional experiences.* It is for many patients a most important corrective experience to be with someone close who represents human compassion and reasonableness; who represents what normal emotional "reality" is about; who is not judgmental nor condemning; who treats them like individuals to be respected; allows, and is prepared to listen to, their feelings and thoughts, wild, "crazy" and "perverse" as these might be; who allows them to learn and develop on their own; and who permits them to arrive at their own conclusions in their own way. As one of my patients said to me, "I am always touched when you talk to me as if I was a person, not some crazy fool. It gives me a sense of being somebody."

Being understood by a therapist is therapeutic in itself. Understanding and the actions that demonstrate it affirm or reinforce the patient's own awarenesses. The patient can thereby get implicit confirmation from the outside for what he senses internally. Learning is enhanced by this complementary input. It is most confusing and disruptive of a developing sense of self when one's awarenesses are not affirmed or reinforced from the outside, as so often happens with patients who have grown up with unrelated psychotic or alcoholic parents. Mrs. C. felt that *she* had to hold the "idea of me" in mind, that if *she* didn't, no one else would, because her parents had no clear image of her in their minds. She felt she would vanish if no one had her in mind. When she came to feel that I "had a clear sober perception" of her, she was "able to relax in some profound way."

The human relationship that we offer patients allows them to identify with the therapist in many ways. They can acquire information from the therapist's models both of the world and of them that may correct their own pathological representations.

In the follow-up interviews, Mrs. A. reported how important it was for her that I seemed to point out that she was as intelligent as she had to be and that she was able to compete with others and often even think more clearly than her exceptionally brilliant husband. For this to have happened, I had to have a model of Mrs. A. that was infinitely more realistic than the one she had of herself. Mrs. B. felt that I was implicitly giving her new "guidelines," appropriate ones for her age and intelligence. Mrs. C. adopted my attitudes to "reality," work, and effort, which differed considerably from those of her mother. Mrs. D. emphasized the importance of a stable, purposeful, working relationship with me. Mr. R. emphasized the sense of peace and safety and of endless time as soon as he entered my office— experiences that undoubtedly did not characterize his early years. For Mr. S. I became one of the very few figures "present in [his] head."

Finally, *the therapeutic process allows healing and normal maturational steps to occur.* Note that I use the word "allows." I believe that therapeutic effectiveness comes about not so much by what the process "does" as by what it "allows." This idea should come as no surprise. The physician who administers an antibiotic does not truly actively heal; he does something that *allows* the organism to heal itself. As the therapeutic process moves on, awareness is increased, relevant informational input is maximized, new learning takes place, corrective emotional experiences occur—healing is allowed. As a result of this "healing," conflicts become resolved, panics and anxiety attenuated, guilt and depression relieved. Patients can find their way, recognize who they are, and perhaps discover new interests and talents. And we can see normal maturational steps taking place, steps that may have been previously arrested. Thus, we can see the changing attitudes characteristic of the phases of a normal life cycle: the interest in sexuality and marriage, the interest in one's children to whom the torch is handed; the reconciliation and adaptation to one's limitations, to advancing years, to illness, and to death—realistic adaptations in many ways. It was impressive to see how some of the patients had adapted. Mrs. A. was able to adapt to her husband and see both his problems and his very great assets.

Is there a prototype for the optimal Freudian analytic process? I believe there may be: in the optimal mother-infant interaction. The empathic mother allows herself to make contact with her child, attempts to meet his needs, allows him to quietly explore, discover his body and the world about, permitting him thereby to "construct" aspects of what we call "self" and "object world." She allows her child to learn that he can learn and explore, with all of the joy that goes with such activities. She presents a benign, tolerant, patient atmosphere which, by her participating in his learning, implicitly reinforces what he is doing. She doesn't negate his efforts, contradict his awarenesses, impose her will, or provoke him to such a state of rage, panic, and anxiety that learning is not possible. She is tolerant of his emotional expressions—tears, rage. Although she must set limits and must frustrate, she is aware of the degree of stress that her child can tolerate. She adapts to her child. She learns from her infant, learns how to "read" him, permits error correction when she goes wrong, and slowly builds up a model of her own individual child and of herself as mother to this particular child. It can indeed be said, as Freud (1913, p. 130) wrote of the analytic process, that a good mother can only "supervise" the process of growth and maturation. The optimal mother-child interactions bear many striking re-

semblances to the therapist-patient interactions in the heuristic analytic process; they can hardly be said to resemble the patient-
therapist relationships in stereotyped approaches.

Thus, behind the issues of "evidence," the "confirmation of hypotheses," and "error-correcting feedback"—all of the terms of "science" in which I have discussed the heuristic approach lies perhaps
the most basic and universal form of early human interaction. Good
science is deeply humanistic and deeply respectful of human
uniqueness. And perhaps we can recognize that much of the enormous objection to the stereotyped forms of Freudian therapy, often
mistakenly called "classical," is not only that they represent poor
science, but also—and perhaps more important—that they violate
our deepest sense of what is humanistically right.

I close with a few brief comments on my personal reactions to the
follow-up interviews. The letter from Mrs. C. was troubling and not
easy to evaluate. Although helped in many ways, she had evidently
also been hurt, more than I had realized. Many strategies I would
now advocate had obviously not been operative, especially during
the early part of her treatment. Nevertheless, the follow-up interviews were one of the most rewarding experiences of my professional career.

We tend to lose perspective as we plod along day by day, hour
after hour. It is difficult to work with patients who have a very wide
range of capabilities, and when often, even in favorable cases, little
seems to be happening for long periods of time or else a great deal is
happening that we do not understand. It is natural to wonder if we
are accomplishing anything at all, if we are on the right track, if we
are perhaps misunderstanding the case completely. The good/effec-
tive hours stand out as markers that perhaps there is movement and
that something is happening. But such hours are only cross sections
of a long-term process. While engaged in the process we cannot tell
if our work will stand up. It was therefore most rewarding to see
what some of my patients had done with their lives. There were
definite limitations to what was accomplished, but there were also
significant gains, and these gains were maintained. Indeed, some of
the patients now had lives that were comparatively free of their
earlier problems—lives that, before treatment, they undoubtedly
never thought were possible for them.

References

Abelson, R. P. (1981). Psychological status of the script concept. *American Psychologist,* 36: 715–729.

Alexander, F., French, T., et al. (1946). *Psychoanalytic Therapy.* New York: Ronald Press.

Arlow, J. A. (1963). Conflict, regression and symptom formation. *International Journal of Psycho-Analysis,* 44: 12–22.

Beck, A. T. (1976). *Cognitive Therapy and the Emotional Disorders.* New York: International Universities Press.

Blanck, G. & Blanck, R. B. (1974). *Ego Psychology.* New York: Columbia University Press.

Blois, M. S. (1980). Clinical judgment and computers. *The New England Journal of Medicine,* 303: 192–197.

Boden, M. (1977). *Artificial Intelligence and Natural Man.* New York: Basic Books.

Bowlby, J. (1969). *Attachment and Loss, Vol. 1, Attachment.* New York: Basic Books.

Bowlby, J. (1973). *Attachment and Loss, Vol. 2, Separation.* New York: Basic Books.

Bowlby, J. (1980). *Attachment and Loss, Vol. 3, Loss.* New York: Basic Books.

Brenner, C. (1976). *Psychoanalytic Technique and Psychic Conflict.* New York: International Universities Press.

Diesing, P. (1971). *Patterns of Discovery in the Social Sciences.* Chicago: Aldine.

DSM-III (*Diagnostic and Statistical Manual of Mental Disorders* 3rd ed.) (1980). Washington, D.C.: American Psychiatric Association.

Erdelyi, M. J. (1974). A new look at the new look: Perceptual defense and vigilance. *Psychological Review,* 81: 1–25.

Ericsson, K. A. & Simon, H. A. (1980). Verbal reports as data. *Psychological Review,* 87: 215–251.

Freud, S. (1899). Screen memories. *Standard Edition* 3: 303–322. London: Hogarth Press, 1962.

Freud, S. (1900). The interpretation of dreams. *Standard Edition,* 4 & 5. London: Hogarth Press, 1953.

Freud, S. (1912). Recommendations to physicians practising psycho-analysis. *Standard Edition,* 12: 109–120. London: Hogarth Press, 1958.

Freud, S. (1913). On beginning the treatment (further recommendations on the technique of psycho-analysis, I). *Standard Edition,* 12: 121–144. London: Hogarth Press, 1958.

Freud, S. (1923). Remarks on the theory and practice of dream-interpretation. *Standard Edition,* 19: 109–121. London: Hogarth Press, 1961.

Greenacre, P. (1973). The primal scene and the sense of reality. *Psychoanalytic Quarterly,* 42: 10–41.

Greenson, R. R. (1967). *The Technique and Practice of Psychoanalysis.* New York: International Universities Press.

Greenspan, S. I. & Sharfstein, S. S., (1981). Efficacy of psychotherapy. *Archives of General Psychiatry,* 38: 1213–1219.

Isakower, O. (1938). A contribution to the psychopathology of phenomena associated with falling asleep. *International Journal of Psycho-Analysis,* 19: 331–345.

Kaplan, A. (1964). *The Conduct of Inquiry.* New York: Crowell.

Kohut, H. (1959). Introspection, empathy, and psychoanalysis. In *The Search for the Self.* ed. P. Ornstein. New York: International Universities Press, 1978, pp. 205–232.

Kohut, H. (1979). The two analyses of Mr. Z. *International Journal of Psycho-Analysis,* 60: 3–27.

Kohut, H. & Wolf, E. S. (1978). The disorders of the self and their treatment: An outline. *International Journal of Psycho-Analysis,* 59: 413–425.

Kovel, J. (1978). Things and words: Metapsychology and the historical point of view. *Psychoanalysis and Contemporary Thought,* 1, 21–88.

Kris, E. (1956). On some vicissitudes of insight in psychoanalysis. In *The Selected Papers of Ernst Kris.* New Haven: Yale University Press, 1975, pp. 252–271.

Lindsay, P. H. & Norman, D. A. (1977). *Human Information Processing* 2nd ed. New York: Academic.

Loftus, G. R. & Loftus, E. F. (1976). *Human Memory.* Hillsdale: Lawrence Erlbaum Associates.

Malcove, L. (1975). The analytic situation: Toward a view of the supervisory experience. *Journal of the Philadelphia Association of Psychoanalysis,* 2: 1–19.

Neisser, U. (1976). *Cognition and Reality.* San Francisco: W. H. Freeman.

Peterfreund, E. (1971). *Information, Systems, and Psychoanalysis.* [Psychological Issues Monograph 25/26] New York: International Universities Press.

Peterfreund, E. (1976). How does the analyst listen? On models and strategies in the psychoanalytic process. In *Psychoanalysis and Contemporary Science,* Vol. 4, ed. D. P. Spence. New York: International Universities Press, pp. 59–101.

Peterfreund, E. (1980). On information and systems models for psychoanalysis. *International Review of Psycho-Analysis,* 7: 327–345.

Peterfreund, E. & Franceschini, E. (1973). On information, motivation, and meaning. In *Psychoanalysis and Contemporary Science,* Vol. 2, ed. B. B. Rubinstein, New York: Macmillan.

Ramzy, I. (1974). How the mind of the psychoanalyst works: An essay on psychoanalytic inference. *International Journal of Psycho-Analysis,* 55: 543–553.

Rubinstein, B. B. (1976). On the clinical psychoanalytic theory and its role in the inference and confirmation of particular clinical hypotheses. In *Psychoanalysis and Contemporary Science,* Vol. 4, ed. D. P. Spence. New York: International Universities Press, PP. 3–57.

Rubinstein, B. B. (1980). The problem of confirmation in clinical psychoanalysis. *Journal of the American Psychoanalytic Association,* 28: 397–417.

Simon, H. A. (1962). The processes of creative thinking. In *Models of Thought.* New Haven: Yale University Press, 1979, pp. 144–174.

Webster's (1957). *New World Dictionary of the American Language, College Edition.* Cleveland: The World Publishing Co.

Winograd, T. (1972). Understanding natural language. *Cognitive Psychology,* 3: 1–191.

Wisdom, J. O. (1967). Testing an interpretation within a session. *International Journal of Psycho-Analysis,* 48: 44–52.

Index